Minerals

W9-AXC-324

Minerals of
the World

Walter Schumann

Sterling Publishing Co., Inc.   New York

Translated by Elisabeth E. Reinersmann

Library of Congress Cataloging-in-Publication Data

Schumann, Walter.
    [Mineralien aus aller Welt. English]
    Minerals of the world / Walter Schumann ; [translated by Elisabeth
E. Reinersmann].
        p.   cm.
    Translation of: Mineralien aus aller Welt.
    Includes bibliographical references and index.
    ISBN 0-8069-8570-4
    1. Minerals—Handbooks, manuals, etc.   2. Minerals—
Identification—Handbooks, manuals, etc.   I. Title.
QE366.8.S3813   1992
549—dc20   91-42362
                                                                              CIP

Edited by Rodman P. Neumann

10 9 8 7 6 5 4 3 2 1

First paperback edition published in 1998 by
Sterling Publishing Company, Inc.
387 Park Avenue South, New York, N.Y. 10016
Original edition published in German
under the title *Mineralien aus aller Welt*
© 1990 by BLV Verlagsgesellschaft mbH, München 19
Distributed in Canada by Sterling Publishing
% Canadian Manda Group, One Atlantic Avenue, Suite 105
Toronto, Ontario, Canada M6K 3E7
Distributed in Great Britain and Europe by Cassell PLC
Wellington House, 125 Strand, London WC2R 0BB, England
Distributed in Australia by Capricorn Link (Australia) Pty Ltd.
P.O. Box 6651, Baulkham Hills, Business Centre, NSW 2153, Australia
Printed and bound in Hong Kong

Sterling ISBN 0-8069-8570-4 Trade
              0-8069-8571-2 Paper

Contents

PREFACE

This field guide with its rapid-identification system represents something entirely new. The minerals are organized in categories based on three easily measurable properties: the streak, Mohs' hardness, and specific gravity. These properties are displayed in a multicolored bar on the left margin of the descriptive pages. Identifying individual minerals is made much easier, by using the left margin bar.

Countless minerals that were previously difficult to recognize can now be identified or can—up to a point at least—be classified as belonging to a particular group.

The book covers three main areas. The first part of the introduction explains how to use the rapid-identification system. Next, the many forms and properties of minerals are discussed. And lastly, the reader can use the guide for identification, learning how to apply the properties that can be determined.

The main section, the actual guide for identification, has the multicolored margin bar of properties along the left page. For collectors, this is the heart of the book.

Following the guide for identification, there is an extensive glossary. Combined with the extensive index, this makes the book not only a field guide but also a good reference work.

The glossary carries terms that are not explained in the text. Other concepts are listed in the index.

Many of my friends and colleagues have contributed to the success of this field guide with much enthusiasm. Countless people and several institutes supplied charts and photos. And to all of them, I give my heartfelt thanks.

Walter Schumann

ORGANIZATION

Recognizing Minerals From the approximately 3000 known minerals in the world and their several thousand varieties, well over 500 entities have been carefully chosen.

The choices are not free from subjective judgment. Criteria governing them are how common they are, their degree of popularity as well as their availability on the international market. In fact only a few hundred minerals in the world are found in abundance, are in a condition worthwhile for collecting, and therefore, are of interest to mineral collectors.

Text The text for the guide is brief, often in a telegraphic style, and tailored to the interested collector, novice or expert. The glossary further explains terminology. Primary emphasis is placed on information that is helpful to the user who wants to identify minerals. Included are notations of where an individual mineral is found, to which category it belongs, and what minerals are similar to the one in question. The multicolored bar of properties along the outside margin of the left page—opposite the photos of minerals—corresponds to the group of minerals discussed in the text.

With the text organized on the left and photos on the right, the user can easily compare the written information with the visual example.

Photographs The samples used for the photographs are not one-of-a-kind museum pieces but rather minerals and aggregates that any typical collector could find or buy. The specimens were photographed in such a way that the reader will be able to recognize many distinctive features with the naked eye. Some photographs have been enlarged either to clarify certain information or whenever technical reasons made it necessary to do so. The degree of enlargement is given in the form of a ratio. For instance, 1:3 means the photo is three times larger than actual size; 1:½ means the photo represents one-half the actual size. For larger than actual size, only whole numbers are used, eliminating decimal points for simplicity. If the difference between the photo and actual size is small, no ratio is given.

Drawings of Crystals These drawings are typical, though somewhat idealized. They are meant to give a general impression of the form of a particular crystal. The drawings were taken from scientific literature.

Localities The places where a particular mineral has been found in nature are listed generally either as a region or a country. To find specific localities, other sources must be consulted. When searching for a locality for a particular mineral, it is advisable to investigate several regions or countries of known occurrence as well as places that are of mineralogical, historic, or economic importance.

HOW TO FIND A PARTICULAR MINERAL

The Rapid-Identification System

To identify a mineral, which means distinguishing it from any other, the collector is required to make certain determinations. The identification system of this guide is based on three properties determined in the following order:

1. The streak.
2. The Mohs' hardness.
3. The specific gravity of the particular mineral.

Additional characteristics must be carefully noted, including the lustre, transparency, and cleavage, among others.

With this information, it is possible to determine the mineral group to which a particular specimen belongs. The text, drawings, and photographs in the guide allow an even closer identification. Categories of minerals with similar characteristics are kept small enough so that it is often possible to make a positive identification after inspecting only one or two pages of photographs. Sometimes three pages may need to be consulted, but seldom more than four.

If a specimen displays a streak shading that might fall in more than one category, or if its degree of hardness or specific gravity points to another group, other possibilities are suggested in a boxed footnote on the page where the first group is discussed.

FIRST DETERMINATION: WHAT IS THE STREAK?

A simple method for the rough identification of a mineral is to look at its streak, also called powder color. Because, even if a mineral appears to have more than one color, or shows differing shades of color, its inherent color—or streak—is always the same.

The guide distinguishes among six streak categories: white and colorless, green, grey and black, red and orange, gold and brown, and blue.

Along the outside margin of each left page of the guide is a bar of properties including the streak at the top. The bar corresponds to the group of minerals whose particular properties are discussed on the page.

If a mineral has a streak shading that might fall under two or more of the guide's streak categories, the mineral is discussed under one group and referenced in the footnotes at the bottom of the page to point the reader to the appropriate page. A mineral, for instance, with a blue-green streak might be described in the green group (with photo and identifying characteristics), and cross-referenced in a boxed footnote in the blue group. If

Streak	Streak	Streak	Streak	Streak	Streak
white and colorless	green	grey and black	red and orange	gold and brown	blue

there is any doubt, check all the likely streak categories.

Light grey is used in the margin bar for the white and colorless group. Minerals with a definite grey streak are discussed in the grey and black group. A more detailed discussion of streak can be found on page 16.

SECOND DETERMINATION: WHAT IS THE MOHS' HARDNESS?

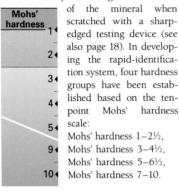

The degree of scratch hardness can be determined by observing the resistance of the mineral when scratched with a sharp-edged testing device (see also page 18). In developing the rapid-identification system, four hardness groups have been established based on the ten-point Mohs' hardness scale:

Mohs' hardness 1–2½,
Mohs' hardness 3–4½,
Mohs' hardness 5–6½,
Mohs' hardness 7–10.

If a particular streak category has only a few minerals in a specific hardness group, then two hardness groups have been combined.

The multicolored margin bar along the left page displays the relative Mohs' hardness scale in the middle section. One glance will tell the reader if the determined scratch hardness of the specimen corresponds to the range given in the scale—of course within the appropriate streak category; if not, continue within the streak category until the hardness is correctly identified. Each streak category progresses through the hardness groups from hardness 1 through 10.

THIRD DETERMINATION: WHAT IS THE SPECIFIC GRAVITY?

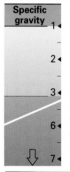

This characteristic—also called "relative density"—is often the one that will make a positive identification of a specimen possible. Specific gravity is the weight of a specific material compared with the weight of the same volume of water. This characteristic and its determination are discussed on pages 20 and 21.

Several ranges of specific gravity are again defined as groups for the lower section of the multicolored margin bar. As many minerals as possible are included in each group.

The lower section of the margin bar is fitted with a scale displaying values from 1 to 7. Values beyond 7 are indicated by an arrow pointing downward at the bottom of the scale.

ADDITIONAL DETERMINATIONS (IF NECESSARY)

Most of the time these three basic properties—streak, Mohs' hardness, and specific gravity—are sufficient for the identification of an unknown mineral. If not, refer to the guide, checking the additional characteristics mentioned for minerals in that group. Perhaps some typical characteristics of a mineral are not well represented in the photograph or are not detectable in the specimen. Another property such as color, lustre, or transparency may give the needed clue; or maybe the shape of the crystal or the discussion of aggregates will clarify the determination.

The three basic properties and other ways of testing a specimen are discussed on pages 16 through 25. The additional characteristics may help narrow the field of possibilities among several minerals with similar streak, Mohs' hardness, and specific gravity.

Example—Fluorite

Rapid identification of a specimen is often possible by matching the information in the multicolored margin bar along the left page.

Determination	Result	Marking on left margin bar	Appropriate Pages
Streak?	white	**Streak** white and colorless	26–128 = 52 pages of photographs
Mohs' hardness?	4 belongs to hardness group 3–4½	**Mohs' hardness** 1◄ 2◄ 3◄ 4◄	52–76 = 13 pages of photographs
Specific gravity?	3.18 belongs to group 3.1–4.0	**Specific gravity** 1◄ – 2◄ 3◄ 4◄	68–72 = 3 pages of photographs

Examining the remaining three pages usually makes it possible to quickly identify the specimen. Additional properties helpful in the decision-making process include the color (here: brownish), transparency (here: clear), shape of the crystal (here: cubic), and additional characteristics mentioned in the text.

EXTERNAL SHAPES OF MINERALS

Structure of Minerals

Minerals are naturally occurring, self-contained components of celestial bodies, whether in the Earth or in the solid parts of other celestial bodies in the universe. They have a definite chemical composition with very definite physical and optical properties, and nearly all have an ordered atomic arrangement. Minerals are usually expressed in chemical formulas, excluding impurities even when they may cause part or all of the mineral's color.

Nine classes of minerals have been established according to their chemical structure: elements; sulfides and related compounds; halides; oxides and hydroxides; nitrates, carbonates, and borates; sulfates; chromates, molybdates, and tungstates; phosphates, arsenates, and vanadates; silicates; and organic compounds.

Synthetic products with the same composition and structure as a naturally occurring mineral are, nevertheless, not considered to be minerals.

There are minerals, however, that have the same chemical composition, but each mineral is its own distinct entity. The reason they are separate minerals is the difference in the crystal form. Such minerals are called polymorphic crystals with modified internal structures. For instance, carbon is a polymorph of graphite and diamond. The minerals quartz, cristobalite, citrine, amethyst, and tridymite, as well as opal, are polymorphs of silica.

Most minerals occur in crystalline form—whether they appear to be shapeless, display crystal faces, or are found in well-rounded pebbles. Each possesses its own internal geometric structure, which may be similar to other mineral crystals of differing compositions. The inner structure determines the physical and optical properties: the outer shape (faces), as well as the hardness, cleavage, type of fracture, specific gravity, refractive index, and optical axes. When this inner structure, the arrangement of atoms, ions, and molecules, appears in a regular, recurring pattern, it is called the spatial or crystal lattice.

Minerals with such a lattice are called crystalline; those without a definite inner arrangement are termed amorphous. Another category is crystals which are isomorphous—components of the lattice can be substituted by other substances without changing their basic crystalline and chemical structure. When such an exchange takes place to a large degree, the isomorphous crystals form a so-called solid solution such as for the calcium sodium feldspars—plagioclase.

It is common to find within a group of monomineralic crystals distinct varieties which, nevertheless, have the same properties. The basic chemical and crystalline structure within each such apparent variety remains essentially fixed, given the conditions for crystal growth in the normal development of the mineral. Some minerals with a certain hardness and variations in color are used as gemstones for jewels.

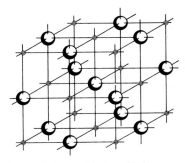

Geometrical crystal lattice of halite (large circles: chlorine; small circles: sodium).

11

Crystal Systems

cubic

tetragonal

hexagonal

trigonal

rhombic

monoclinic

triclinic

Crystal Systems

Most minerals develop orderly geometrical atomic structures that are specific to the particular mineral crystal. The atomic structure controls the symmetry and overall shape of the crystals. In crystallography, crystals are divided into seven such symmetry systems. The difference between them is determined by crystal axes and angles. On the opposite page are diagrams of the seven crystal systems and some typical crystal forms.

Cubic System (Isometric and Regular) All three axes have the same length and intersect at right angles. Typical crystal shapes are the cube and octahedron (8 faces), rhombic dodecahedron (12 square faces), pentagon dodecahedron (12 pentagonal faces), icosi-tetrahedron (24 faces), and hexoctahedron (48 faces).

Tetragonal System All three axes intersect at right angles; two are of the same length and are in the same plane while the third (main axis) is either shorter or longer. Typical crystal shapes are four-sided prisms and pyramids, trapezohedrons and eight-sided pyramids as well as double pyramids.

Hexagonal System Three of four axes are in the same plane, are of equal length and intersect at an angle of 120° (respectively 60°). The fourth axis of differing length is at right angles to the others. Typical crystal shapes are hexagonal prisms and dipyramids as well as dihexagonal dipyramids and double pyramids.

Trigonal System (Rhombohedral) Axes and angles are similar to the preceding system and often the two systems are combined as the hexagonal. The difference is one of symmetry. In the hexagonal system, the cross section of the prism base is six-sided; in the trigonal system, it

is three-sided. The hexagonal shape is formed when the corners of the triangles are bevelled. Typical crystal forms are three-sided prisms and pyramids, rhombohedra, and scalenohedra.

Rhombic System (Orthorhombic) Three axes of unequal length are at right angles. Typical crystal shapes are basal pinacoids, rhombic prisms and pyramids as well as rhombic double pyramids.

Monoclinic System Two of the three axes—all unequal in length—are at right angles to each other; the third is inclined. Typical crystal forms are basal pinacoids and prisms with inclined end faces.

Triclinic System All three axes are of different length and inclined towards each other. Typical crystal forms are paired faces.

The Law of Constant Angles

Each crystal may seem to be different, even when they belong to the same group.

Most crystals are not regularly shaped: Some are large, some small; some narrow, some wide; some straight, some angled. As the crystal grows naturally, some crystal faces develop better and are more pronounced.

The form of each crystal in the group appears to be irregular with the size and relationship of faces seeming to be different. However, the angles between the faces always remain constant among minerals belonging to the same group. Whenever identifying an unknown mineral on the basis of crystal shape, try to imagine the ideal form while inspecting the real crystal shape. Some minerals occur in combinations of crystal forms such as octahedron and cube.

Twinning in Crystals

Where two or more crystals of the same group and the same shape are intergrown according to certain laws, it is called twinning. Depending on whether the individual crystals simply grow together or are intergrown, it is either contact twinning or penetration twinning, respectively. Depending on the number of individual members, it is also referred to as tripling, quadrupling, etc. Twinning of many individual crystals is often called multiple twinning.

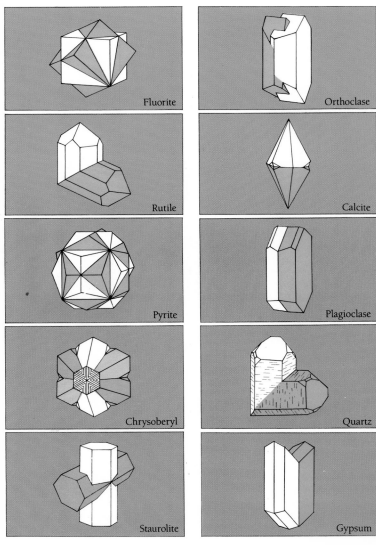

Fluorite

Orthoclase

Rutile

Calcite

Pyrite

Plagioclase

Chrysoberyl

Quartz

Staurolite

Gypsum

Mineral Aggregates

When several minerals—in sizes anywhere from millimetres to many metres—are irregularly intergrown, they are called aggregates. The individual minerals need not belong to the same group. Large units of aggregate are called rocks. An aggregate with several well-defined surface crystals is called a terrace.

1

2

3

4

5

6

7

8

9

The photographs above show some typical examples of mineral aggregates.

1 **skeletal** bearing some resemblance to dendrites, moss, branching trees, wire, knitting (copper);
2 **flaky** foliated, bearing some resemblance to scales, rose petals, rosettes (gypsum rose);
3 **radial** bearing some resemblance to radial filaments or striae (pyrite—so-called marcasite tubers);
4 **granular** recognizable with the naked eye, grainy-textured aggregate (olivine);

5 **crusty** bearing some resemblance to bark, thin coating of a cavity (pyromorphite);
6 **glass bead–like** reniform, botryoidal, wart-like, mammillary (red hematite);
7 **parallel fibrous** bearing some resemblance to tufts, bundles (amianthus/actinolite);
8 **disordered fibrous** bearing some resemblance to a tangled radiating texture, matted (actinolite);
9 **oolitic** pisolitic (pea-shaped concretions), bearing some resemblance to roe, shells (aragonite).

15

Color of Minerals and Streak

Only a very few minerals come in a single, characteristic color such as green malachite, red cinnabar, blue azurite or yellow phosphor. Most minerals exhibit many different colors; some even have all the colors of the spectrum. Color alone is seldom a useful characteristic by which to identify an unknown specimen.

The streak, also called powder color, on the other hand, is a good, objective means for identification. The inherent color—or streak—can be seen whenever a mineral is pulverized. While the apparent coloring of a mineral variety is produced by impurities or the result of a disturbed crystal structure (thereby not the inherent color), the streak is always a distinct and constant color for a particular mineral. It is inherent—in other words, characteristic. The finely ground powder acts like thin, transparent platelets. The streak color of fluorite (see page 10) is always white, even if the mineral appears to be yellow, green, blue, violet or black.

The inherent color can be determined by streaking the mineral on an unglazed porcelain tile, the streak plate. In the absence of an actual streak plate, the unglazed portion on the underside of a porcelain bowl or vase, the surface of an electrical fuse, or the back of a glazed wall tile will do just fine.
Pulverizing the mineral by rubbing it across the plate will produce the streak. If

Streak.   Top, left to right: orpiment, pyrite, cinnabar.

          Bottom, left to right: hematite, azurite, malachite.

no streak is detectable, the mineral's streak is said to be white or colorless.

Sometimes—for more accurate identification—it is advisable to compare a visible streak on the streak plate with the "streak" of the edge of another streak plate. But such hints are mentioned in the description of individual minerals in the guide for identification.

When the hardness of the specimen is greater than that of the streak plate (above Mohs' hardness 6), a small portion must first be pulverized. The powder is then rubbed onto the tile.

Use only fresh fractures when performing the streak test; avoid those parts that have been oxidized or discolored.

Streak test on a porcelain streak plate. Brass-yellow pyrite produces a greyish-black streak.

Pleochroism

Some transparent minerals appear to show a different color or depth of color when viewed from different angles. The reason is that light is absorbed differently depending on the direction it travels through the mineral. Pleochroism is the collective term for any such phenomena.

If two main colors can be observed, it is often called dichroism; three colors, trichroism. Dichroism is possible only in tretragonal, hexagonal, and trigonal crystal systems; trichroism only in rhombic, monoclinic, and triclinic systems. Amorphus minerals and those belonging to the cubic crystal system do not show pleochroism. The presence of pleochroism can be either weak, distinct, vivid, or very strong.

Light Effects and Surface Lustre

With some minerals, specific striated light effects and surface color effects (lustre) can only be observed after the mineral has been shaped or polished. These effects are not related to the mineral's color or streak and are not caused by impurities or chemical composition, but are caused by the reflection, interference, and refraction of light.

Asterism Asterism occurs when light rays form a star; the rays meet at one point, crossing each other at given angles, depending on the symmetry of the crystal structure.

Cat's Eye Effect (Chatoyancy) An effect similar to the shape and glow of a cat's eye results when light rays are reflected by parallel fibres, needles, or channels.

Opalescence The milky blue or pearly appearance of common opal is caused by the reflection of light.

Opalization A speckled play of color of opal is observed and changes according to the angle of observation. It is the result of light reflection and interference.

Labradorescence A play of color in metallic hues produces a sheen, which is most probably caused by interference phenomena. Blue and green effects are often found, particularly in labradorite.

17

Mohs' Hardness

When a mineral collector speaks of hardness, the reference is actually to scratch hardness. In essence this is a practical determination of the ability of the specimen to resist scratches that the collector is trying to make using a sharp-edged test mineral.

The scratch hardness test was invented by the Viennese mineralogist Friedrich Mohs (1773–1839). He developed a scale of ten minerals of increasing hardness. Mohs' scale is still a standard tool in use throughout the world. Scratch hardness 1 represents the softest mineral, 10 the hardest.

Some minerals show different hardness on different faces or in different directions. In general, however, the differences are so small that a collector need not be concerned.

Only in a few cases where the differences are very great must they be taken into consideration. Kyanite, for instance, has a Mohs' hardness value of 4 to 4½ in the long direction of the crystal, while across it is 6 or 7.

Mohs' scratch hardness is a relative scale. It only shows which mineral scratches another. An absolute value of increasing hardness within the scale is not possible with Mohs' scale.

RELATIVE AND ABSOLUTE HARDNESS SCALE

Mohs' hardness	Mineral	Simple testing devices	Absolute hardness
1	talc	fingernail: rubbing	0.03
2	gypsum	fingernail: scratching possible	1.25
3	calcite	copper coin: scratching possible	4.5
4	fluorite	knife: scratching easily possible	5.0
5	apatite	knife: scratching still possible	6.5
6	orthoclase	steel file: scratching possible	37
7	quartz	will scratch window glass	120
8	topaz		175
9	corundum		1000
10	diamond		140,000

Each mineral in the series of ten scratches the previous one, and can be scratched by the following one. Minerals with equal hardness cannot scratch each other. By comparative application of Mohs' hardness scale, every mineral can be assigned a hardness. In the course of time half degrees of hardness have been added to the scale; but they are always written as ½, and not as 0.5.

Every book dealing with minerals uses Mohs' scale to designate the hardness of a mineral. Minerals with a scratch hardness of 1 and 2 are considered soft, 3 to 6 medium hard, over 6 hard.

Mohs' scale is only a relative measurement and lacks the necessary accuracy for strict scientific evaluation. A technically involved process has been established for determining "absolute" hardness. In the table above, the absolute values are compared to the relative Mohs' hardness. It is easy to see substantial differences between the two descriptions. However, the Mohs' hardness scale is indispensable to the collector—if only because it is so practical. Determining an absolute value of hardness is intractable for the layperson and not necessary for the identification of minerals.

Tools for Testing the Scratch Hardness

Implements to test the Mohs' hardness of specimens are readily available such as kits of mineral samples or handy metal holders in which mineral chips are set. In the absence of such kits, a few simple devices can be used for a rough determination: A fingernail will scratch up to hardness 2; a copper coin to 3; a good steel pocketknife to as high as 5½. Steel files are even harder and will scratch to hardness 6. Quartz, Mohs' hardness 7, will visibly scratch window glass. Quite easily and simply a rough evaluation can be made in the field.

When a scratch test is made, it is important to make sure that only a sharp-edged test piece is used on an unbroken mineral face. Uneven formation, foliated or chipped crystals, and weathered surfaces can give a false lower hardness.

After the test scratch, a powder-like residue will remain on the surface of the unknown mineral. This residue might be either the test mineral or the mineral being tested. Therefore, wipe the dust off with a finger. If the dust can be removed revealing no scratch mark, the test mineral is softer than the unknown mineral.

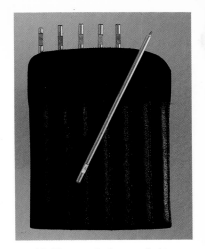

Metal holders in which mineral chips are set for testing scratch hardness.

If a scratch mark is revealed, the test mineral is harder. If no clear result can be detected with the naked eye, suggesting that the test mineral and the unknown mineral may have the same hardness, a magnifying glass might help decide the issue.

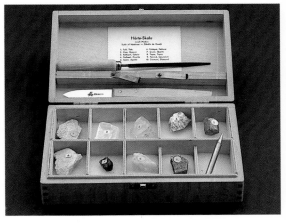

Mohs' hardness test kit of sample minerals, steel file, and knife.

Specific Gravity

Specific gravity—also called "relative density"—is the weight of a specific material compared with the weight of the same volume of water. For instance, quartz with a density of 2.65 is 2.65 times as heavy as the same volume of water.

The specific gravity of minerals varies between 1 and 20. Values under 2 are considered light (amber 1.1); those from 2 to 4 normal (calcite 2.7); and those above 4 are heavy (lead 7.5). In mining practice, minerals with a value above 2.9 are called heavy.

Precious stones and precious metals have a specific gravity that is clearly higher than the ordinary rock-forming minerals that make up sand such as quartz and feldspar. This is the principle of panning and explains why they settle—in moderately moving waters—before the lighter sand minerals in river and coastal deposits.

Specific gravity is established according to the following formula.

$$\text{Specific gravity} = \frac{\text{Weight of the Mineral}}{\text{Volume of the Mineral}}$$

The weight of the mineral is established on a scale. The more accurate the weight the more accurate will be the identification of the specimen. Experts work with 1/100 gram precision.

Volume can be determined in several different ways: water displacement measured in a graduated cylinder or weight determined with a hydrostatic balance.

The first method requires the following procedure: The specimen is placed in a graduated cylinder that is halfway filled with water. The narrower the cylinder the more accurate the volume measurement. The amount of water displacement (the difference in the level of the water surface before and after the mineral is placed in the cylinder) is the volume of the object.

This method is not very good for small specimens since water displacement is minimal. In addition, reading the difference is made more difficult by a capillary effect; the surface of the water is higher at the edge of the cylinder than it is in the center (see illustration below). Always try to read from the lowest point of the water's surface.

Best results are obtained with a hydrostatic balance. It is based on Archimedes' Principle: The rise in the water level is equal to the volume of the water that has been displaced by the mineral. First weigh the specimen in air and then in water.

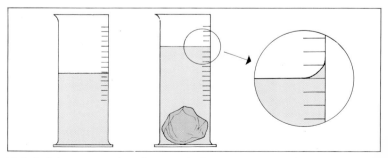

Method of determining volume by water displacement.

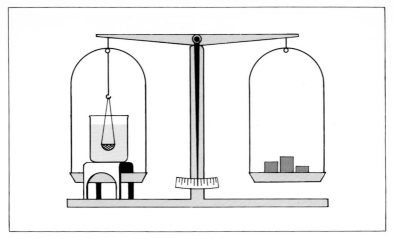

Method of determining volume with a hydrostatic balance.

The difference is equal to the weight of the displaced water and therefore also to the volume of the mineral.

Example:	
Weight in air	5.2g
Weight in water	3.3g
Difference = Volume	1.9
Specific gravity = $\dfrac{\text{Weight}}{\text{Volume}}$	$\dfrac{5.2}{1.9} = 2.7$

The specific gravity of the specimen is 2.7. Based on this value, the specimen could be calcite.

It is important that the mineral—when weighed in air—is dry and free of any foreign substances. Some minerals, however, are naturally "contaminated"—if only slightly—or are subject to variation in the combination of their components. Either would mean that the specific gravity would be variable depending on the particular specimen.

In gemology, in addition to the hydrostatic balance, a so-called heavy liquid, or

suspension, method is used to determine the specific gravity of a precious stone. It rests on the idea that by definition an object will remain suspended in a liquid of the same specific gravity; it will neither sink to the bottom nor float to the surface. The specimen is put into a liquid with a high specific gravity. The liquid is diluted—and the degree of dilution is recorded—until the specimen is suspended. Control indicators of known specific gravity, such as pieces of glass or minerals, can also be used to match the specific gravity of the diluted liquid. In either case, the result is the specific gravity of the specimen.

The suspension method is recommended when certain precious stones have to be separated from a group of unknown stones, or where synthetic stones or imitations have to be identified.

Lustre

Many minerals have their own characteristic lustre. It is the result of light reflected back from the surface and is dependent on the refractive index and the nature of the surface, but not on the color.

When describing minerals, one speaks of vitreous (glassy), waxy, and resinous as well as silky, mother-of-pearl, adamantine (diamond), greasy, and metallic.

Minerals without lustre are described as dull.

Vitreous lustre is the most common among minerals—accounting for about two-thirds of all minerals. Metallic lustre is only found in opaque minerals, particularly those of the pure metals, sulfides, and oxides. Silky lustre is found in fibrous minerals as well as mineral aggregates. Mother-of-pearl and greasy lustres are mostly found on the plane of cleavage.

Tarnish, discolorations, and weathering are all able to detract from the lustre of a mineral. Therefore, only examine a specimen that has not been otherwise altered, and only in bright light.

Transparency

Transparency is the ability of light to penetrate a mineral. There are transparent, semi-transparent, and opaque minerals. In very thin sections many opaque minerals are transparent or semi-transparent.

All metals are opaque, regardless of how thin the sample might be. Granular, fibrous, or dendritic minerals, as well as all aggregates, are always opaque.

Double Refraction

Double refraction occurs when a ray of light enters the crystal and separates into two rays. All transparent minerals, except those that are cubic and amorphous, show some degree of double refraction. Calcite found in Iceland shows double refraction especially clearly. It is also easily seen in zircon and sphene, where double refraction at the lower edge of the crystal can be observed with the naked eye. In general, however, a special instrument is needed in order to detect double refraction.

Cleavage

In mineralogy cleavage refers to the quality of a crystallized substance of splitting along definite planes. The crystal lattice of a mineral—the cohesive property of the atoms—determines if cleavage is possible. If the components of the lattice are arranged in such a way that (theoretically)

Double refraction in calcite from Iceland.

a flat object could pass through without touching any, cleavage is possible; if not, the attempt would result in fractures which create irregular surfaces.

The ease with which a crystal can be cleaved depends on the cohesive strength of the atoms as well as their arrangement. In the guide for identification, degrees of cleavability are differentiated as perfect, complete, incomplete, and none.

Some minerals can only be split along one plane; others allow separation along two or more. Miners in the past would call minerals with very good cleavability spar. Examples include feldspars, river spar (sapphire), spar calcite or Iceland spar, and heavy spar (barite).

A cleavage plane of a mineral is unrelated to its external shape (e.g., crystal growth faces) and depends only on the structure of the crystal lattice. Different minerals that possess the same crystal symmetry may produce very similar cleavage forms—even if the original shapes were quite different. Cleavage of galena and halite will always produce cubes; calcite: rhombohedra; fluorite: octahedra. The cleavage angle (the angle between two edges of a cleavage plane) is a characteristic property of a mineral.

Crystal growth faces usually do not have the same lustre and are seldom as smooth as cleavage planes. Crystal faces typically show tiny flaws, patterns, and indentations.

Fracture

Whenever a mineral is accidentally broken (due to pressure or a blow) producing irregular surfaces, it is called fracture; however, if the resulting pieces have flat, smooth surfaces, it is called cleavage. The loosening of contact twins is not cleavage but separation. A fracture may be conchoidal (resembling the impression left by a seashell), uneven, smooth, fibrous, dendritic, hook-shaped, splintery, or crumbly (like crumbled earth).

Tenacity

Tenacity in mineralogy refers to a mineral's brittleness (brittle, soft, easily cut), flexibility (malleable, pliable, flexible), and elasticity (elastic inelastic).

It is sometimes useful as an identifying characteristic. In specific instances this property is mentioned in the guide for identification.

Magnetism

Magnetic behavior varies for different minerals. For instance, some minerals (such as magnetite) have magnetic properties of their own, while others (such as magnesite) are attracted by a magnet. The balance of minerals are magnetically neutral. Inherent magnetism and being attracted to a magnet are mineral properties that are easily determined with a directional compass.

The suspended magnetized needle in a compass is sensitive to even slight magnetic influence. Position the specimen at rest next to the compass needle and observe any changes. Small specimens and those with weaker magnetic forces are tested by moving them back and forth over the compass—as close as possible. For some minerals the degree of magnetism varies according to the locality as well as their iron content.

Conchoidal fracture with well-expressed shell-like depressions (obsidian).

23

Fluorescence

Fluorescence is the ability of a substance to glow (luminesce) when exposed to ultraviolet light. Many minerals will only give off a white light; others produce a color in one of many hues. The name fluorescence comes from the mineral fluorite, which was the substance in which this phenomenon was first observed. If the object continues to glow after the ultraviolet light has been turned off, the effect is called phosphorescence—after the well-known glow of phosphorous.

Luminescence is the collective term for the phenomena of substances glowing regardless of the physical or chemical reaction or rays that are illuminating them, with the exception of heat radiation. The cause of these phenomena are the incorporation of impurities and other structural discrepancies within the crystal. Some minerals will react only to short waves (2800–2000 Å), others only to long waves (4000–3150 Å). Some react to both long wave (designated 3650 Å) and short wave (designated 2537 Å) ultraviolet light.

For identification purposes, fluorescence is only of limited use, because specimens of the same mineral group can produce entirely different shades of color, while others do not react at all. At times fluorescence might be a helpful characteristic when a particular locality from which a mineral originated needs to be identified. Some localities yield very distinct fluorescent colors for a particular mineral.

Fluorescence is particularly useful in recognizing synthetic and imitation specimens. The glue used to join mineral pieces, for instance, has a different fluorescence than the mineral itself.

Flame-Test Color

Since some elements have the ability to change the color of a flame, a flame test can be useful in determining the chemical components of an unknown mineral. A gas flame is preferred over a candle flame because the gas is easily regulated so that the flame's own color is not visible. It is best to darken the room when conducting a flame test. Strontium produces a purplish red flame, lithium a carmine red, calcium a brick red, sodium a yellow, barium a yellowish green, boron a green, copper a blue, and potassium a violet flame.

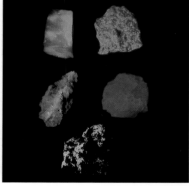

Fluorescent minerals under white light (left) and under ultraviolet light (right).

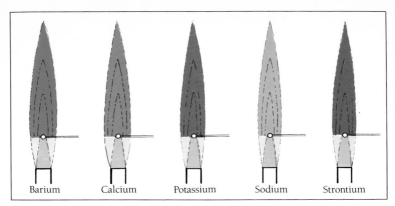

Flame color as a method of identifying minerals.

Only a small sliver of the material is necessary for a flame test. Hold the sliver—with a pair of tweezers or a platinum loop—in the flame until the sliver begins to glow. It is important to make sure that the piece to be tested is not contaminated.

Other Characteristics

Sometimes the identification process can be greatly assisted by very simple tests, such as smelling (sulphurous, earthy), tasting (salty, bitter), or touching (greasy, cold—which means that it is a good conductor of heat). Water solubility and reactions to acid or base can also be helpful.

Experts must sometimes undertake very specific tests under particular circumstances, such as when dealing with precious stones or when a potentially economic mineral vein has been located. Among the properties that can be tested are the optical dispersion of white light into its spectral colors, absorption and absorption spectra, microscopic studies of reflection as well incident and penetrating light, fusibility, and radioactivity.

Borax

$Na_2[B_4O_5(OH)_4] \cdot 8\ H_2O$

① Boron, California/USA
② Boron, California/USA

Streak white. **Mohs' hardness** 2–2½. **Specific gravity** 1.7–1.8. **Characteristics:** white, yellowish, seldom bluish, greenish. Weathered surface: grey. Lustre: greasy, vitreous, resinous, weathered surface dull; transparent to opaque. Cleavage: complete. Fracture: conchoidal; brittle; easily soluble in water. Taste: bitter-sweet. Crystals: (monoclinic) short-prismatic, thick-columned, also tabular. **Aggregates:** rough, grainy, fibrous, crumbly, powdery, as crust; present in salt lake beds, hot spring deposits, and volcanic vents. **Accompanied by:** halite, soda, gypsum, calcite, colemanite, kernite, ulexite. **Found in:** Nevada/USA; Tibet/China; Kashmir/Pakistan/India; Kazakhstan/USSR; Iran. **Similar to:** kernite, colemanite, sassolite, soda, trona.

Sassolite   boric acid

$B(OH)_3$

③ Death Valley, California/USA

Streak white. **Mohs' hardness** 1. **Specific gravity** 1.48. **Characteristics:** white to grey, occasionally colorless, yellow to brown. Lustre: vitreous, cleavage surfaces mother-of-pearl; transparent. Cleavage: perfect. Malleable; greasy to the touch; soluble in warm water. Taste: sour. Low melting point; flame test: green. Crystals: (triclinic) psuedo-hexagonal, tabular, sometimes acicular. **Aggregates:** flaky, scaly, crusty, powdery; present as hot spring deposits and from sublimation associated with volcanic vents. **Found in:** Tuscany, Vesuvius/Italy; Kamchatka/USSR; Ladakh/India; California, Nevada/USA. **Similar to:** borax, kernite.

Sal Ammoniac

Ammonium Chloride
NH_4Cl

④ Paricutin/Mexico

Streak white. **Mohs' hardness** 1–2. **Specific gravity** 1.53. **Characteristics:** colorless, white, sometimes yellow to brown. Lustre: opaque; transparent. Cleavage: incomplete. Fracture: conchoidal, crumbly, moderate, malleable but tough; easily soluble in water. Taste: stinging, salty. Crystals: (cubic) cubic, octahedral; rare and small. **Aggregates:** rough, crusty, skeletal, stalactitic, botryoidal, fibrous and crumbly; present at volcanic vents, on burning coal fields, as layers of minable ore and coal, in guano. **Accompanied by:** phosphorite. **Found in:** Saarland; Ruhr valley; Saxony; Vesuvius, Etna/Italy; Hekla/Iceland; Hawai, California/USA; Chile; Peru. **Similar to:** alunite.

Epsonite   bitter salt

$Mg[SO_4] \cdot 7\ H_2O$

⑤ California/USA

Streak white. **Mohs' hardness** 2–2½. **Specific gravity** 1.68. **Characteristics:** white, sometimes greenish, reddish, yellowish. Lustre: transparent to translucent. Cleavage: complete. Fracture: conchoidal, brittle; easily soluble in water. Taste: bitter–salty. Crystals: (rhombic) prismatic, acicular, filamentary, fibrous; rare. **Aggregates:** fibrous with silky lustre, radial, stalactitic, grainy, crumbly as cottony rosettes, crusty as deposits in salt springs or ore bodies; present as deposits in salt lakes and in arid steppe regions. **Accompanied by:** anhydrite, carnallite, gypsum, halite, calcite. **Found in:** Lower Saxony/Germany; Czechoslovakia; Yugoslavia; Surrey/England; Colorado/USA; Kazakhstan, Crimea/USSR. **Similar to:** Kieserite.

26

sulfur pg. 38, sepiolithe pg. 38, serpentine pg. 44, chrysocolla pg. 130

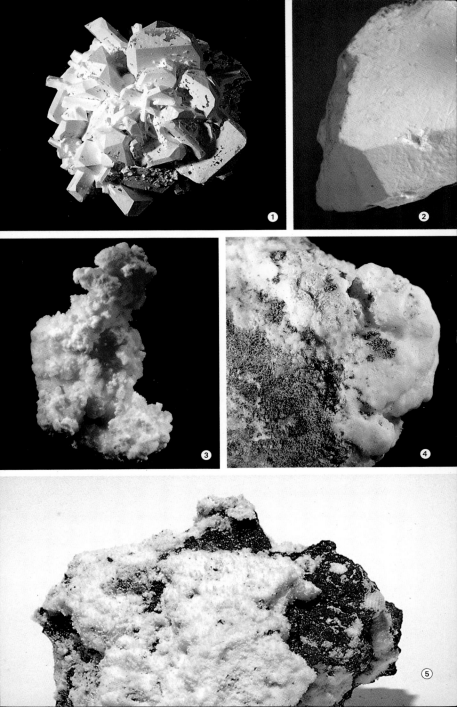

Streak

white and
colorless

Mohs'
hardness 1 ◄

2 ◄

3 ◄

4 ◄

5 ◄

6 ◄

7 ◄

8 ◄

9 ◄

10 ◄

Specific
gravity 1 ◄

2 ◄

3 ◄

4 ◄

5 ◄

6 ◄

7 ◄

Ozokerite   earth wax   ① Pribram/Czechoslovakia 1:3
Mixture of hydrocarbons

Streak white, also brown. **Mohs' hardness** 2–2½. **Specific gravity** 1.6. **Characteristics:** yellow to greenish, brown to black. Lustre: greasy, opaque. Cleavage: none. Fracture: shallow conchoidal to hook-shaped. Malleable to brittle. Odor: waxy. Melting point: between 50–100°C. Crystals: none, amorphous. **Aggregates:** rough, fibrous, tabular, botryoidal; present as impregnations or in the poor space of sandstone and slate. **Found in:** Galizia/Poland, Romania; Trinidad; Venezuela.

Mellite   honey stone   ② Thuringia 1:2
$Al_2[C_{12}O_{12}] \cdot 18\ H_2O$

Streak white. **Mohs' hardness** 2–2½. **Specific gravity** 1.6 **Characteristics:** honey to wax-yellow, brown to reddish, seldom white. Lustre: vitreous; greasy; translucent. Cleavage: incomplete. Fracture: conchoidal, somewhat brittle. Blue fluorescence under ultraviolet light; soluble in nitric acid and potassium hydroxide. Crystals: (tetragonal) dipyramidal, small, often convex, rough faces; isolated intergrowth and surficial crystals; rare. **Aggregates:** rough, small, fine-grained or nodular; present in crevices and cavities in lignite and anthracite, sometimes in sandstone. **Accompanied by:** ordinary coal. **Found in:** Thuringia, Saxony/Germany; Czechoslovakia; Seine/France, Tula/USSR. **Similar to:** amber.

Kernite   ③ Kern Co., California/USA
$Na_2[B_4O_6(OH)_2] \cdot 3\ H_2O$

Streak white. **Mohs' hardness** 2½–3. **Specific gravity** 1.9. **Characteristics:** when fresh colorless and transparent, but usually white and opaque. Lustre: vitreous, on cleavage surface silky to mother-of-pearl. Fracture: dendritic, splintery, brittle. Flame test: yellow. Crystals: (monoclinic) prismatic, pyramidal, wedge-shaped, tabular mass; rare. **Aggregates:** rough, coarsely spar-like with fibrous structure; present in tabular or irregular masses, in borate deposits. **Accompanied by:** borax, colemanite, ulexite. **Found in:** California, Argentina, Turkey, Catalonia/Spain. **Similar to:** borax, sassoline.

Sylvite   ④ with yellowish halite;
KCl   Kern Co., California/USA

Streak white. **Mohs' hardness** 1½–2. **Specific gravity** 1.9–2.0. **Characteristics:** colorless, grey, white, yellowish to reddish, seldom blue or violet. Lustre: greasy–vitreous; transparent, also often cloudy. Cleavage: complete. Fracture: uneven, brittle. Taste: bitter, pungent, salty. Flame test: violet. Easily water-soluble; when contaminated hygroscopic; good heat conductor. Crystals: (cubic) cubic, octahedral in geodes and crevices. **Aggregates:** granular, rough, dense, seldom dendritic; found in potassium hydroxide salt deposits, with halite to form rock (sylvinite), on crevices in halite and anhydrite rocks; rarely found associated with volcanic vents or as deposits in deserts and steppe regions. **Accompanied by:** halite, gypsum and anhydrite, carnallite, polyhalite, kieserite, kainite. **Found in:** Lower Saxony, Baden, eastern Harz mountains/Germany; Galicia/Poland; Urals/USSR; Alsace-Lorraine/France; Vesuvius Etna/Italy; Saskatchewan/Canada; New Mexico; Texas/USA; Chile; Peru; India. **Similar to:** halite, anhydrite.

28

Streak

white and
colorless

Mohs'
hardness 1 ◀

2 ◀

3 ◀

4 ◀

5 ◀

6 ◀

7 ◀

8 ◀

9 ◀

10 ◀

Specific
gravity 1 ◀

2 ◀

3 ◀

4 ◀

5 ◀

6 ◀

7 ◀

Carnallite
$KMgCl_3 \cdot 6\ H_2O$

① Hattorf, Philippsthal, Hesse/Germany
② Röbling, Halle/Germany 1:½

Streak white. **Mohs' hardness** 1–2. **Specific gravity** 1.6. **Characteristics:** yellow to white, reddish, seldom white, colorless or blue. Lustre: greasy–vitreous, usually with a metallic sheen, turning dull soon after exposure to air; translucent to transparent. Cleavage: none. Fracture: conchoidal, brittle; highly hygroscopic; dissolves easily in water (with a crackling sound). Generally highly fluorescent. Taste: biting, bitter; Crystals: (rhombic) pseudohexagonal, barrel-shaped, tabular mass, scattered, or in pore space; rare. **Aggregates:** rough, grainy, sometimes fibrous; present in rock-forming carnallite as important source of potassium in potash mines; as concretions and as recent deposits in salt lakes; **Accompanied by:** anhydrite, halite, kainite, kieserite, sylvite, boracite, polyhalite. **Found in:** Lower Saxony, Hesse, near the towns of Magdeburg, Halle, Erfurt/Germany; Galicia and Catalonia/Spain; Urals/USSR; Iran; Libya; Saskatchewan/Canada; New Mexico, Texas, Utah/USA.

Aluminite
$Al_2[(OH)_4|SO_4] \cdot 7\ H_2O$

③ More, Halle/Germany 1:2

Streak white. **Mohs' hardness** 1–2. **Specific gravity** 1.6. **Characteristics:** white to yellow, grey. Lustre: dull; transparent to opaque. Cleavage: indiscernible. Fracture of aggregate crumbly, soft, easy to crush; soluble in acid. Crystals: (rhombic or mono-clinic) indiscernible. **Aggregates:** botryoidal, reniform, tuberous, crumbly, minutely flaky, occasionally spherolitic; present in layered clay, sand, and gypsum deposits, and in coal ore. **Found in:** Saxony/Germany; Bohemia/Czechoslovakia; Sussex/England; vicinity of Paris/France; Punjab/Pakistan; Colorado, Missouri, Utah/USA. **Similar to:** alunite.

Natrite   soda
$Na_2CO_3 \cdot 10\ H_2O$

④ Kazakhstan/USSR; 1:½

Streak white. **Mohs' hardness** 1–1½. **Specific gravity** 1.42–1.47. **Characteristics:** colorless, grey-white, yellowish. Lustre: vitreous, dull; transparent to translucent. Cleavage: complete. Fracture: conchoidal, crumbly. Flame test: yellow; melts at 32°C. Easily soluble in water. Crystals: (monoclinic) large crystals unknown in nature. **Aggregates:** granular, dendritic, acicular, as a crust and dusting; present in salt lake deposits, deposits covering the soil in arid regions, and volcanic vent deposits. **Found in:** region around Vesuvius Etna/Italy; Hungary; Armenia; Kazakhstan/USSR; Egypt; Tanzania; Gobi desert/Mongolia; Tibet/China; California, Nevada/USA. **Similar to:** borax, colemanite.

Struvite
$(NH_4)Mg[PO_4] \cdot 6\ H_2O$

⑤ Hamburg/Germany

Streak white. **Mohs' hardness** 1½–2. **Specific gravity** 1.7. **Characteristics:** color: yellow or brownish, seldom colorless, white after dehydration. Lustre: vitreous, after dehydration dull; transparent to translucent. Cleavage: complete. Fracture: uneven, moderate; piezo-, and pyroelectric. Crystals: (rhombic) short prismatic, wedge-shaped, also in a tabular mass. **Aggregates:** present in recent sediments with a high proportion of organic matter, also in guano, cesspits, and ditches. **Found in:** Hamburg/Germany; Limfjord/Denmark; Victoria/Australia; Papland/South Africa; Ré-union island/Indian Ocean.

Amber   succinite   ① Palmnicken/Poland 1:2
Approximately $C_{10}H_{16}O$

Streak white. **Mohs' hardness** 2–2½. **Specific gravity** 1.05–1.30. **Characteristics:** light yellow to brown, also red to almost colorless, green, blue, and black, occasionally cloudy or streaky. Lustre: greasy, resinous; transparent to translucent, usually cloudy. Cleavage: none. Fracture: conchoidal, brittle; becomes electrically charged when rubbed, attracting small particles. Can be ignited by a match, giving off a resinous smell; floats on the surface of a saline solution. Crystals: none, amorphous; amber is the fossilized, hardened resin of the pine tree, *Pinus succinifera*, formed in the Eocene period about 50 million years ago. **Aggregates:** tuberous, stalactitic, layered; often containing inclusions of insects and parts of plants; present in so-called blue earth amber-bearing clay and coastal deposits. **Found in:** Samland/Poland; Atlantic coast/USA, Dominican Republic. **Similar to:** resins, synthetics, yellow glass, ambriod, mellite.

Gaylussite   ② Amboseli-Sea/Kenya 1:2
$CaNa_2[CO_3]_2 \cdot 5\ H_2O$

Streak white. **Mohs' hardness** 2½–3. **Specific gravity** 1.99 **Characteristics:** white, colorless, grey, yellowish. Lustre: dull–vitreous; transparent to translucent. Cleavage: complete. Fracture: conchoidal, brittle; easily soluble in water. Crystals: (monoclinic) flat, elongated wedge-shaped, octohedral, faces usually rough. **Aggregates:** rough, grainy, dispersed; present in salt lakes, desert sands, or in saline-rich soil (such as marshlands). **Found in:** California, Wyoming, Nevada/USA; Venezuela; Gobi desert/Mongolia; Madrid/Spain.

Halotrichite   ③ Colorado/USA
$FeAl[SO_4]_4 \cdot 22\ H_2O$

Streak white. **Mohs' hardness** 1½. **Specific gravity** 1.73–1.79. **Characteristics:** white, colorless, greyish, yellowish. Lustre: vitreous to silky; translucent. Cleavage: none. Fracture: fibrous, brittle; easily water soluble. Taste: pungent. Crystal: (monoclinic) acicular and fibrous. **Aggregates:** rough, grainy, dispersed; present in brown coal, ore mines, and slate containing pyrite; byproduct in fumeroles. **Found in:** Rhineland/Germany; Czechoslovakia; Campania/Italy; Urals/USSR; Iran; Chile; California, New Mexico/USA.

Ulexite   ④ Boron, California/USA
$NaCa[B_5O_6(OH)_6] \cdot 5\ H_2O$ ⑤ Ihn, Hemmersdorf, Saarland/Germany

Streak white. **Mohs' hardness** 1–2½. **Specific gravity** 1.96. **Characteristics:** crystals colorless with vitreous lustre, white fibrous aggregates with silky sheen, otherwise dull; transparent to translucent. Cleavage: complete. Fracture: fibrous, soft; water soluble. Flame test: yellow. Crystals: (triclinic) acicular, scaly, short prismatic; very rare and very small. **Aggregates:** cottony fibrous; small aggregates with parallel fibrous structure have light conducting abilities, so called television stone; present in terraced salt deposits, rarely as deposits associated with volcanic springs. **Accompanied by:** gypsum, anhydrite, glauberite, halite, borax, trona, colemanite, calcite. **Found in:** Tuscanny/Italy; Kaps region/USSR; California, Nevada/USA; Atacama/Chile; Argentina; Peru. **Similar to:** colemanite, datolite.

32

Gypsum selenite
CaSO$_4$ · 2 H$_2$O

① Tuscanny/Italy
② Thüringia/Germany
③ Sahara/Tunisia
④ Valencia/Spain

Streak white. **Mohs' hardness** 2½. **Specific gravity** 2.03. **Characteristics:** colorless, white, multicolored. Lustre: vitreous, cleavage surfaces mother-of-pearl, fibrous aggregates display silky sheen; transparent to translucent. Cleavage: perfect. Fracture: conchoidal, fibrous, soft to brittle, malleable but not flexible; poor heat conductor; turns cloudy when heated; sometimes fluorescent and phosphorescent under ultraviolet light. Crystals: (monoclinic) prismatic, tabular, lenticular; occurring intergrown and as surficial growth; frequent twinning and pseudomorphs. **Aggregates:** rough, granular, parallel fibrous (fibrous gypsum), scaly, dense (alabaster); rosette-shaped (desert-, gypsum-, or sandrose), with strong snake-like layers, often contaminated with bitumen (stink gypsum), rock-forming, leaf-layered, transparent shapes are called "lady's ice" or "Mary's glass"; present in salt lakes, salt and iron ore mines, as concretions in clay-rich rock formations, deposits in deserts, and old ore mines. **Accompanied by:** anhydrite, halite, aragonite, dolomite, boracite. **Found in:** Harz mountains, Thüringia/Germany; Tyrol/Austria; Alsace, region around Paris/France; Tunisia; Morocco; Usbekistan, western Ural region/USSR, Utha, New Mexico/USA; Chile. **Similar to:** anhydrite, gypsum, calcite, marble, talc, muscovite, brucite, glauberite, celestite.

Artinite
Mg$_2$[(OH)$_2$ | CO$_3$] · 3 H$_2$O

⑤ San Bernito Co., California/USA

Streak white. **Mohs' hardness** 2½. **Specific gravity** 2.03. **Characteristics:** white, greyish, seldom colorless. Lustre: crystals are vitreous, fibrous aggregates silky; transparent. Cleavage: complete. Fracture: fibrous, brittle; soluble in cold hydrochloric acid (foaming). Crystals: (monoclinic) acicular to thin tabular; always surficial growth. **Aggregates:** small fibrous, radial tufts, also crusty, and in thin-fibrous masses; present on crevices in serpentinite and serpentinized peridotite. **Accompanied by:** hydromagnesite, actinolite, aragonite, brucite, dolomite, natrolite, serpentine. **Found in:** Steiermark/Austria; Lombardy/Italy; California, Nevada, Pennsylvania/USA; Urals/USSR. **Similar to:** hydromagnesite, actinolite, aragonite, natrolite.

Brucite
Mg(OH)$_2$

⑥ Pennsylvania/USA

Streak white. **Mohs' hardness** 2½. **Specific gravity** 2.03. **Characteristics:** white, grey, greenish, bluish, yellow to brown. Lustre: vitreous, on cleavage surfaces mother-of-pearl; transparent to translucent. Cleavage: perfect. Fracture: flaky, soft, malleable; greasy to the touch; easily soluble in acid. Crystals: (trigonal) tabular, pointed prismatic; rare. **Aggregates:** rough, bladed, scaly, small fibrous, granular; present in zones of serpentinization, marble, cloritic and dolomitic slate. **Accompanied by:** hydromagnesite, aragonite, calcite, chlorite, dolomite, magnesite, periclase, serpentine, talc. **Found in:** Steiermark/Austria; Trient/Italy; Sweden; Quebec/Canada; California, Nevada, Pennsylvania/USA; Urals/USSR. **Similar to:** alunite, chlorite, gibbsite, gypsum, pyrophilite, talc, muscovite.

34 pharmacolite pg. 42, serpentine pg. 44, gibbsite pg. 58

Streak

white and
colorless

Mohs'
hardness 1 ◄

—

2 ◄

3 ◄

4 ◄

5 ◄

6 ◄

7 ◄

—

8 ◄

9 ◄

10 ◄

Specific
gravity 1 ◄

—

2 ◄

3 ◄

4 ◄

—

5 ◄

6 ◄

7 ◄

Halite
NaCl

① Heringen, Hesse/Germany 1:2

Streak white. **Mohs' hardness** 2. **Specific gravity** 2.1–2.2. **Characteristics:** colorless to white, reddish, yellow, blue, grey to black. Lustre: vitreous to opaque. Cleavage: complete. Fracture: conchoidal, somewhat brittle; good heat conductor. Flame test: yellow. Taste: salty; easily soluble in water, hygroscopic when contaminated. Crystals: (cubic) cubes, rarely octahedral; usually surficial growth. **Aggregates:** rough, granular, fibrous, dense, crusty; present in drusy cavities, as surficial growth, by-product of volcanic sublimation; rock-forming (rock salt); **Accompanied by:** anhydrite, sylvenite, carnallite, kainite, kieserite, gypsum. **Found in:** Lower Saxony, Magdeburg/Germany; Salzkammergut/Austria; Alsace/France; Caspian Sea; Turkey; Iran; Utah, California, southern states/USA. **Similar to:** sylvenite, carnellite, fluorite, boracite.

Trona
Na₃H[CO₃]₂·2 H₂O

② California/USA 1:2

Streak white. **Mohs' hardness** 2½–3. **Specific gravity** 2.1–2.2. **Characteristics:** colorless, white, greyish, yellow, brownish. Lustre: vitreous to silky, dull; transparent to translucent. Cleavage: perfect. Fracture: conchoidal to uneven, brittle; soluble in hydrochloric acid. Crystals: (monoclinic) tabular, prismatic. **Aggregates:** granular, dendritic crusts; developing on surfaces, also in layers; present in salt lakes, on desert surfaces, in lava pockets. **Accompanied by:** borax, soda, hanksite, thenardite, glauberite. **Found in:** Egypt; Libya; Kenya; Wyoming, California/USA; Venezuela; Iran; Tibet/China; Manchuria. **Similar to:** borax.

Kainite
KMg[Cl I SO₄]·3 H₂O

② Buggingen, Feiburg im Breisgau/
Germany   1 : ½

Streak white. **Mohs' hardness** 2½–3. **Specific gravity** 2.1–2.2. **Characteristics:** colorless to white, red, yellowish, grey, blue. Lustre: translucent. Cleavage: complete. Fracture: splintery, brittle; easily soluble in water. Flame test: orange–yellow. Taste: bitter–salty. Crystals: (monoclinic) thick tabular, pyramid-shaped; rare. **Aggregates:** rough, fine- or sugar-grained, dense, fibrous; rock-forming with hailite (kainitite); present in slate quarries. **Accompanied by:** sylvenite, halite, carnallite, kieserite, polyhalite, anhydrite. **Found in:** Lower Saxony, Hesse, Magdedurg/Germany; Galicia/Poland; Ukraine/USSR; New Mexico, Texas/USA. **Similar to:** carnallite, kieserite.

Palygorskite
(Mg,Al)₂[OH I Si₄O₁₀]·2 H₂O + 2 H₂O

④ Hüttenberg, Carinthia/Austria

Streak white. **Mohs' hardness** 2–2½. **Specific gravity** 2.1–2.3. **Characteristics:** white, grey, yellowish, brownish. Lustre: vitreous, silky, dull; translucent to opaque. Cleavage and fracture: indeterminable; maleable in thin layers, highly porous. Crystals: (monoclinic or rhombic) microscopically small. **Aggregates:** finely fibrous, fine-grained, felt-like (so-called mountain leather, mountain cork, and mountain wood is matted polygorskite, chrysotile, or actinolite); present in tailings of weathered serpentinite or granitic rocks. **Accompanied by:** calcite, baryte, chalcedony, opal, chlorite, magnesite. **Found in:** Wallis/Switzerland; Czechoslovakia; Shetland Island/Scotland; Ukraine/USSR; Morocco; Georgia/USA. **Similar to:** sepiolite, chrysotile.

36 chrysocolla pg. 130, chalcanthite pg. 206

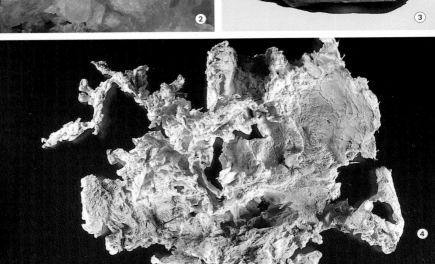

Streak

white and
colorless

Mohs'
hardness 1 ◄
             –
          2 ◄

          3 ◄

          4 ◄
             –
          5 ◄
             –
          6 ◄
             –
          7 ◄
             –
          8 ◄
             –
          9 ◄

         10 ◄

Specific
gravity 1 ◄

          2 ◄

          3 ◄
             –
          4 ◄
             –
          5 ◄
             –
          6 ◄
             –
          7 ◄

Sulphur
S

① with calcite, Sicily/Italy

Streak white. **Mohs' hardness** 2. **Specific gravity** 2.0–2.1. **Characteristics**: white, yellow, brownish black. Lustre: adamantine. Fracture: resinous to greasy; translucent. Cleavage: incomplete. Fracture: conchoidal to uneven, very brittle. Extensive double-refraction; negatively charged when rubbed. Flame of a match: will melt sulphur when held into flame. Body temperature: (holding sulphur in the palm of the hand) will cause mineral to shatter; soluble in carbon disulphide. Crystals: (rhombic) dipyramidal, tabular; surficial growth. **Aggregates**: rough, grainy, fibrous, crumbly, powdery, dense, stalactitic, as surficial growth and impregnation; present in association with volcanic vents, thermal springs, salt mines, ore as well as coal mines. **Accompanied by**: calcite, gypsum, anhydrite, celestite, aragonite, halite. **Found in**: Liparian Islands, Sicily/Italy; Japan; Indonesia; Don River region, middle Asia/USSR; Texas, Louisiana/USA; Mexico. **Similar to**: realgar, sphalerite, wulfenite, orpiment, uranophane.

Whewellite
Ca[C₂O₄]·H₂O

② Burgk, Dresden/Germany

Streak white. **Mohs' hardness** 1½–3. **Specific gravity** 2.2. **Characteristics**: colorless, white, yellowish. Lustre: vitreous to mother-of-pearl; transparent to translucent. Cleavage: complete. Fracture: conchoidal; easily soluble in acid. Crystals: (monoclinic) columnar, tabular, large well-developed faces; often with twinning. **Aggregates**: star-shaped; present in rock formations near coal, and oil deposits, in ore mines. **Accompanied by**: barite, calcite, siderite, ankerite, pyrite, marcasite, magnatite. **Found in**: Saxony/Germany; Bohemia/Czechoslovakia; Alsace/France; Tuscany, Sardinia/Italy; Rumania, Kuban and Transbaikal region/USSR; Utah, Ohio/USA. **Similar to**: barite.

Nitratite   Chile salt peter

③ Chile 1:10

NaNO₃

Streak white. **Mohs' hardness** 1½–2. **Specific gravity** 2.2–2.3. **Characteristics**: colorless, white, also grey, yellow, brownish, reddish. Lustre: vitreous to dull; transparent. Cleavage: complete. Fracture: conchoidal, brittle. Taste: bitter–salty, cooling. Flame test: yellow. Easily soluble in water, somewhat hygroscopic. Crystal: (trigonal) rhombohedral; very rare; often twinning. **Aggregates**: rough, fine-grained; present in Chile where mineral deposits are well-developed, otherwise occurs as crusts and other surficial deposits. **Accompanied by**: halite, glauberite, epsomite, gypsum, anhydrite. **Found in**: Chile, Bolivia; Peru; Egypt; India; trans-Caspian region/USSR; California/USA. **Similar to**: calcite.

Sepiolite   meerschaum

④ Eskishehir/Turkey

Mg₄[(OH)₂ | Si₆O₁₅]·2 H₂O + 4 H₂O

Streak white. **Mohs' hardness** 2–2½. **Specific gravity** 2.0–2.3. **Characteristics**: white, grey, yellowish, blue-green, reddish. Lustre: dull, opaque. Cleavage: indeterminable. Fracture: conchoidal, moderate. When wet: soft; when dry: hard. Feels like soap; sticks to tongue. Floats on water; soluble in acid. Crystals: (rhombic) microscopically small. **Aggregates**: rough, tuberous, small-particled; present as concretions in serpentinite. **Accompanied by**: magnesite, chlorite, chalcedony, opal. **Found in**: Anatolia/Turkey, Samos island/Greece; Madrid/Spain; Morocco; Tanzania; Kenya; Crimea/USSR; Texas, New Mexico/USA. **Similar to**: palygorskite.

38

Streak

white and
colorless

Mohs'
hardness 1 ◄

2 ◄

3 ◄

4 ◄

5 ◄

6 ◄

7 ◄

8 ◄

9 ◄

10 ◄

Specific
gravity 1 ◄

2 ◄

3 ◄

4 ◄

5 ◄

6 ◄

7 ◄

Paragonite
NaAl₂[(OH,F)₂ | AlSi₃O₁₀]

① with blue kyanite 1:2

Streak white. **Mohs' hardness** 2–2½. **Specific gravity** 2.8–2.9. **Characteristics:** white, light grey, also colorless. Lustre: mother-of-pearl; transparent to translucent. Cleavage: perfect. Fracture: flaky, elastic. Crystals: (monoclinic) unknown. **Aggregates:** finely scaled to dense; small blades scattered throughout; present in schist, gneiss, common quartz deposits, fine-grained sediments; slates. **Accompanied by:** staurolite, kyanite, actinolite, muscovite, biotite, quartz, tremolite. **Found in:** Tessin/Switzerland; Tyrol/Austria; Piemonte/Italy; Urals/USSR; Colorado, Virginia/USA. **Similar to:** sericite.

Zinnwaldite
KLiFeAl[(F,OH)₂ | AlSi₃O₁₀]

② Zinnwald, Erzgebirge/Germany

Streak white. **Mohs' hardness** 2–3. **Specific gravity** 2.9–3.2. **Characteristics:** yellowish to brown, grey, also violet, green, black. Lustre: vitreous, on cleavage surface mother-of-pearl; transparent to opaque. Cleavage: perfect. Fracture: flaky, elastic; soluble in acid. Flame test: red. Crystals: (monoclinic) flat, hexagonal surfaces; rare. **Aggregates:** scaly, foliated; present in granite pegmatite, granite, greisen, zinc-ore deposits. **Accompanied by:** scheelite, wolframite, topaz, fluorite, quartz. **Found in:** Bavarian Forest, Saxony/Germany; Bohemia/Czechoslovakia; Cornwall/England; Virginia/USA. **Similar to:** lepidolite.

Lepidolite
KLi₂Al[(F,OH)₂ | Si₄O₁₀]

③ Minas Gerais/Brazil

Streak white. **Mohs' hardness** 2–3. **Specific gravity** 2.8–2.9. **Characteristics:** pink to soft-violet, seldom white, grey, yellow, greenish. Lustre: vitreous, on cleavage surface mother-of-pearl; transparent to translucent. Cleavage: perfect. Fracture: flaky, elastic. Flame test: carmine red. Crystals: (monoclinic) foliated tabular, hexagonal surfaces; rare. **Aggregates:** scaly, foliated, fine-grained, tabular; present in granite pegmatite, granite, geodes in distintegrated weathered granite, zinc ore deposits. **Accompanied by:** tourmaline, topaz, spodumene, amblygonite, feldspar, quartz, muscovite, beryl, kassiterite, fluorite. **Found in:** Saxony; Mahren/Czechoslovakia; Elba/Italy; Sweden; Urals/USSR; California, Maine/USA; Quebec/Canada; Madagascar; Namibia. **Similar to:** zinnwaldite, muscovite.

Phlogopite
KMg₃[(F,OH)₂ | AlSi₃O₁₀]

④ Templeton, Ontario/Canada

Streak white. **Mohs' hardness** 2–2½. **Specific gravity** 2.75–2.97. **Characteristics:** reddish brown to brownish red, yellowish, green, also grey, white, colorless. Lustre: vitreous, on cleavage surfaces mother-of-pearl; transparent to translucent. Cleavage: perfect. Fracture: flaky, elastic; often asterismic; soluble in sulphuric acid. Crystals: (monoclinic) tabular, with six-sided surfaces, seldom prismatic. **Aggregates:** foliated, scaly, rough; present in ultrabasic magmatite, pegmatite, marble. **Accompanied by:** diopside, scapolite, apatite, feldspar, garnet, wollastonite, forsterite, spinel, graphite, calcite. **Found in:** Tessin/Switzerland; Sweden; Finland; Italy; Baikal region/USSR; Ontario/Canada; California, Colorado/USA; Madagascar; South Africa. **Similar to:** biotite, diaspore, astrophyllite.

40

biotite pg. 46, muscovite pg. 46, kämmererite pg. 64, vivianite pg. 206

Streak

white and
colorless

Mohs'
hardness 1◀

2◀

3◀
_

4◀
_

5◀
_

6◀
_

7◀

8◀
_

9◀

10◀

Specific
gravity 1◀

_

2◀

_

3◀

4◀

_

5◀

_

6◀

7◀

Glauberite
CaNa₂[SO₄]₂

① Boron, California/USA

Streak white. **Mohs' hardness** 2½–3. **Specific gravity** 2.7–2.8. **Characteristics**: grey, colorless, yellowish, red. Lustre: vitreous to greasy, on cleavage surfaces mother-of-pearl; translucent to transparent. Cleavage: complete. Fracture: conchoidal, brittle. Flame test: yellow. Exposed to air: powdery; soluble in water and hydrochloric acid. Taste: bitter–salty. Crystals: (monoclinic) tabular, prismatic, dipyramidal. **Aggregates**: granular, dense, crumbly, bladed, crusty, layered; present in and associated with salt beds, nitrate deposits, cavities associated with dormant volcanoes, fumeroles. **Accompanied by**: halite, gypsum, anhydrite, silvenite, polyhalite, thenardite, sassoline, sodium nitrate. **Found in**: Lower Saxony, Magdeburg/Germany; Salzburg/Austria; Lothringen/France; Liparian Islands/Italy; India; Ukraine/USSR; California, Arizona/USA. **Similar to**: gypsum, thenardite.

Pharmacolite
CaH[AsO₄]·2 H₂O

② Richelsdorf, Hesse/Germany

Streak white. **Mohs' hardness** 2–2½. **Specific gravity** 2.5–2.7. **Characteristics**: white, grey, colorless, greenish, reddish. Lustre: silky; transparent to translucent. Cleavage: complete. Fracture: uneven. Crystals: (monoclinic) acicular. **Aggregates**: radial, botryoidal, as surficial growth or dusting; present in arsenic ore deposits. **Accompanied by**: erythrite, skutterudite, nickeline, chloantite, annabergite. **Found in**: Black Forest, Harz mountains/Germany; Bohemia/Czechoslovakia; Alsace/France; California, Nevada/USA. **Similar to**: arsenolite.

Talc
Mg₃[(OH)₂|Si₄O₁₀]

③ Futu Pass, Florence/Italy

Streak white. **Mohs' hardness** 1. **Specific gravity** 2.7–2.8. **Characteristics**: green, yellow, brownish, white, colorless. Lustre: mother-of-pearl, greasy; translucent to transparent. Cleavage: perfect. Fracture: uneven, inelastic malleable, poor heat conductor; greasy to the touch. Crystals: (monoclinic) very small, pseudohexagonal or rhombic, pseudomorphic. **Aggregates**: scaly–foliated, conchoidal, dense (steatite); present in limestone or dolomite, metamorphic rocks. **Accompanied by**: magnesite, serpentine, dolomite, chlorite, apatite, magnetite, pyrite, quartz. **Found in**: Fichtel mountains, Saxony/Germany; Piemonte/Italy; Transvaal/South Africa; Madras/India; California, Arizona/USA. **Similar to**: pyrophylite, brucite, muskovite, biotite, gypsum, chlorite, serpentine.

Cyrolite
Na₃[AlF₆]

④ with galena; Ivigtut/Greenland
⑤ Ivigtut/Greenland

Streak white. **Mohs' hardness** 2½–3. **Specific gravity** 2.95. **Characteristics**: white, colorless, brownish, reddish, grey to black. Lustre: vitreous; transparent. Cleavage: none. Fracture: uneven. Flame test: reddish-yellow. Easily soluble in sulfuric acid. Crystals: (monoclinic) cubic, short-columned; usually with twinning. **Aggregates**: rough, with flat, parquet-like crystals, spar-like, coarse-grained to dense; present in pegmatite, associated with granite. **Accompanied by**: siderite, quartz, fluorite, barite, galena, topaz, zircon, pyrite, sphalerite, chalcocite, kassiterite, wolframite, columbite. **Found in**: west Greenland; Colorado/USA; Urals/USSR; Nigeria. **Similar to**: fluorite, barite, topaz, anhydrite.

Streak

white and
colorless

**Mohs'
hardness** 1 ◀

2 ◀

3 ◀

4 ◀
–
5 ◀
–
6 ◀
–
7 ◀
–
8 ◀
–
9 ◀

10 ◀

**Specific
gravity** 1 ◀

2 ◀

3 ◀
–
4 ◀
–
5 ◀
–
6 ◀

7 ◀

Serpentine
$Mg_6[(OH)_8 | Si_4O_{10}]$

① Chrysotile; Quebec/Canada
② Antigorite; Norway

Streak white. **Mohs' hardness** 2½–4. **Specific gravity** 2.0–2.6. **Characteristics:** green, grey to black, white, brownish. Lustre: greasy to silky, dull; transparent to opaque. Cleavage: complete. Fracture: conchoidal, splintery, moderate, fibrous pieces inelastic, malleable; soluble in hydrochloric and sulfuric acid. Crystals: (monoclinic) unknown; fibrous serpentine (chrysotile); foliated serpentine (antigorite); dense and very finely fibrous (asbestos); pseudomorphic. **Aggregates:** fine-grained, dense, foliated, fibrous, crusty. So-called mountain leather (mountain wood, mountain cork) is often felted chrysotile; present in layers within slate limestone and marble; serpentinite. **Accompanied by:** chlorite, olivine, chromite, magnetite, dolomite, talc, quartz, opal. **Found in:** Fichtel mountains, Thüringen, Saxony/Germany; Tirol/Austria; Urals/USSR; Quebec/Canada; South Africa; Zimbabwe. **Similar to:** palygorskite, chlorite, talc, tremolite, actinolite, garnierite.

Annabergite
$Ni_3[AsO_4]_2 \cdot 8\, H_2O$

③ Laurio/Greece 1:10

Streak white. **Mohs' hardness** 2. **Specific gravity** 3.0–3.1. **Characteristics:** green, white, grey. Lustre: dull; transparent to opaque. Cleavage: complete. Fracture: bladed, moderate, small blade-shaped pieces are malleable; soluble in acid. Crystals: (monoclinic) prismatic, tabular, acicular foliated; rare. **Aggregates:** rough, dense, crumbly, crusty; present in nickel deposits. **Accompanied by:** chloanthite, nickeline, erythrite, pharmacolite, proustite, siderite, barite, calcite. **Found in:** Siegerland, Hesse, Harz mountains, Saxony/Germany; Dauphiné/France; Sardinia/Italy; Spain; Ontario/Canada; Nevada/USA. **Similar to:** malachite, chrysocolla.

Thenardite
Na_2SO_4

④ California/USA

Streak white. **Mohs' hardness** 2½–3. **Specific gravity** 2.7. **Characteristics:** colorless, grey, brownish, reddish. Lustre: vitreous and resinous; transparent to translucent. Cleavage: complete. Fracture: uneven, brittle; easily soluble in water. Flame test: yellow. Taste: salty. Crystals: (rhombic) dipyramidal, tabular; often with twinning. **Aggregates:** granular, crumbly, as crust and as bloom; present in salt lakes, deserts, terrestrial salt mines, associated with volcanic vents. **Accompanied by:** glauberite, gypsum, epsom, halite, soda, sodium nitrate. **Found in:** Sicily/Italy; Kazakhstan/USSR; California, Arizona/USA; Chile; Peru. **Similar to:** glauberite.

Pyrophylite
$Al_2[(OH)_2 | Si_4O_{10}]$

⑤ Indian Gulch, California/USA

Streak white. **Mohs' hardness** 1–1½. **Specific gravity** 2.7–2.9. **Characteristics:** white, yellow, green. Lustre: mother-of-pearl, dull; translucent to opaque. Cleavage: complete. Fracture: uneven, gentle, malleable; greasy to the touch. Crystals: (monoclinic) tabular, foliated, never individually. **Aggregates:** radial, foliated, rough, dense; present in slate, quartz veins, veins of ore, cavities associated with dormant volcanoes. **Accompanied by:** quartz, kyanite, sillimanite, amblygonite, andalusite, kassiterite, mica, hematite, lazulite. **Found in:** Eifel mountains, Saxony/Germany; Switzerland; Urals/USSR; California, Georgia/USA; Brazil; South Africa. **Similar to:** talc, brucite, margarite, jadeite.

Streak

white and
colorless

Mohs'
hardness 1◄

2◄

3◄

4◄

5◄

6◄

7◄

8◄

9◄

10◄

Specific
gravity 1◄

2◄

3◄

4◄

5◄

6◄

7◄

Hydrozincite   zinc blossom   ① Yazd/Iran 1:2
$Zn_5[(OH)_3 | CO_3]_2$

Streak white. **Mohs' hardness** 2–2½. **Specific gravity** 3.2–3.8. **Characteristics:** white, grey, pink, colorless. Lustre: vitreous to silky, dull; transparent to opaque. Cleavage: complete. Fracture: crumbly, brittle; soluble in hydrochloric acid. Light-blue fluorescence under ultraviolet light. Crystals: (monoclinic) tabular, very small. **Aggregates:** rough, crumbly, dense, botryoidal, crusty; stalactitic, as dusting on crusts; present in oxidized zones in zinc mines. **Accompanied by:** mica, smithsonite, hemimorphite, wulfenite. **Found in:** Black Forest, Westfalia/Germany; Kärnten/Austria; Santander/Spain; Nevada/USA; West Australia. **Similar to:** smithsonite.

Biotite   ② Miask, Urals/USSR
$K(Mg,Fe)_3 [(OH,F)_2 | AlSi_3O_{10}]$

Streak white. **Mohs' hardness** 2½–3. **Specific gravity** 2.7–3.3. **Characteristics:** black, dark brown, bronze-colored. Lustre: vitreous, on cleavage surface mother-of-pearl; translucent to opaque. Cleavage: perfect, with hexagonal contour. Fracture: foliated, elastic malleable. Strong pleochroism; easily soluble in sulfuric acid. Crystals: (monoclinic) tabular, foliated, and columnar; intergrown and surficial growth. **Aggregates:** bladed, foliated; present particularly in granitic rocks, pegmatite, gneiss, mica slate. **Accompanied by:** muscovite, amphibole (hornblende), quartz, feldspars. **Found in:** Alps/Austria; Vesuvius/Italy; Scandinavia; Scotland; Urals/USSR; California, Idaho/USA. **Similar to:** phlogopite, muscovite, chlorite, gold.

Arsenolite   ③ St. Andreasberg, Harz mountains,
As_2O_3 Lower Saxony/Germany 1:10

Streak white. **Mohs' hardness** 1½. **Specific gravity** 3.88. **Characteristics:** white, colorless, yellowish, bluish. Lustre: vitreous; transparent to opaque. Cleavage: complete. Fracture: conchoidal; soluble in warm water and hydrochloric acid; very poisonous. Crystals: (cubic) octohedral, very small. **Aggregates:** powdery, radial-fibrous, as crust; present in deposits of arsenic minerals, ore veins. **Accompanied by:** arsenopyrite, skutterudite. **Found in:** Black Florest, Saxony/Germany; Bohemia/Czechoslovakia; Alsace/France; California, Nevada/USA. **Similar to:** pharmacolite.

Muscovite   ④ Urals/USSR 1:2
$KAl_2[(OH,F)_2 | AlSi_3O_{10}]$

Streak white. **Mohs' hardness** 2–3. **Specific gravity** 2.7–3.88. **Characteristics:** colorless, yellowish, greenish (fuchsite), silvery. Lustre: vitreous, on cleavage surfaces mother-of pearl; transparent to translucent. Cleavage: perfect. Fracture: foliated, elastic malleable. Crystals: (monoclinic) tabular with hexagonal contours, individual pyramidal; intergrown and surficial growth. **Aggregates:** foliated (sericite), dense; present in pegmatites, rock-forming particularly in granite, phyllite, mica slate, gneiss, sandstone. **Accompanied by:** biotite, lepidolite, feldspar, quartz, topaz, wolf-ramite, kassiterite. **Found in:** Taunus mountains/Germany; Tirol/Austria; Tessin/Switzerland; South Tyrol/Italy; Urals, middle Siberia/USSR; Bihar/India; Transvaal/South Africa; Ontario/Canada; New Hampshire, South Dakota/USA. **Similar to:** biolite, phogopite, paragonite, lepidolite, margarite, chlorite, brucite, gypsum.

---

46   zinnwaldite pg. 40, annabergite pg. 44, kammererite pg. 64, autunite pg. 188, aurichalcite pg. 208

Streak
white and colorless

Mohs' hardness	
	1 ◄
	2 ◄
	3 ◄
	4 ◄
	5 ◄
	6 ◄
	7 ◄
	8 ◄
	9 ◄
	10 ◄

Specific gravity	
	1 ◄
	2 ◄
	3 ◄
	4 ◄
	5 ◄
	6 ◄
⇓	7 ◄

Stolzite
PbWO$_4$

① New South Wales/Australia 1:6
② New South Wales/Australia 1:2

Streak white. **Mohs' hardness** 2½–3. **Specific gravity** 7.9–8.2. **Characteristics:** reddish, grey, yellow, brown, green. Lustre: greasy to resinous; transparent. Cleavage: incomplete. Fracture: conchoidal, brittle. Crystals: (tetragonal) dipyramidal, massive tabular, short columnar; intergrown and surficial growth. **Aggregates:** rough, spherical, conical; present in oxidized zones of wolframite deposits. **Accompanied by:** scheelite, quartz, fluorite. **Found in:** Saxony/Germany; Bohemia/Czechoslovakia; Piemonte/Italy; England; Nigeria; Arizona, Utah/USA; New South Wales/Australia. **Similar to:** scheelite, wulfenite.

Leadhillite
Pb$_4$[(OH)$_2$|SO$_4$|(CO$_3$)$_2$]

③ Tsumeb/Namibia

Streak white. **Mohs' hardness** 2½. **Specific gravity** 6.45–6.55. **Characteristics:** colorless, white, grey, blue. Lustre: adamantine, mother-of-pearl, greasy; transparent to translucent. Cleavage: complete. Fracture: conchoidal, brittle; soluble in diluted nitric acid. Crystals: (monoclinic) pseudohexagonal, tabular, also pseudorhombohedral. **Aggregates:** rough, granular, scaly, crusted; present in oxidized zones of lead-ore deposits. **Accompanied by:** cerussite, galena, anglesite, phosgenite. **Found in:** Kärten/Austria; Sardinia/Italy; Scotland; Tunisia; Namibia; Arizona, Utah, Nevada/USA. **Similar to:** cerussite, anglesite.

Silver
Ag

④ Cobalt, Ontario/Canada 1:2
⑤ Freiberg, Saxony/Germany 1:2

Streak white. **Mohs' hardness** 2½–3. **Specific gravity** 9.6–12.0. **Characteristics:** silver-white, yellowish, brown, grey or black tarnish. Lustre: metallic, in thin layers blue transparent, otherwise opaque. Cleavage: none. Fracture: hook-shaped, very malleable, supple; soluble in nitric acid and in concentrated hydrochloric acid; good heat conductor. Crystals: (cubic) cubic, octahedral, dodecahedral, usually distorted; pseudomorphic. **Aggregates:** rough as clumps and grains; loose and wire-shaped as pure metal; moss-like, dendritic as inclusions; present in ore veins, occasionally in placers. **Accompanied by:** argenite (silver sulphide), proustite, pyrargyrite, stephanite, polybasite, siderite, chloanthite, copper, galena, cerussite, pyrite, barite, fluorite, calcite. **Found in:** Saxony, Harz mountains/Germany; Bohemia/Czechoslovakia; Norway; Ontario/Canada; Colorado/USA; Mexico; Bolivia; Peru; Chile; Altai/USSR; Australia. **Similar to:** dyscrasite, argenite, pure antimony, platinum, pure arsenic.

Senarmontite
Sb$_2$O$_3$

⑥ Djebel Hamimat/Algeria 1:2

Streak white. **Mohs' hardness** 2–2½. **Specific gravity** 5.6. **Characteristics:** colorless, white to grey. Lustre: adamantine, greasy; translucent to transparent. Cleavage: incomplete. Fracture: conchoidal, brittle; often high degree of double refraction; soluble in hydrochloric acid. Crystals: (cubic) octahedral, often with curved surfaces; rare; dimorph with valentinite. **Aggregates:** rough, granular, dense, crusty; present in oxidized zones of antimony ore deposits. **Accompanied by:** valentinite, antimonite, kermesite, boulangerite. **Found in:** Saxony/Germany; Bohemia/Czechoslovakia; Isére/France; Sardinia/Italy; Algeria; Quebec/Canada; California, South Dakota/USA. **Similar to:** boracite.

bismutite pg. 164, calomel pg. 190, aurichalcite pg. 208, caledonite pg. 208

Streak

white and
colorless

Mohs'
hardness   1 ◀
              ‒
          2 ◀
              ‒
          3 ◀
          4 ◀
              ‒
          5 ◀
              ‒
          6 ◀
              ‒
          7 ◀
              ‒
          8 ◀
              ‒
          9 ◀
         10 ◀

Specific
gravity   1 ◀
              ‒
          2 ◀
              ‒
          3 ◀
              ‒
          4 ◀
              ‒
          5 ◀
              ‒
          6 ◀

⇓   7 ◀

Valentinite
Sb$_2$O$_3$

① Pezinok, Czechoslovakia 1:10

Streak white. **Mohs' hardness** 2½–3. **Specific gravity** 5.6–5.8. **Characteristics:** colorless, white, grey, yellowish. Lustre: adamantine, on cleavage surface mother-of-pearl; transparent. Cleavage: complete. Fracture: uneven, brittle, fragile; easily soluble in acid. Crystals: (rhombic) prismatic to acicular, tabular, multifaceted; sometimes pseudomorphic; dimorph with senarmontite. **Aggregates:** rough, granular, radial, fibrous, fan-shaped as deposits; present in oxidized zones, particularly in antimony-bearing ore. **Accompanied by:** senarmontite, antimonite. **Found in:** Harz mountains, Saxony/Germany; Bohemia/Czechoslovakia; Dauphiné/France; Sardinia/Italy; Algeria; Bolivia; Quebec/Canada; California, Oregon/USA. **Similar to:** cerussite.

Chlorargyrite
AgCl

② St. Andreasberg, Harz mountains,
Lower Saxony/Germany 1:2

Streak white. **Mohs' hardness** 1½–2. **Specific gravity** 5.5–5.6. **Characteristics:** initially colorless with adamantine lustre and translucent, under light becoming grey, brownish to black with metallic, waxy lustre or dull horn-like, opaque. Cleavage: none. Fracture: hook-shaped, supple, can be cut with a knife; soluble in ammonia. Crystals: (cubic) cube-like, very small and very rare. **Aggregates:** rough, crusty, reniform, stalactitic, dendritic, parallel-fibrous; present in oxidized zones of silver-bearing ore deposits, particularly as impregnations in sandstone. **Accompanied by:** silver, argenite, cerussite, baryte, calcite. **Found in:** Saxony/Germany; Bohemia/Czechoslovakia; Nevada, Idaho/USA; Atacama/Chile; Bolivia; New South Wales/Australia; Altai/USSR. **Similar to:** calomel, pure silver.

Phosgenite
Pb$_2$[Cl$_2$ I CO$_3$]

③ Monte Poni, Sardinia/Italy 1:2

Streak white. **Mohs' hardness** 2–3. **Specific gravity** 6.0–6.3. **Characteristics:** white, grey, yellow, also colorless and greenish. Lustre: greasy, adamantine; translucent to transparent. Cleavage: complete. Fracture: conchoidal and gentle; soluble in diluted nitric acid. Sometimes yellow fluorescence under ultraviolet light. Crystals: (tetragonal) prismatic, pyramidal, tabular, often multifaceted; usually surficial deposits. **Aggregates:** rough, granular; present in oxidized zones of lead ore deposits. **Accompanied by:** cerussite, anglesite. **Found in:** Upper Silesia/Poland; Derbyshire/England; Sardinia/Italy; Greece; Namibia; Colorado, California/USA; Argentina. **Similar to:** cerussite, anglesite, barite.

Mercury
Hg

④ Almadén/Spain 1:4

Streak white. **Mohs' hardness** none. **Specific gravity** 13.6. **Characteristics:** zinc-white, often with a grey coating. Lustre: strongly metallic; opaque. Fumes very poisonous. Crystals: none. Liquid solidifies at 38.9°C to form rhombohedral crystals in the tetragonal crystal system. **Aggregates:** impregnation or single droplets on the surface of the source stone, particularly cinnabar; present in oxidized zones of mercury ore deposits; occasionally in ore veins or associated with volcanics. **Accompanied by:** cinnabar. **Found in:** Rhine Palatinate/Germany; Cuidad/Spain; Croatia, Serbia/Yugoslavia; Tuscany/Italy; Texas, California/USA; Peru.

Streak

white and
colorless

Mohs'
hardness 1

2

3

4

5

6

7

8

9

10

Specific
gravity 1

2

3

4

5

6

7

Laumontite
Ca[AlSi$_2$O$_6$]$_2$·4 H$_2$O

① Unterberg, southern Tirol/Italy 1:2

Streak white. **Mohs' hardness** 3–3½. **Specific gravity** 2.25–2.35. **Characteristics:** colorless, white, yellow, reddish. Lustre: vitreous, on cleavage surfaces mother-of-pearl. Will turn dull when exposed to air, crumbly, transparent to opaque. Cleavage: complete. Fracture: uneven, brittle; soluble in hydrochloric acid. Crystals: (monoclinic) narrow columnar, vertically striped. **Aggregates:** stalk-like, fibrous, rough; present in crevices and pore space of magmatites and metamorphic rocks, occasionally in veins of ore. **Accompanied by:** heulandite, stilbite, chabazite, analcite, prehnite, apophyllite, chlorite, albite, quartz, calcite. **Found in:** Rheinland-Pfalz, Saxony/Germany; Tessin/Switzerland; southern Tirol/Italy; New Jersey, California/USA. **Similar to:** feldspars.

Hydromagnesite
Mg$_5$[OH | (CO$_3$)$_2$]$_2$·4 H$_2$O

② San Benito Co., California/USA

Streak white. **Mohs' hardness** 3½. **Specific gravity** 2.2. **Characteristics:** white, colorless. Lustre: vitreous; transparent to translucent. Cleavage: complete, brittle. Soluble in diluted hydrochloric acid, effervescence. Greasy to the touch. Crystals: (monoclinic) pseudorhombic, acicular, tabular, usually very small. **Aggregates:** rough, radial filaments, wart-like, crusty, crumbly; present as a product of weathering in serpentinites and other magnesium-rich deposits, in cavities in volcanic rocks. **Accompanied by:** brucite, artinite, opal, calcite and dolomite. **Found in:** Steiermark/Austria; Mähren/Czechoslovakia; Trentino/Italy; Iran; British Columbia/Canada; New York, California, Nevada/USA. **Similar to:** artinite.

Gyrolite
Ca$_2$[Si$_4$O$_{10}$]·4 H$_2$O

③ with acicular okenite, Poona/India

Streak white. **Mohs' hardness** 3–4. **Specific gravity** 2.3–2.4. **Characteristics:** colorless, white. Lustre: vitreous; transparent to translucent. Cleavage: complete. Fracture: uneven, brittle. Crystals: (trigonal or hexagonal) not known. **Aggregates:** rough, fibrous, radial, as concretion; present in cavities of weathered calc-silicate rocks. **Accompanied by:** apophyllite, prehnite. **Found in:** Bohemia/Czechoslovakia; Northern Ireland; Skye/Scotland; Nova Scotia/Canada; California/USA; India. **Similar to:** prehnite.

Variscite
Al[PO$_4$]·2 H$_2$O

④ Perth/Australia 1:2

Streak white. **Mohs' hardness** 4–5. **Specific gravity** 2.5. **Characteristics:** green, white, bluish, colorless; transparent to opaque. Cleavage: incomplete. Fracture: conchoidal, brittle; greasy to the touch. Crystals: (rhombic) tabular, short prismatic, small, rare. **Aggregates:** rough, dense, tuberous, crusty; present in crevices and pore space in aluminum-rich deposits, particularly greywacke and slate. **Accompanied by:** wavellite, strengite, quartz. **Found in:** Vogtland/Germany; Steiermark/Austria; Arkansas, Utah/USA; Bolivia; Queensland/Australia. **Similar to:** wavelite, strengite, chalcedony, opal, chysoprase, chrysocolla, turquoise, wardite.

52 | kernite pg. 28, gaylussite pg. 32, serpentine pg. 44, chrysocolla pg. 130

Phillipsite
KCa[Al$_3$Si$_5$O$_{10}$]·6 H$_2$O

① Tuscany/Italy 1:2

Streak white. **Mohs' hardness** 4–4½. **Specific gravity** 2.2. **Characteristics:** colorless, white, grey, yellowish, reddish. Lustre: vitreous; transparent to translucent. Cleavage: incomplete. Fracture: uneven, brittle; soluble in acid. Crystals: (monoclinic) tabular, columnar, small; usually twinning and quadrupling; almost always surficial covering. **Aggregates:** radial, spherical, rough, present in cavities of basaltic rock, in terrestrial salt lakes, in deep ocean floor sediments. **Accompanied by:** chabazite, harmotome, natrolite, analcite. **Found in:** Vogelsberg, Kaiserstuhl/Germany; Bohemia/Czechoslovakia; Ireland; Iceland; Vesuvius/Italy; California, Hawaii/USA; Chile; Pacific Ocean basin. **Similar to:** harmotome, heulandite, stibite, chabazite.

Okenite
CaH$_2$[Si$_2$O$_6$]·H$_2$O

② Poona/India 1:2

Streak white. **Mohs' hardness** 4½–5. **Specific gravity** 2.3. **Characteristics:** white, yellow, bluish. Lustre: vitreous to mother-of-pearl; translucent to transparent. Cleavage: complete. Fracture: uneven, brittle. Flame test: orange. Crystals: (triclinic) flat–acicular. **Aggregates:** small fibrous, radial, rough; present in cavities of volcanic rocks. **Accompanied by:** prehnite, gyrolite. **Found in:** Iceland; Greenland; USA; Chile; Bombay/India; Faeroe Islands/Denmark. **Similar to:** natrolite.

Apophyllite
KCa$_4$[F | (Si$_4$O$_{10}$)$_2$]·8 H$_2$O

③ Poona/India 1:2

Streak white. **Mohs' hardness** 4½–5. **Specific gravity** 2.3–2.4. **Characteristics:** colorless, white, yellow to brown, reddish, greenish. Lustre: mother-of-pearl, vitreous; transparent to translucent. Cleavage: perfect. Fracture: uneven, brittle; soluble in hydrochloric acid. Flame test: violet. Crystals: (tetragonal) dipyramidal, prismatic, cubic, tabular; often rough, uneven surfaces: almost always surficial growth. **Aggregates:** bladed, scaly, granular, dense; present in volcanic rock, ore veins and alpine crevices. **Accompanied by:** analcite, prehnite, heulandite, natrolite, scolecite, stilbite, calcite. **Found in:** Harz mountains, Siebengebirge/Germany; Bohemia/Czechoslovakia; Dolomite Alps/Italy; Norway; Bombay/India; New Jersey/USA; Mexico; Brazil. **Similar to:** chabazite, heulandite, fluorite, ludlamite, datolite.

Heulandite
Ca[Al$_2$Si$_7$O$_{18}$]·6 H$_2$O

④ Poona/India

Streak white. **Mohs' hardness** 3½–4. **Specific gravity** 2.2. **Characteristics:** colorless, white, grey, yellowish, red. Lustre: on cleavage surface mother-of-pearl; transparent to translucent. Cleavage: perfect. Fracture: uneven, brittle; easily soluble in hydrochloric acid. Crystals: (monoclinic) tabular, short columnar; surficial growth. **Aggregates:** bladed, scaly, radial, also rough, sparlike; present in cavities of volcanic rocks, in crevices of metamorphic rocks, less often in ore veins. **Accompanied by:** stilbite, chabazite, scolecite, pectolite, calcite, quartz. **Found in:** Rheinland-Pfalz, Harz mountains/Germany; Wallis, Switzerland; Dolomite Alps/Italy; Iceland; Norway; Ukraine/USSR; Bombay/India; New Jersey/USA. **Similar to:** phillipsite, apophyllite, stilbite, feldspar.

kainite pg. 36, trona pg. 36, serpentine pg. 44, whevellite pg. 38

Harmotome
Ba[Al$_2$Si$_6$O$_{16}$] · 6 H$_2$O

① Strontian/Scotland 1:2

Streak white. **Mohs' hardness** 4½. **Specific gravity** 2.44–2.50. **Characteristics:** colorless, white, grey, yellowish, pink. **Lustre:** vitreous; transparent to translucent; dull. **Cleavage:** incomplete. **Fracture:** uneven to conchoidal, brittle; easily soluble in hydrochloric acid. **Crystals:** (monoclinic) columnar, usually interpenetration twinning; surficial growth. **Aggregates:** radial; present in ore veins, in cavities in volcanic rocks. **Accompanied by:** heulandite, stilbite, galena, barite, sphalerite, calcite. **Found in:** Harz mountains/Germany; Bohemia/Czechoslovakia; Norway; Scotland; Saskatchewan, Ontario/Canada; New York/USA. **Similar to:** phillipsite.

Gonnardite
(Ca,Na)$_3$[(Al,Si)$_5$ O$_{10}$]$_2$ · 6 H$_2$O

② Schellkopf, Eifel/Germany

Streak white. **Mohs' hardness** 4½–5. **Specific gravity** 2.25. **Characteristics:** white, colorless. **Lustre:** vitreous to silky; transparent. **Cleavage:** none. **Fracture:** fibrous, brittle. **Crystals:** (rhombic) fibrous, acicular, usually very small; rare. **Aggregates:** dense, fibrous, radial; present in cavities in volcanic rock. **Accompanied by:** phillipsite, thomsonite, wollastonite, pyrite, calcite. **Found in:** Vogelsberg, Eifel/Germany; Steiermark, Austria; Sicily/Italy; Auvergne/France; Norway; California/USA. **Similar to:** thomsonite, scolecite, natrolite.

Stilbite
Ca[Al$_2$Si$_7$O$_{18}$] · 7 H$_2$O

③ St. Andreasberg, Harz mountains
Lower Saxony, Germany 1:2

Streak white. **Mohs' hardness** 3½–4. **Specific gravity** 2.1–2.2. **Characteristics:** colorless, white, grey, yellowish, reddish. **Lustre:** on cleavage surface mother-of-pearl; translucent to transparent. **Cleavage:** complete. **Fracture:** uneven, brittle; soluble in hydrochloric acid. **Crystals:** (monoclinic) columnar, tabular; usually combined in sheaflike bundles of interpenetration twinnings. **Aggregates:** dendritic, radial; present in cavities of magmatics and metamorphic rocks, in ore veins. **Accompanied by:** chabacite, laumontite, scolecite, heulandite, calcite. **Found in:** Harz mountains/Germany; Tessin/Switzerland; Scotland; Faeroe Islands/Denmark; Iceland; Norway; Bombay/India; Washington, Oregon, California/USA. **Similar to:** heulandite, prehnite, phillipsite.

Chabazite
(Ca,Na$_2$)[Al$_2$Si$_4$O$_{12}$] · 6 H$_2$O

④ Nova Scotia/Canada

Streak white. **Mohs' hardness** 4–5. **Specific gravity** 2.1. **Characteristics:** colorless, white, reddish, brown. **Lustre:** transparent to translucent. **Cleavage:** incomplete. **Fracture:** uneven, brittle; soluble in hydrochloric acid. **Crystals:** (trigonal) cubic, rombohedral; always surficial growth; often twinning. **Aggregates:** rough, crusty; present in drusy cavities and in crevices of magmatites, particularly basalt and phonolite; also as deposits in hot springs. **Accompanied by:** natrolite, stilbite, heulandite, analcite, orthoclase, albite, quartz, fluorite, epidote, calcite, phillipsite. **Found in:** Vogelsberg, Westerwald, Rheinland-Pfalz/Germany; Bohemia/Czechoslovakia; Iceland; Faeroe Islands/Denmark; Vogesen/France; Südtirol/Austria; Elba, Sardinia/Italy; New Jersey, Oregon/USA; New Zealand. **Similar to:** apophyllite, fluorite, calcite, dolomite.

chrysoberyl pg. 130, serpierite pg. 210

Wavellite
$Al_3[(OH)_3 \mid (PO_4)_2] \cdot 5\ H_2O$

① Arkansas/USA

Streak white. **Mohs' hardness** 3½–4. **Specific gravity** 2.3–2.4. **Characteristics:** green, yellowish, grey, colorless. Lustre: vitreous to silky; transparent. Cleavage: incomplete. Fracture: uneven, brittle; soluble in hydrochloric acid. Crystals: (rhombic) prismatic, thin acicular; rare. **Aggregates:** radial, spheroidal, reniform, crusty; present in crevices and layers of siliceous schist, sandstone, zinc ore veins and phosphate deposits. **Accompanied by:** strengite, hematite, limonite, pyrolusite. **Found in:** Hesse, Thüringen, Sachsen/Germany; Cornwall, Devonshire/England; Arkansas, Pennsylvania/USA; Brazil; Bolivia. **Similar to:** variscite, natrolite, gibbsite, prehnite, calcite, aragonite.

Gmelinite
$(Na_2,Ca)[Al_2Si_4O_{12}] \cdot 6\ H_2O$

② Glenarm, Antrim/Ireland 1:3

Streak white. **Mohs' hardness** 4½. **Specific gravity** 2.1. **Characteristics:** white, yellowish, reddish, also colorless. Lustre: vitreous; transparent to translucent. Cleavage: incomplete. Fracture: uneven, brittle. Crystals: (hexagonal) dipyramidal, thick tabular; often twinning. **Aggregates:** isolated crystal groups; present in cavities in volcanic rock. **Accompanied by:** chabazite, analcite, phillipsite, thomsonite. **Found in:** Siegerland, Harz mountains/Germany; Antrim/Ireland; Skye/Scotland; Vincenza/Italy; Nova Scotia/Canada; New Jersey, Oregon/USA; Victoria/Australia.

Gibbsite
hydrargillite
$Al(OH)_3$

③ Laurion/Greece

Streak white. **Mohs' hardness** 2½–3½. **Specific gravity** 2.3–2.4. **Characteristics:** colorless, white, grey, greenish, bluish. Lustre: vitreous, on cleavage surface mother-of-pearl; transparent to translucent. Cleavage: perfect. Fracture: uneven, tough; malleable in thin layers. Crystals: (monoclinic) pseudohexagonal–tabular; often twinning; small and very rare. **Aggregates:** radial fibrous, scaly, botryoidal, wart-like, crusty; present in talc and serpentine deposits, also found mixed with bauxite and on the floor of tropical forests. **Accompanied by:** diaspore, boehmite, natrolite, limonite, calcite. **Found in:** Vogelsberg, Rhön/Germany; southern France; Hungary; Guinea; Jamaica; California, Arizona, Arkansas/USA; northern Australia. **Similar to:** wavellite, brucite, chalcedony.

Colemanite
$Ca[B_3O_4(OH)_3] \cdot H_2O$

④ Ankara/Turkey

Streak white. **Mohs' hardness** 4–4½. **Specific gravity** 2.4. **Characteristics:** colorless, white, yellowish, grey. Lustre: vitreous to adamantine; transparent to translucent. Cleavage: complete. Fracture: uneven, conchoidal, brittle; soluble in warm hydrochloric acid. Flame test: green. Crystals: (monoclinic) short to long columnar, tabular. **Aggregates:** rough, granular, dense, dendritic, bladed; present in dried salt beds. **Accompanied by:** ulexite, borax, boracite, kernite, realgar, celestite, halite, gypsum, calcite. **Found in:** Anatolia/Turkey; Kazakhstan/USSR; California, Nevada/USA; Chile; Argentina. **Similar to:** ulexite, datolite, borax, soda, danburite.

Calcite
CaCO₃

① Namibia; 1:2
② Berchtesgaden/Germany
③ Chihuahua/Mexico

Streak white. **Mohs' hardness** 3. **Specific gravity** 2.6–2.8. **Characteristics:** colorless, white, grey, yellow to brown, reddish, seldom green, bluish, black. Lustre: vitreous; translucent to transparent. Cleavage: perfect; rhombohedral cleavage fragments. Fracture: conchoidal, brittle; high double refraction. Fluorescence under ultraviolet light: red, yellow, blue. Easily soluble in cold, diluted hydrochloric acid (effervescent). Crystals: (trigonal) occurring in several hundred crystallographic forms and several thousand combinations thereof; basic shapes are rhombohedral, prismatic; almost always surficial growth, particularly in drusy cavities and other hollow spaces; often twinning, pseudomorphic. **Aggregates:** rough, granular, dense, sparlike, dendritic, fibrous, crumbly, stalactitic, oolitic, as concretions and contributing to the fossilization process; rock-forming; principal constituent in limestone, calcprecipitates, marble, carbonatite; as cement in many other rocks. **Accompanied by:** quartz, mica, dolomite, sulfur, many ore minerals. **Found in:** northern and southern Calcite Alps; Jura mountains/France, Switzerland, southern Germany; Harz mountains, Erzgebirge/Germany; Bohemia/Czechoslovakia; Champagne/France; Cumberland/England; Ireland; Ontario/Canada; Missouri, South Dakota, Colorado/USA; Mexico; Crimea, middle Siberia/USSR. **Similar to:** dolomite, aragonite, gypsum, anhydrite, quartz, barite, fluorite, chabazite.

Alunite
KAl₃[(OH)₆ | (SO₄)₂]

④ Taiwan

Streak white. **Mohs' hardness** 3½–4. **Specific gravity** 2.6–2.9. **Characteristics:** colorless, white, grey, yellowish, reddish. Lustre: vitreous; on cleavage face mother-of-pearl; translucent to transparent. Cleavage: complete. Fracture: conchoidal, brittle, splintery; soluble in potassium leach and hot sulfuric acid. Crystals: (trigonal) rhombohedral, tabular, small and rare. **Aggregates:** rough, dense, granular, crumbly, fibrous; present in cavities in volcanic rock, bauxite, and on floor of tropical forests. **Accompanied by:** quartz, opal, sulphur, ammonium chloride, gypsum. **Found in:** Latium, Tuscany/Italy; Hungary; Greece; Uzbekistan, Azerbaijan/USSR; Nevada, Colorado/USA; Australia. **Similar to:** aluminite, sal ammoniac, brucite.

Coral
CaCO₃

⑤ Calabria/Italy
⑥ Sicily/Italy

Streak white. **Mohs' hardness** 3–4. **Specific gravity** 2.6–2.7. **Characteristics:** red, pink, white. Lustre: usually dull, sometimes waxy; translucent. Cleavage: none. Fracture: uneven, splintery, brittle; soluble in acid (effervescence). Crystals: (trigonal) microcrystalline. **Aggregates:** rough, dense, dendritic; present in reefs, atolls, and coral banks; skeletal deposits. **Found in:** coast of the western Mediterranean countries; Gulf of Biscay; Canary Islands; Malayan archipelago; Midway Islands; Japan; Hawaii/USA. **Similar to:** glass, horn, (Indian) rubber, bones, synthetic substances. The very rare blue and black corals are organic substances and are found in the Malayan archipelago, along the coast of north Australia and the Red Sea.

lepidolite pg. 40, zinnwaldite pg. 40, glauberite pg. 42, cryolite pg. 42

Aragonite
CaCO₃

① Arizona/USA
② Morocco 1:2
④ Karlsbad/Czechoslovakia

Streak white. **Mohs' hardness** 3½–4. **Specific gravity** 2.95. **Characteristics:** colorless, white, grey, yellow-green, bluish, reddish. Lustre: on cleavage face greasy; translucent to transparent. Cleavage: incomplete. Fracture: conchoidal, brittle; easily soluble in hydrochloric acid (effervescent). Crystals: (rhombic) prismatic, tabular, acicular, intergrown, and surficial growth; often twinning and quadrupling, pseudomorphic. **Aggregates:** rough, crusty, dendritic, radial, stalactitically branched; striped, oolitic, powdery; present in crevices and cavities in younger volcanic rocks, aragonitic muds, in ore veins, as deposits in hot springs, in supporting structures of molluscs, material of pearls. **Accompanied by:** natrolite, chabazite, harmotome, gypsum, sulfur, limonite, siderite. **Found in:** Kaiserstuhl, Kärnten/Austria; Bohemia/Czechoslovakia; Aragonia/Spain; Vesuvius, Sicily/Italy; southwest France; Arizona, New Mexico/USA; New Zealand. **Similar to:** calcite, strontianite, celestite, barite, natrolite.

Anhydrite
CaSO₄

③ Mexico

Streak white. **Mohs' hardness** 3½. **Specific gravity** 2.9–3.0. **Characteristics:** colorless, white, grey, bluish, reddish. Lustre: vitreous and mother-of-pearl; transparent. Cleavage: complete, square-shaped fragments. Fracture: conchoidal, splintery, brittle; volume increases and turns slowly into gypsum under humid conditions. Not easily soluble in acid; easily soluble as a powder in sulfuric acid. Flame test: dull red. Crystals: (rhombic) cubic, prismatic, tabular, intergrown, and surficial growth. **Aggregates:** rough, granular, sparlike, fibrous, dense, often contaminated; present in salt beds, ore deposits, in pegmatites, and alpine crevices; also as exhalation product of volcanic activities, and rock-forming as alteration product. **Accompanied by:** halite, gypsum, sylvanite, carnallite, kainite, polyhalite, kieserite, boracite, dolomite. **Found in:** lower Saxony, eastern Harz mountains/Germany; Tessin/Switzerland; Kärnten/Austria; Urals/USSR; Louisiana, Texas/USA; Chile; western Australia. **Similar to:** gypsum, calcite, cryolite, barite.

Magnesite
MgCO₃

⑤ Tuscany/Italy

Streak white. **Mohs' hardness** 4–4½. **Specific gravity** 2.9–3.1. **Characteristics:** colorless, white, yellow to brown, also grey to black. Lustre: vitreous to dull; transparent to translucent. Cleavage: perfect. Fracture: conchoidal, brittle; in powder form soluble in warm hydrochloric acid; occasionally green or blue fluorescence under ultraviolet light. Crystals: (trigonal) rombohedral, columnar, thick tabular; mostly intergrowth; rare. **Aggregates:** rough, granular, sparlike, dendritic, dense, crumbly; present in talc and chlorite slate, serpentinite, dolomite, in individual layers in veins, rarely in pegmatites. **Accompanied by:** calcite, aragonite, dolomite, serpentine, chlorite, talc, opal, chalcedony, gypsum. **Found in:** Tyrol, Kärnten, Steiermark/Austria; Mähren/Czechoslovakia; Euboea/Greece; Piemonte, Tuscany/Italy; Norway; Sweden; Urals/USSR; Manchuria/China; Nevada, California/USA. **Similar to:** calcite, dolomite, siderite, ankerite.

serpentine pg. 44, thenardite pg. 44, biotite pg. 46, muscovite pg. 46

Streak	

Streak

white and
colorless

Dolomite
$CaMg[CO_3]_2$

① with calcite; Durham/England
② Arkansas/USA

Streak white, light grey. **Mohs' hardness** 3½–4. **Specific gravity** 2.85–2.95. **Characteristics:** white, grey, yellow to brown, reddish, also colorless to black. Lustre: vitreous to mother-of-pearl; transparent to translucent. Cleavage: complete. Fracture: conchoidal and brittle; easily soluble in warm hydrochloric acid, in powder form also in cold hydrochloric acid. Crystals: (trigonal) rhombohedral, intergrown and surficial growth; parallel twinning, pseudomorphic. **Aggregates:** rough, granular, sparlike, dendritic, dense; present in ore and mineral veins, in chlorite and talc slate; rock-forming. **Accompanied by:** calcite, gypsum, quartz, pyrite, realgar, tremolite, wollastonite, ankerite. **Found in:** northern Bavaria, Eifel, Erzgebirge/Germany; Tyrol/Austria; Wallis/Switzerland; Dolomite Alps/Italy; Cornwall/England; Urals/USSR; Quebec/Canada; Missouri, Iowa/USA; Mexico. **Similar to:** calcite, magnasite, chabazite, siderite, gypsum, hydrite, quartz.

Polyhalite
$K_2Ca_2Mg[SO_4]_4 \cdot 2\,H_2O$

③ Hallein/Austria 1:½

Streak white. **Mohs' hardness** 3–3½. **Specific gravity** 2.8. **Characteristics:** red, yellow, white, grey. Lustre: greasy, vitreous, resinous; transparent. Cleavage: perfect. Fracture: fibrous, brittle. Taste: bitter. Flame test: violet. Soluble in water. Crystals: (triclinic) prismatic; mostly intergrowth; small and rare; often twinning. **Aggregates:** rough, fibrous, rarely dendritic, bladed, granular; present in salt mines. **Accompanied by:** halite, anhydrite, gypsum, kieserite, carnallite. **Found in:** Lower Saxony, upper Bavaria, Magdeburg/Germany; Salzkammergut/Austria; Lothringen/France; Texas, New Mexico/USA; Chile. **Similar to:** kieserite, gypsum.

Kämmererite
$(Mg,Cr)[(OH)_2 | AlSi_3O_{10}] \cdot Mg_3(OH)_6$

④ Guleman/Turkey

Streak white. **Mohs' hardness** 2–3. **Specific gravity** 2.6–3.3. **Characteristics:** red, violet. Lustre: vitreous, mother-of-pearl, dull; transparent to translucent. Cleavage: complete. Fracture: bladed, in thin layers nonelastic, malleable; soluble in hydrochloric and sulfuric acid. Crystals: (monoclinic) columnar, barrel-shaped, pyramidal. **Aggregates:** bladed, crumbly, as surficial deposit; present in chromite deposits. **Accompanied by:** chromite, uvarovite. **Found in:** Steiermark/Austria; Silesia/Poland; Piemonte/Italy; Turkey; Urals, Caucasus/USSR; California, Texas/USA.

Ankerite
$CaFe[CO_3]_2$

⑤ Sunk, Steiermark/Austria

Streak white, also light grey and light brown. **Mohs' hardness** 3½–4. **Specific gravity** 2.9–3.8. **Characteristics:** yellow to brown, white, grey. Lustre: vitreous to mother-of-pearl; transparent to translucent. Cleavage: complete. Fracture: uneven, brittle. Soluble (effervescent) in warm hydrochloric acid; occasional yellowish or red fluorescence under ultraviolet light. Crystals: (trigonal) rhombohedral. **Aggregates:** rough, sparlike, granular, dense; present in ore veins and alpine crevices. **Accompanied by:** calcite, siderite, quartz, dolomite, galena. **Found in:** Steiermark, Kärnten/Austria; Hungary; Lancashire/England; South Dakota/USA. **Similar to:** dolomite, magnesite, siderite.

64

margarite pg. 68, wollastonite pg. 90, serpierite pg. 210

Streak

white and
colorless

Mohs'
hardness 1 ◄

2 ◄

3 ◄

4 ◄

5 ◄

6 ◄

7 ◄

8 ◄

9 ◄

10 ◄

Specific
gravity 1 ◄

2 ◄

3 ◄

4 ◄

5 ◄

6 ◄

7 ◄

Kieserite
MgSO$_4$·H$_2$O

① Hanover/Germany

Streak white. **Mohs' hardness** 3½. **Specific gravity** 2.57. **Characteristics:** colorless, white, yellowish, grey, reddish. Lustre: vitreous; transparent, dull. Cleavage: complete. Difficult to dissolve in water. Crystals: (monoclinic) dipyramidal; rarely well developed; usually dispersed. **Aggregates:** rough, fine-grained, rarely large-grained; present either layered or scattered in salt mines, particularly in potassium salt mines; **Accompanied by:** halite, polyhalite, sylvite, anhydrite, carnallite, kainite. **Found in:** Lower Saxony, Hessia, Magdeburg/Germany; Salzburg/Austria; Poland; Sicily/Italy; Utah, Texas, New Mexico/USA; Punjab/India. **Similar to:** epsomite, polyhalite, kainite.

Hanksite
KNa$_{22}$[Cl | (CO$_3$)$_2$ | (SO$_4$)$_9$]

② Boron, California/USA 1:2

Streak white. **Mohs' hardness** 3–3½. **Specific gravity** 2.56. **Characteristics:** colorless, white, yellow, grey to black. Lustre: vitreous; transparent to translucent. Cleavage: perfect. Fracture: uneven, brittle. Taste: salty. Sometimes yellow fluorescence under ultraviolet light. Crystals: (hexagonal) tabular to short prismatic, dipyramidal; often penetration twinning. **Aggregates:** in groups with interpenetrating crystals; present in salt mines, specifically in borax, and soda mines. **Accompanied by:** borax, soda, halite, trona. **Found in:** California/USA. **Similar to:** quartz.

Strangite
Fe[PO$_4$]·2 H$_2$O

③ Svappavaara/Sweden

Streak white. **Mohs' hardness** 3–4½. **Specific gravity** 2.8–2.9. **Characteristics:** red, violet, white, yellow, greenish, and almost colorless. Lustre: vitreous; transparent to translucent. Cleavage: perfect. Fracture: conchoidal to uneven, brittle; soluble in hydrochloric acid. Crystals: (rhombic) pseudohexagonal, tabular, short prismatic, often multifaceted; rare. **Aggregates:** radial, spherical, botryoidal, as crusts and surface covering; present in drusy cavities of phosphate-bearing pegmatites and ore deposits. **Accompanied by:** vavelite, vivianite, dufrenite, cacoxenite, limonite, quartz. **Found in:** Hesse, Oberpfalz, Thüringen/Germany: Portugal; Lappland/Sweden; California, Alabama/USA. **Similar to:** varicite, amethyst, scorodite.

Pectolite
Ca$_2$NaH[Si$_3$O$_9$]

④ Rauschermühle/Germany

Streak white. **Mohs' hardness** 4½–5. **Specific gravity** 2.8–2.9. **Characteristics:** white, grey, sometimes greenish, yellowish, colorless. Lustre: vitreous; transparent to translucent. Cleavage: perfect. Fracture: conchoidal to uneven, brittle; soluble in hydrochloric acid. Flame test: yellow. Crystals: (triclinic) occasionally columnar, commonly dendritic, fibrous, acicular; rare. **Aggregates:** rough, dense, radial, spheroidal; also parallel fibrous; present in crevices and drusy cavities in basic volcanic rocks, sometimes in metamorphic rocks. **Accompanied by:** natrolite, laumontite, heulandite, thomsonite, prehnite, diopside, calcite. **Found in:** Rheinland-Pfalz/Germany; Bohemia/Czechoslovakia; Skye/Scotland; Quebec, Ontario/Canada; New Jersey, New York/USA. **Similar to:** wollastonite, tremolite.

Ludlamite
Fe$_3$[PO$_4$]$_2$·4 H$_2$O

① Trepca/Yugoslavia

Streak white. **Mohs' hardness** 3–4. **Specific gravity** 3.1–3.2. **Characteristics:** light to apple green, seldom colorless. Lustre: vitreous; transparent to translucent. Cleavage: perfect. Fracture: uneven, brittle; soluble in acid. Flame test: green. Crystals: (monoclinic) tabular. **Aggregates:** rough, granular, sparlike; present in oxidation zones of ore veins, in granite pegmatites. **Accompanied by:** vivianite, triphylite. **Found in:** northern Bavaria/Germany; Cornwall/England; Yugoslavia; New Hampshire, Idaho/USA. **Similar to:** apophyllite, chalcedony.

Astrophyllite
(K,Na)$_3$(Fe,Mn)$_7$[Ti,Zr)$_2$[Si$_8$(O,OH)$_{31}$]

② Mt. St. Hilaire/Canada 1:2

Streak white, also brownish. **Mohs' hardness** 3–3½. **Specific gravity** 3.3–3.4. **Characteristics:** yellow to brown, olive. Lustre: vitreous; cleavage face mother-of-pearl; transparent to translucent. Cleavage: complete. Fracture: bladed, brittle; obvious pleochroism; slowly soluble in acid. Crystals: (triclinic) tabular, bladed; rare. **Aggregates:** radial; present in basic plutonites. **Accompanied by:** quartz, feldspars, mica, aegerine, zircon, titanite. **Found in:** Norway; Quebec/Canada; Colorado/USA; Kola/USSR. **Similar to:** muscovite, biotite, phlogopite.

Margarite
CaAl$_2$[(OH)$_2$ |Al$_2$Si$_2$O$_{10}$]

③ Chester, Massachusetts/USA

Streak white. **Mohs' hardness** 4–4½. **Specific gravity** 3.0–3.1. **Characteristics:** grey, white, reddish, yellow, green. Lustre: mother-of-pearl; translucent. Cleavage: perfect. Fracture: bladed, brittle; somewhat soluble in warm hydrochloric acid. Crystals: (monoclinic) tabular with hexagonal contours; very rare. **Aggregates:** bladed, scaly, granular; present in schists, emery deposits; **Accompanied by:** corundum, staurolite, tourmaline, emerald, magnatite, rutile. **Found in:** Tyrol/Austria; St. Gotthard/Switzerland; southern Tirol/Italy; Naxos/Greece; Turkey; Urals/USSR; Pennsylvania/USA. **Similar to:** pyrophyllite, muscovite.

Fluorite
CaF$_2$

④ with baryte: Oberpfalz/Bavaria
⑤ Pöla, Erzgebirge/Germany

Streak white. **Mohs' hardness** 4. **Specific gravity** 3.1–3.2. **Characteristics:** violet, blue, black, yellow to brown, green, pink, often zoned colors, seldom colorless. Lustre: vitreous; transparent to translucent. Cleavage: complete. Fracture: conchoidal, splintery, brittle. Flame test: dull red. Often violet, blue, or green fluorescence under ultraviolet light. Crystals: (cubic) cubic, octahedral, rhombododecahedral; usually surface growth. **Aggregates:** rough, sparlike, macrocrystalline to dense, rarely dendritic or crumbly; present in veins, pegmatites, and alpine crevices, as by-product of many rocks. **Accompanied by:** barite, apatite, calcite, tourmaline, topaz, quartz, siderite, galena, sphalerite, kieserite. **Found in:** Harz mountains, eastern Bavaria, Thüringen/Germany; Tauern/Austria; St. Gotthard/Switzerland; Derbyshire/England; Spain; Urals, Kazakhstan/USSR; Illinois/USA; Namibia. **Similar to:** apatite, barite, chalcedony, calcite, halite, apophyllite.

 zinnwaldite pg. 40, biotite pg. 46, muscovite pg. 46, magnesite pg. 62

Streak

white and
colorless

Mohs'
hardness 1 ◀

2 ◀

3 ◀

4 ◀

5 ◀

6 ◀

7 ◀

8 ◀

9 ◀

10 ◀

Specific
gravity 1 ◀

2 ◀

3 ◀

4 ◀

5 ◀

6 ◀

7 ◀

Betafite

① Antsirabe/Madagascar 1:3

$(Ca,U)_2(Nb,Ti,Ta)_2O_6(O,OH,F)$

Streak white, sometimes grey and yellowish. **Mohs' hardness** 3–5½. **Specific gravity** 3.7–5.2. **Characteristics:** greenish brown to black, yellowish. Lustre: resinous, on cleavage face greasy; transparent to opaque. Cleavage: none. Fracture: conchoidal, uneven, brittle, soluble in acid; strongly radioactive. Crystals: (cubic) octahedral and dodecahedral, tabular. **Aggregates:** crusty, granular, dense; present in granite pegmatites. **Accompanied by:** fergusonite, euxenite, allanite. **Found in:** Norway; Baikal Lake/USSR; Madagascar; Ontario/Canada; Colorado/USA; Brazil. **Similar to:** pyrochlore, magnesite, scheelite, euxenite, uraninite.

Triphylite

② Hagendorf, Bavaria/Germany

$Li(Fe,Mn)[PO_4]$

Streak grey–white. **Mohs' hardness** 4–5. **Specific gravity** 3.4–3.6. **Characteristics:** greenish, blue, brownish. Lustre: vitreous, greasy; transparent to translucent. Cleavage: complete. Fracture: splintery, uneven, brittle. Flame test: red. Easily soluble in hydrochloric acid. Crystals: (rhombic) prismatic; always intergrown; rare. **Aggregates:** dense, rough–granular, sparlike; present in granite pegmatites, tin ore veins; **Accompanied by:** cassiterite, spodumene, amblygonite, apatite, beryl. **Found in:** northern Bavaria/Germany; Portugal; Sweden; Namibia; Manitoba/Canada; South Dakota, Connecticut/USA; Tasmania/Australia.

Kyanite   disthene

③ Alpe Spondar,
Tessin/Switzerland 1:2

$Al_2[O \mid SiO_4]$

Streak white. **Mohs' hardness** 4–4½ vertically, 6–7 horizontally. **Specific gravity** 3.5–3.7. **Characteristics:** blue, yellowish, green, white, pink, seldom colorless. Lustre: vitreous, mother-of-pearl; transparent to translucent. Cleavage: complete. Fracture: fibrous, uneven, brittle. Crystals: (triclinic) linearly columnar, mostly intergrown. **Aggregates:** irregularly radial, bladed, seldom dense; present in metamorphic rocks, pegmatites, sand and gravel deposits. **Accompanied by:** staurolite, andalusite, corundum, mica, garnet, tourmaline, quartz. **Found in:** Tyrol/Austria; Tessin/Switzerland; southern Tirol/Italy; Assam/India; western Australia; Virginia/USA; Brazil. **Similar to:** sillimanite, dumortierite, actinolite, glaucophane.

Celestite

④ Madagascar

$SrSO_4$

Streak white. **Mohs' hardness** 3–3½. **Specific gravity** 3.9–4.0. **Characteristics:** light blue, white, yellowish, grey, colorless, seldom reddish and greenish. Lustre: vitreous to mother-of-pearl; transparent to translucent. Cleavage: complete. Fracture: conchoidal, uneven, brittle. Flame test: carmine red. Soluble as powder in concentrated hydrochloric acid. Crystals: (rhombic) prismatic, tabular, mostly surficial growth. **Aggregates:** granular, sparlike, dense, dendritic, small, tuberous; present in limestone and gypsum stone, in cavities in volcanic rocks, in veins. **Accompanied by:** calcite, aragonite, gypsum, anhydrite, sulfur, galena, sphalerite. **Found in:** Kaiserstuhl, Thüringen/Germany; Sicily, Vicenza/Italy; Granada/Spain; southwest England; Madagascar; Tennessee/USA; Turkestan/USSR. **Similar to:** barite, gypsum, calcite, aragonite, strontianite, cerussite.

ankerite pg. 64, kämmererite pg. 64, scorodite pg. 136, sphalerite pg. 194

Streak
white and colorless

Boehmite
AlOOH

① Le Duc, Provence, France

Streak white. **Mohs' hardness** 3. **Specific gravity** 3.07. **Characteristics**: colorless, white, yellowish to brown. Lustre: vitreous, mother-of-pearl, dull; transparent. Cleavage: perfect. Fracture: uneven, brittle. Crystals: (rhombic): microscopically small and tabular. **Aggregates**: rough and crumbly; present with bauxite. **Accompanied by**: diaspore, gypsite, limonite. **Found in**: southern France; Yugoslavia; Hungary; Urals/USSR; California, Georgia/USA; Jamaica; Surinam/Indonesia. **Similar to**: diaspore.

Mohs' hardness	1 ◀
	2 ◀
	3 ◀
	4 ◀
	5 ◀
	6 ◀
	7 ◀
	8 ◀
	9 ◀
	10 ◀

Siderite
FeCO$_3$

② Iron ore, Steiermark/Austria

Streak white. **Mohs' hardness** 4–4½. **Specific gravity** 3.7–3.9. **Characteristics**: yellowish to brown, black, seldom white; occasionally tarnished in different colors. Lustre: vitreous, mother-of-pearl; transparent to translucent. Cleavage: complete. Fracture: conchoidal, sparlike, brittle; easily soluble in warm hydrochloric acid; occasional lemon-yellow fluorescence under ultraviolet light. Crystals: (trigonal) rhombohedral, scalenohedral. **Aggregates**: rough, sparlike, granular, dense, radial, botryoidal, oolitic; as concretion (clay ironstones) present in peat bogs. **Accompanied by**: quartz, barite, calcite, galena, sphalerite, ankerite. **Found in**: Siegerland, northern Bavaria, Saxony/Germany; Kärnten, Steiermark/Austria; Czechoslovakia; Cornwall/England; Lorraine/France; Spain; Connecticut/USA. **Similar to**: calcite, dolomite, smithsonite, sphalerite, ankerite.

Rhodochrosite
MnCO$_3$

③ St. Luis, Argentina
④ Saxony/Germany

Streak white. **Mohs' hardness** 3½–4. **Specific gravity** 3.3–3.6. **Characteristics**: pink, grey, brown to black, seldom colorless. Lustre: vitreous; transparent to opaque. Cleavage; complete. Fracture: uneven, brittle; easily soluble in warm hydrochloric acid. Crystals: (trigonal) rhombohedral, scalenohedral; surface growth. **Aggregates**: rough, granular, sparlike, dense, radial, botryoidal, stalactitic, crusty; occasionally with ragged rings; present in oxidized zones of ore veins, as stalagmites in abandoned mines. **Accompanied by**: rhodonite, manganite, quartz, fluorite, barite, limonite. **Found in**: Saxony, Siegerland/Germany; Romania; Huelva/Spain; Pyrenees/France; South Africa; Montana, Colorado/USA; Mexico; Argentinia; Urals/USSR. **Similar to**: rhodonite, calcite, dolomite, siderite, ankerite.

Specific gravity	1 ◀
	2 ◀
	3 ◀
	4 ◀
	5 ◀
	6 ◀
	7 ◀

Strontianite
SrCO$_3$

⑤ on barite, Koenitz,
Thüringen/Germany

Streak white. **Mohs' hardness** 3½. **Specific gravity** 3.7–3.8. **Characteristics**: colorless, grey, white, yellow, green, reddish. Lustre: vitreous, on cleavage face greasy; transparent to translucent. Cleavage: incomplete. Fracture: conchoidal, brittle. Flame test: red. Easily soluble in warm hydrochloric acid (effervescence). Occasional blue fluorescence under ultraviolet light. Crystals: (rhombic) acicular, prismatic, tabular. **Aggregates**: rough, radial, crusty, reniform, as concretions; present in ore veins, limestone, and marl. **Accompanied by**: calcite, barite, galena, pyrite, celestite. **Found in**: Harz mountains, Münsterland, Saxony/Germany; Steiermark/Austria; Scotland; California, Arizona/USA. **Similar to**: aragonite, calcite, natrolite, barite, celestite.

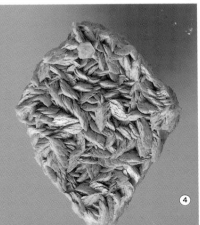

Streak

white and colorless

Mohs'
hardness 1 ◄
–
2 ◄

3 ◄
4 ◄

5 ◄
–
6 ◄
–
7 ◄
–
8 ◄

9 ◄

10 ◄

Specific
gravity 1 ◄

–

2 ◄

3 ◄

–

4 ◄

–

5 ◄

6 ◄

–

⇓⇓ 7 ◄

Mimetite
Pb₅[Cl I (AsO₄)₃]

① Tsumeb/Namibia 1:2
② Mexico

Streak white. **Mohs' hardness** 3½–4. **Specific gravity** 7.1. **Characteristics:** yellow, greenish, sometimes colorless, grey, white, brown, reddish. Lustre: adamantine, greasy; transparent to translucent. Cleavage: none. Fracture: conchoidal to uneven, brittle; soluble in nitric acid and potassium leach. Crystals: (hexagonal) prismatic, tabular, acicular, surface growth. **Aggregates:** botryoidal, crusty, reniform, crumbly; present in oxidized zones of lead ore veins. **Accompanied by:** galena, cerussite, anglesite, pyromophite, wulfenite, limonite. **Found in:** Erzgebirge/Germany; Czechoslovakia; Cornwall, Cumberland/England; Sweden; Sardinia/Italy; Turkestan/USSR; Namibia; Nevada/USA; Mexico. **Similar to:** pyromophite, vanadinite, apatite, wulfenite, crocoite.

Cerussite
PbCO₃

③ Tsumeb/Namibia 1:2

Streak white. **Mohs' hardness** 3–3½. **Specific gravity** 6.4–6.6. **Characteristics:** colorless, white, grey, yellow, brown, black. Lustre: adamantine, greasy, vitreous; transparent to opaque. Cleavage: incomplete. Fracture: conchoidal, very brittle; soluble in nitric acid (effervescence); blue-green fluorescence under ultraviolet light. Crystals: (rhombic) tabular, prismatic, dipyramidal, acicular; twinning and pseudomorphic. **Aggregates:** dense, rough, crusty, reniform, dendritic, crumbly; present in oxidized zones of lead ore veins. **Accompanied by:** galena, anglesite, pyromorphite, hemimorphite, smithsonite. **Found in:** Siegerland/Germany; Czechoslovakia; Sardinia/Italy; Zambia; Namibia; Colorado/USA; Altai mountains/USSR; Australia. **Similar to:** anglesite, celestite, barite, phosgenite, scheelite.

Adamite
Zn₂[OH I AsO₄]

④ Mapimi/Mexico

Streak white. **Mohs' hardness** 3½. **Specific gravity** 4.3–4.5. **Characteristics:** colorless, white, yellow, green, pink to violet. Lustre: vitreous; transparent to translucent. Cleavage: complete. Fracture: conchoidal, uneven, brittle; distinct pleochroism; easily soluble hydrochloric acid; sometimes lemon-yellow fluorescence under ultraviolet light. Crystals: (rhombic) prismatic to acicular, tabular; surface growth. **Aggregates:** fine-grained, radial, crusty, crumbly; present in oxidized zones of zinc veins. **Accompanied by:** smithsonite, hemimorphite, azurite. **Found in:** Attica/Greece; Var/France; Namibia; Utah/USA; Mexico; Chile. **Similar to:** olivene, libethenite.

Witherite
BaCO₃

⑤ Alston Moore/England

Streak white. **Mohs' hardness** 3–3½. **Specific gravity** 4.3. **Characteristics:** colorless, white, grey, yellowish. Lustre: vitreous or dull, on cleavage face greasy; transparent to translucent. Cleavage: incomplete. Fracture: uneven, brittle. Flame test: yellowish green. Soluble in diluted hydrochloric acid (effervescence). **Witherite is poisonous in powder form.** Crystals: (rhombic) prismatic, dipyramidal; penetration twinning. **Aggregates:** rough, botryoidal, radial, bladed, crusty; present in veins. **Accompanied by:** barite, galena, sphalerite, calcite. **Found in:** Steiermark/Austria; England; Turkmenia/USSR; California, Illinois/USA. **Similar to:** strontianite, cerussite, quartz.

silver pg. 48, stolzite pg. 48, vallentinite pg. 50, phosgenite pg. 50, betafite pg. 70, scheelite pg. 110, bismutite pg. 164, platinum pg. 164

Anglesite
PbSO₄

① Tsumeb, Namibia

Streak white. **Mohs' hardness** 3–3½. **Specific gravity** 6.3–6.4. **Characteristics:** colorless, grey to blackish, brownish. Lustre: adamantine, greasy; transparent to translucent. Cleavage: incomplete. Fracture: conchoidal, brittle; soluble in potassium leach and warm sulfuric acid. Crystals: (rhombic) prismatic and tabular; surface growth. **Aggregates:** rough, granular, crusty, reniform, crumbly; present in oxidized zones of galena deposits, as a volcanic sublimation product. **Accompanied by:** galena, cerussite, phosgenite, sphalerite, smithsonite, limonite. **Found in:** Siege Germany; Kärnten/Austria; Sardinia/Italy; Wales; Scotland; Spain; Urals Namibia; Missouri/USA. **Similar to:** cerussite, scheelite, barite, phosgenite.

Barite   baryte
BaSO₄

② chalcosite, Alston Moore/England
④ baryte rose, Rockenberg, Hesse/Germany

Streak white. **Mohs' hardness** 3–3½. **Specific gravity** 4.48. **Characteristics:** colorless, white, yellow to brown, reddish, blue, green, grey to black. Lustre: on cleavage face mother-of-pearl; translucent to transparent. Cleavage: complete. Fracture: conchoidal, uneven, brittle. Flame test: yellow-green. Slowly soluble in concentrated sulfuric acid. Crystals: (rhombic) tabular, prismatic; surface growth. **Aggregates:** rough, bladed, sparlike, reniform, rosette-like (barite rose), granular, dense, as concretions; present in ore veins, sandstone, magmatites. **Accompanied by:** galena, siderite, sphalerite, quartz, fluorite. **Found in:** Westphalia, Harz mountains/Germany; Czechoslovakia; England; Urals/USSR; Colorado/USA; western Australia. **Similar to:** aragonite, feldspars, anglesite.

Pyromorphite
Pb₅[Cl i (PO₄)₃]

③ Freihung/Germany

Streak white. **Mohs' hardness** 3½–4. **Specific gravity** 6.7–7.1. **Characteristics:** green (green alteration of galena), brown (brown alteration of galena), yellow, reddish, white and colorless, also zoned colors. Lustre: adamantine, greasy; transparent to translucent. Cleavage: none. Fracture: conchoidal to uneven, brittle; soluble in nitric acid and potassium leach. Crystals: (hexagonal) prismatic, tabular, acicular, dipyramidal, often barrel-shaped; pseudomorphic. **Aggregates:** botryoidal, radial, rough; present in oxidized zones of lead deposits. **Accompanied by:** mimetite, cerussite, galena, wulfenite. **Found in:** Harz mountains, Siegerland, Saxony/Germany; Czechoslovakia; England; Colorado/USA; Mexico; Sambia. **Similar to:** mimetite, apatite, vanadinite.

Wulfenite   yellow lead ore
PbMoO₄

⑤ Mexico/Yugoslavia

Streak white. **Mohs' hardness** 3. **Specific gravity** 6.7–6.9. **Characteristics:** yellow, orange, colorless, grey. Lustre: adamantine, resinous; transparent to translucent. Cleavage: incomplete. Fracture: conchoidal to uneven, brittle; slowly soluble in hydrochloric acid. Crystals: (tetragonal) tabular, pyramidal, acicular; usually surficial growth. **Aggregates:** rough, dense, crusty; present in oxidized zones of lead-ore deposits. **Accompanied by:** galena, cerussite, pyromorphite, hydrozincite, smithsonite, calcite. **Found in:** Kärnten/Austria; Czechoslovakia; Yugoslavia; Morocco; Zaire; Namibia; Utah, Arizona/USA; Mexico; Australia. **Similar to:** stolzite, sulfur, mimetite.

76

vanadinite pg. 194, sphalerite pg. 194, powellite pg. 196, caledonite pg. 176

Streak

white and
colorless

Mohs'
hardness

Specific
gravity

Opal
SiO$_2$·nH$_2$O

① fire opal; Mexico
② prose opal; Mexico
③ precious opal; Andamooka/Australia 1:2
④ petrified wood opal; Oregon/USA
⑤ liver opal; Hungary

Streak white. **Mohs' hardness** 5½–6½. **Specific gravity** 1.0–2.5. **Characteristics:** colorless, white, yellow to brown, red to orange (fire opal), green (prose opal), grey to black, occasionally rainbow colored (precious opal). Lustre: vitreous, waxy, mother-of-pearl; transparent (hyalite) to opaque (common opal), often cloudy (milky opal). Cleavage: none. Fracture: conchoidal, splintery, brittle; easily soluble in potassium leach. Noncrystalline: amorphous; only a very small occurrence of fine-crystalline cristobalite and tridymite, rarely represented in the quartz group. **Aggregates:** reniform, tuberous, botryoidal, crusty, layered, crumbly (siliceous earth), as concretions (chert or flint); present as filling in volcanic rock, often in sandstone or limestone, as deposits in hot springs (geyserite), as fossilization product (among others petrified wood). **Accompanied by:** zeolite, chalcedony, limonite. **Found in:** Hungary; Iceland; Turkey; Libya; Egypt; Tanzania; Kazakhstan/USSR; Nevada, Wyoming, Montana/USA; Hidalgo, Queretaro/Mexico; New South Wales, southern Australia, Queensland/Australia; New Zealand; New Caledonia. **Similar to:** chalcedony, variscite, smithsonite, hemimorphite, porcelain, glass, synthetic materials.

Scapolite
⑥ Baikal Lake/USSR

Mineral group series
between marialite and meionite
(marialite) Na$_8$[(Cl$_2$,SO$_4$,CO$_3$) | (AlSi$_3$O$_8$)$_6$]
(meionite) Ca$_8$[(Cl$_2$,SO$_4$,CO$_3$)$_2$ | (Al$_2$Si$_2$O$_8$)$_6$]

Streak white. **Mohs' hardness** 5–6½. **Specific gravity** 2.5–2.8. **Characteristics:** colorless, white, grey, yellow, green, blue, red to violet. Lustre: vitreous, greasy; transparent to opaque. Cleavage: complete. Fracture: conchoidal, brittle; sometimes orange–yellow fluorescence in ultraviolet light. Crystals: (tetragonal) prismatic–pyramidal; surficial and intergrowth. **Aggregates:** rough, granular, dendritic, acicular, dense; present in magmatites, pegmatites, by-product of volcanic eruptions; in metamorphic rocks. **Accompanied by:** garnet, apatite, idocrase, epidote, augite, wollastonite. **Found in:** Eifel, eastern Bavaria/Germany; Tessin/Switzerland; Kärnten/Austria; Scandinavia; Kenya; Tanzania; Madagascar; Karelia, Baikal Lake/USSR; Burma; Ontario/Canada; New York, California/USA; Brazil. **Similar to:** feldspars, idocrase, amblygonite, petalite, apatite, chrysoberyl.

Charoite
⑦ Jakutia/USSR

K(Ca,Na)$_2$[(OH,F) | Si$_4$O$_{10}$]·H$_2$O

Streak white. **Mohs' hardness** 5½–6. **Specific gravity** 2.5. **Characteristics:** violet. Lustre: vitreous, silky; transparent to opaque. Cleavage: incomplete. Fracture: fibrous, tough. Crystals: (monoclinic) unknown. **Aggregates:** fibrous, dense; present in quartzite, as riverspar (fluorite). **Accompanied by:** aegirine, orthoclase. **Found in:** only eastern Siberia/USSR. **Similar to:** sodalite, azurite, lapis lazuli, lazulite.

variscite pg. 52, apophyllite pg. 54, okenite pg. 54, chabazite pg. 56

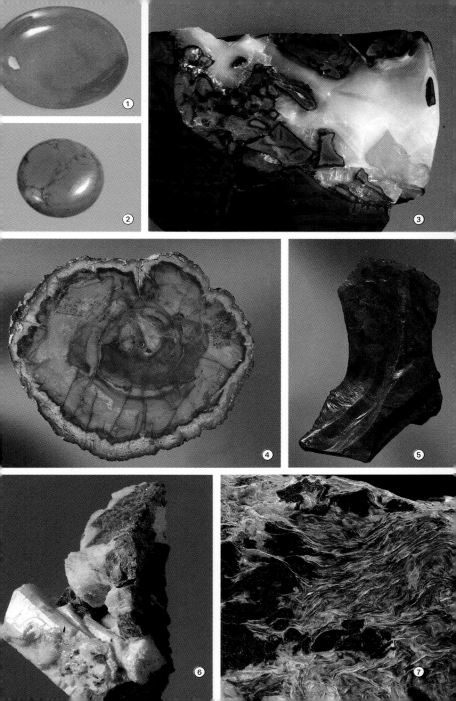

Thomsonite
$NaCa_2[Al_5Si_5O_{20}] \cdot 6\ H_2O$

① Giant's Causeway, Northern Ireland 1:3

Streak white. **Mohs' hardness** 5–5½. **Specific gravity** 2.3–2.4. **Characteristics:** white, grey, yellow, reddish, sometimes colorless, green. Lustre: vitreous, on cleavage face mother-of-pearl; transparent to translucent. Cleavage: complete. Fracture: uneven to conchoidal, brittle; soluble in hydrochloric acid. Crystals: (rhombic) prismatic, columnar, tabular, vertical striped; rare and small, sometimes cross-shaped twinnings. **Aggregates:** rough, radial, dendritic, reniform, spheroidal; present in young, basic volcanics, rarely in sedimentary deposits. **Accompanied by:** natrolite, chabazite, phillipsite, calcite, analcite. **Found in:** Eifel, Erzgebirge/Germany; Czechoslovakia; Vesuvius/Italy; Skye/Scotland; Faeroe Islands/Denmark; Iceland; Nova Scotia/Canada; Oregon, California, Colorado/USA; India. **Similar to:** natrolite, phillipsite, gonnardite.

Cancrinite
in series with vishnevite
$Na_2Ca_2[(CO_3)_2 | (AlSiO_4)_6]$

② Blue Mountain, Ontario/Canada

Streak white. **Mohs' hardness** 5–6. **Specific gravity** 2.4–2.5. **Characteristics:** colorless, yellowish, pink, white. Lustre: on cleavage face mother-of-pearl, vitreous; transparent to translucent. Cleavage: complete; Fracture: uneven, brittle; soluble in hydrochloric acid (effervescence). Crystals: (hexagonal) prismatic, short columnar, acicular; mostly intergrowth. **Aggregates:** rough, granular, dendritic; present as by-product in residual crystallization and of volcanic eruptions. **Accompanied by:** zeolite, nepheline, sanidine, sodalite, calcite. **Found in:** Eifel/Germany; Siebenbuergen/Romania; Norway; Sweden; Kola, Urals/USSR; Ontario/Canada; Maine, Colorado/USA. **Similar to:** nepheline, chondrodite, humite.

Mesolite
$Na_2Ca_2[Al_2Si_3O_{10}]_3 \cdot 8\ H_2O$

③ with hydrous scolecite; India

Streak white. **Mohs' hardness** 5–5½. **Specific gravity** 2.2–2.4. **Characteristics:** colorless, white. Lustre: vitreous, silky, dull; transparent to translucent. Cleavage: complete. Fracture: conchoidal, brittle. Crystals: (monoclinic) long prismatic to acicular. **Aggregates:** delicately fibrous, also crumbly; present in cavities of volcanics. **Accompanied by:** other zeolites, apophyllite. **Found in:** Thüringen/Germany; Northern Ireland; Faeroe Islands/Denmark; Skye/Scotland; Iceland; Greenland; Nova Scotia/Canada; Oregon, California/USA; Australia. **Similar to:** natrolite, scolecite.

Sodalite
$Na_8[Cl_2 | (AlSiO_4)_6]$

④ with white calcite, Canada 1:2

Streak white. **Mohs' hardness** 5–6. **Specific gravity** 2.1–2.3. **Characteristics:** blue, grey, white, colorless. Lustre: vitreous, on cleavage face greasy; translucent to opaque. Cleavage: complete. Fracture: uneven, conchoidal, brittle; soluble in hydrochloric and nitric acid. Flame test: yellow. Crystals: (cubic) rhombododecahedral, surface growth, occasional twinning. **Aggregates:** rough, granular, dense; present in metasomatized rocks, by foyaite (syenite), product of volcanic eruptions. **Accompanied by:** nepheline, leucite, cancrinite, augite, sanidine, zircon, titanite, hematite, barite. **Found in:** Eifel/Germany; Vesuvius, Alban mountains/Italy; Siebenbuergen/Rumania; Portugal; Ukraine, Kola/USSR; Maine, Arkansas/USA; Bolivia; Brazil. **Similar to:** analcite, leucite, lapis lazuli, lazulite, haüynite, charoite.

gonnardite pg. 56, milarite pg. 92, orthoclase pg. 94, chalcedony pg. 118

Haüynite
(Na,Ca)$_{8-4}$[(SO$_4$)$_{2-1}$ I (AlSiO$_4$)$_6$]

① Italy 1:2
② Mendig, Eifel/Germany

Streak white. **Mohs' hardness** 5½–6. **Specific gravity** 2.4–2.5. **Characteristics:** blue, occasionally grey, white, yellowish, reddish, seldom colorless, green. Lustre: vitreous, on cleavage face greasy; transparent to translucent. Cleavage: complete. Fracture: conchoidal, uneven, brittle; easily soluble in hydrochloric acid. Crystals: (cubic) rhombododecahedral; sometimes octahedral; intergrowth and surface growth; very rare, small. **Aggregates:** rough, granular, in basic volcanics, and ejected blocks from volcanic eruptions. **Accompanied by:** nepheline, leucite, nosean, mellite, sanidine, augite, hornblende, idocrase. **Found in:** Eifel, Erzgebirge/Germany; Vesuvius, Alban mountains/Italy; Auvergne/France; Baikal Lake/USSR; Morocco; Quebec/Canada; Montana, South Dakota/USA. **Similar to:** sodalite, lapis lazuli, nosean.

Leucite
K[AlSi$_2$O$_6$]

③ Resina/Italy

Streak white. **Mohs' hardness** 5½–6. **Specific gravity** 2.5. **Characteristics:** white-grey, seldom colorless, usually dull. Lustre: on cleavage face vitreous and greasy; translucent to opaque. Cleavage: none. Fracture: conchoidal to uneven, brittle; soluble in hydrochloric acid. Crystals: (tetragonal) icositetrahedral; mostly intergrowth, pseudomorphic. **Aggregates:** rough, granular, rare; present in young basic magmatites, particularly in foyaite (syenite). **Accompanied by:** nepheline, apatite, augite, biotite, sanidine. **Found in:** Eifel, Kaiserstuhl/Germany; Czechoslovakia; Vesuvius, Alban mountains/Italy; Turkestan, western Siberia/USSR; British Columbia/Canada; Arkansas, Wyoming/USA; Sao Paulo/Brazil. **Similar to:** analcite, sodalite, garnet.

Nosean
Na$_8$[SO$_4$ I (AlSiO$_4$)$_6$]

④ Laarcher Lake, Eifel/Germany 1:3

Streak white. **Mohs' hardness** 5½. **Specific gravity** 2.3–2.4. **Characteristics:** grey, yellow to brown, blue, green, black, seldom white. Lustre: vitreous and greasy; transparent to opaque. Cleavage: complete. Fracture: conchoidal, brittle; soluble in acid. Crystals: (cubic) rhombododecahedral, mostly intergrown; small and rare. **Aggregates:** rough, granular; present in young basic volcanics. **Accompanied by:** nepheline, leucite, haüynite, sanidine, biotite, zircon, augite. **Found in:** Eifel, Baden/Germany; Vesuvius, Alban mountains/Italy; Cornwall/England; Colorado, South Dakota/USA; northern China. **Similar to:** sodalite, haüynite, zircon.

Petalite   castor
Li[AlSi$_4$O$_{10}$]

⑤ reddish aggregate; Meldon,
Devon/England 1:2

Streak white. **Mohs' hardness** 6–6½. **Specific gravity** 2.4. **Characteristics:** colorless, white, grey, reddish, green. Lustre: vitreous, on cleavage face mother-of-pearl; transparent to translucent. Cleavage: complete. Fracture: conchoidal and brittle. Flame test: carmine red. Crystals: (monoclinic) columnar, tabular; mostly scattered; very rare and small. **Aggregates:** rough, sparlike, granular, bladed, dense; present in granite pegmatites. **Accompanied by:** lepidolite, spodumene, tourmaline, quartz, arsenopyrite, pollucite. **Found in:** Elba/Italy; Sweden; Finland; Zimbabwe; South Africa; Namibia; Manitoba/Canada; Massachusetts, Maine/USA; western Australia. **Similar to:** spodumene, amblygonite, scapolite, feldspars, glass.

Streak

white and
colorless

Mohs'
hardness 1 ◀

2 ◀

3 ◀
–
4 ◀

5 ◀
–
6 ◀

7 ◀

8 ◀

9 ◀

10 ◀

Specific
gravity 1 ◀
–
2 ◀

3 ◀
–
4 ◀

5 ◀
–
6 ◀

7 ◀

Analcite   analcime
Na[AlSi₂O₆] · H₂O

① Farmsen/Germany

Streak white. **Mohs' hardness** 5–5½. **Specific gravity** 2.2–2.3. **Characteristics:** colorless, white, grey, yellow, reddish, green. Lustre: vitreous; transparent to translucent. Cleavage: none. Fracture: uneven, conchoidal, brittle. Flame test: yellow. Crystals: (cubic) icositetrahedral, also hexahedral; usually surface growth; pseudomorphic. **Aggregates:** rough, granular, dense, crumbly, crusty; present in basalt, ore veins. **Accompanied by:** leucite, natrolite, nepheline, thomsonite, chabazite, stilbite, apophyllite, prehnite, chlorite, calcite. **Found in:** Harz mountains/Germany; Czechoslovakia; Trient, Sicily/Italy; Faeroe Islands/Denmark; Norway; Urals, Caucasus/USSR; New Jersey, Colorado/USA. **Similar to:** leucite, sodalite, garnet.

Tridymite
SiO₂

② Colli Euganei/Italy 1:4

Streak white. **Mohs' hardness** 6½–7. **Specific gravity** 2.27. **Characteristics:** colorless, white, grey. Lustre: vitreous; transparent to translucent. Cleavage: none. Fracture: conchoidal, brittle; soluble in hot soda solution. Crystals: (hexagonal–rhombic) tabular with hexagonal contours; surface growth, often twinning and tripling. **Aggregates:** scaly, fanlike, spheroidal, rough; present in cavities of acidic volcanics, by-product after volcanic eruptions, in sandstone. **Accompanied by:** quartz, sanidine, hematite, augite, hornblende. **Found in:** Siebengebirge, Eifel/Germany; Hungary; Auvergne/France; Scotland; Colorado, Oregon/USA; Mexico. **Similar to:** sanidine.

Scolecite
Ca[Al₂Si₃O₁₀] · 3 H₂O

③ with pink stilbite and green apophylite; Poona/India

Streak white. **Mohs' hardness** 5–5½. **Specific gravity** 2.3–2.4. **Characteristics:** colorless, white. Lustre: vitreous and silky; transparent. Cleavage: perfect. Fracture: conchoidal, brittle; soluble in hydrochloric acid. Crystals: (monoclinic) prismatic to acicular. **Aggregates:** radial, fibrous; present in drusy cavities in granite and syenite, in alpine and young volcanic crevices. **Accompanied by:** laumontite, heulandite, stilbite, apophyllite. **Found in:** Iceland; Faeroe Islands/Denmark; Scotland; Vesuvius, Trient/Italy; Urals, Caucasus/USSR; Bombay/India; Colorado, California/USA; Rio Grande do Sul/Brazil. **Similar to:** natrolite, mesolite, gonnardite.

Natrolite
Na₂[Al₂Si₃O₁₀] · 2 H₂O

④ Westerwald/Germany

Streak white. **Mohs' hardness** 5–5½. **Specific gravity** 2.2–2.3. **Characteristics:** white, yellowish to brown, reddish, colorless. Lustre: vitreous, silky, mother-of-pearl; transparent to translucent. Cleavage: complete. Fracture: conchoidal, brittle; will melt in flame of a candle. Flame test: yellow. Soluble in hydrochloric acid. Occasional orange fluorescence under ultraviolet light. Crystals: (rhombic) prismatic to acicular, filamentary; usually surface growth. **Aggregates:** radial, spheroidal, rough, powdery; present in cavities in volcanics, in ore veins. **Accompanied by:** zeolite, benitoite, neptunite, andesine, apophyllite, calcite. **Found in:** Baden, Hesse, Harz mountains, Erzgebirge/Germany; Czechoslovakia; Auvergne/France; southern Tirol/Italy; Iceland; Faeroe Islands/Denmark; Kola, Urals/USSR; New Jersey, California/USA. **Similar to:** mesolite, scolecite, thomsonite, wavellite, aragonite, gonnardite.

Streak

white and
colorless

Mohs'
hardness 1

2

3

4

5

6

7

8

9

10

Specific
gravity 1

2

3

4

5

6

7

Tremolite
$Ca_2Mg_5[OH|Si_4O_{11}]_2$

① Campolungo, Tessin/Switzerland 1:2

Streak white. Mohs' hardness 5½–6. Specific gravity 2.9–3.1. Characteristics: white, grey, greenish. Lustre: vitreous, silky; transparent to opaque. Cleavage: complete. Fracture: fibrous, brittle. Crystals: (monoclinic) long prismatic, acicular. Aggregates: dendritic, radial, feltlike (asbestos); present in marble, talc slate, serpentine. Accompanied by: calcite, dolomite, talc, serpentine, diaspore. Found in: eastern Bavaria/Germany; Tessin/Switzerland; Tyrol/Austria; Novara/Italy; Finland; Urals, Baikal Lake/USSR; Namibia; Ontario, Quebec/Canada; New York, Arizona/USA. Similar to: wollastonite, pectolite, zoisite, clinozoisite, diaspore, serpentine.

Amblygonite
$(Li,Na)Al[(F,OH)|PO_4]$

② Viitaniemi/Finland 1:½

Streak white. Mohs' hardness 6. Specific gravity 3.0–3.1. Characteristics: white, grey, yellow to brown, greenish, bluish. Lustre: vitreous, on cleavage face mother-of-pearl; transparent to translucent. Cleavage: complete. Fracture: uneven to conchoidal, brittle. Flame test: carmine red. Soluble in sulfuric acid. Crystals: (triclinic) dipyramidal–distorted; rare, sometimes twinning. Aggregates: rough, sparlike, granular; present in pegmatites, granite. Accompanied by: cassiterite, apatite, feldspars, quartz, spodumene, lepidolite. Found in: Creuse/France; Estremadura/Spain; Finland; Sweden; Kazakhstan/USSR; Namibia; South Dakota, Maine/USA; Brazil. Similar to: feldspars, petalite, spodumene, calcite, brazilianite.

Pollucite
$(Cs,Na)[AlSi_2O_6] \cdot \frac{1}{2} H_2O.$

③ Bernic Lake, Manitoba/Canada

Streak white. Mohs' hardness 6½. Specific gravity 2.9. Characteristics: colorless, white, grey. Lustre: vitreous; transparent to dull-translucent. Cleavage: none. Fracture: conchoidal to uneven, brittle; difficult to dissolve in hydrochloric acid. Crystals: (cubic) cubes; rare. Aggregates: rough, coarse- to fine-grained; present in crevices of granite and pegmatites. Accompanied by: petalite, lepidolite, amblygonite, spodumene, quartz, microcline. Found in: Elba/Italy; Sweden; Kazakhstan/USSR; Namibia; Manitoba, Quebec/Canada; Maine, South Dakota/USA. Similar to: quartz, hyalite.

Bertrandite
$Be_4[(OH)_2|Si_2O_7]$

④ Aschamalm/Austria 1:8

Streak white. Mohs' hardness 6½–7. Specific gravity 2.60. Characteristics: colorless, white, light yellow. Lustre: vitreous, mother-of-pearl; transparent to translucent. Cleavage: complete. Fracture: bladed, brittle. Crystals: (rhombic) tabular, prismatic; usually small; heart-shaped twinning; sometimes pseudomorphic. Aggregates: only groups of crystals; present in acidic volcanics, pegmatites, rarely in lead-ore veins. Accompanied by: beryl, phenakite, aegirine, riebeckite, barite, fluorite, tourmaline, apatite, adularia, opal, calcite. Found in: eastern Bavaria/Germany; Salzburg/Austria; Czechoslovakia; western France; Murcia/Spain; Norway; Namibia; eastern Siberia/USSR; Queensland/Australia; Colorado, Maine/USA; Chihuahua/Mexico. Similar to: barite, albite, muscovite, quartz.

86

pectolite pg. 66, scapolite pg. 78, fassaite pg. 98, lazulite pg. 102

Eudialyte

(Na,Ca,Fe)$_6$Zr[(OH,Cl) | (Si$_3$O$_9$)$_2$]

① Kola/USSR 1:2

Streak white. **Mohs' hardness** 5–5½. **Specific gravity** 2.8–3.1. **Characteristics:** reddish brown, red, pink, yellow. Lustre: transparent. Cleavage: incomplete. Fracture: uneven, brittle; will corrode in acid. Crystals: (trigonal) thick tabular, sometimes prismatic; usually intergrowth; seldom well-developed. **Aggregates:** rough, granular to dense; present in foyaites (syenites), and pegmatites. **Accompanied by:** zircon, nepheline, sodalite, molybdenite, aegirine, microcline. **Found in:** Norway; Kola/USSR; Greenland; Quebec/Canada; Arkansas, Montana/USA; Minas Gerais, Sao Paulo/Brazil; Transvaal/South Africa; Madagascar. **Similar to:** zircon, garnet.

Datolite

CaB[OH | SiO$_4$]

② with danburite; Charcas/Mexico

Streak white. **Mohs' hardness** 5–5½. **Specific gravity** 2.9–3.0. **Characteristics:** colorless, white, yellow, greenish, seldom grey, reddish. Lustre: vitreous, on cleavage face greasy; transparent to translucent. Cleavage: none. Fracture: uneven to conchoidal, brittle. Flame test: green. Lightly corrosive in hydrochloric acid. Crystals: (monoclinic) short prismatic, thick tabular, multifaceted; usually surficial growth. **Aggregates:** rough, granular to dense, fibrous, radial, reniform, crusty; present in cavities of base magmatites and metamorphic rocks; less often granitic rocks, ore deposits, alpine crevices. **Accompanied by:** prehnite, apophyllite, wollastonite, diopside, magnetite, pure copper, quartz, calcite, chabazite, stilbite, heulandite. **Found in:** Harz mountains, Black Forest/Germany; southern Tirol/Italy; Czechoslovakia; Norway; Urals, Transbaikal region/USSR; Tazmania/Australia; New Jersey, Michigan/USA. **Similar to:** ulexite, colemanite, prehnite, danburite, apophyllite.

Beryllonite

NaBe[PO$_4$]

③ Newry, Maine/USA

Streak white. **Mohs' hardness** 5½. **Specific gravity** 2.8. **Characteristics:** colorless, white, yellowish. Lustre: vitreous, mother-of-pearl; translucent to transparent. Cleavage: complete. Fracture: conchoidal, brittle. Crystals: (monoclinic) short prismatic, tabular, multifaceted; occasional twinning. **Aggregates:** only in groups of crystals; present in granite pegmatites. **Accompanied by:** tourmaline, albite, muscovite, smoky quartz. **Found in:** Finland; Zimbabwe; Maine/USA. **Similar to:** many of the colorless minerals, apatite, glass.

Wardite

NaAl$_3$[(OH)$_4$ | (PO$_4$)$_2$]·2 H$_2$O

④ Yukon Co./Canada 1:2

Streak white. **Mohs' hardness** 5. **Specific gravity** 2.8. **Characteristics:** blue-green, white, colorless. Lustre: vitreous, greasy, dull; transparent to translucent. Cleavage: complete. Fracture: uneven, conchoidal, brittle. Crystals: (tetragonal) pyramidal, occasionally horizontally stripped. **Aggregates:** rough, granular, fibrous, crusty, radial–tuberous; present in drusy cavities and crevices of pagmatites and phosphate-rich sedimentary rocks. **Accompanied by:** variscite, vivianite, amblygonite, lazulite, apatite. **Found in:** Creuse/France; Utah, South Dakota, California, New Hampshire/USA; Paraiba/Brazil. **Similar to:** turquoise, variscite.

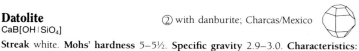

88

Wollastonite
Ca$_3$[Si$_3$O$_9$]

① Auerbach, Bergstrasse, Hesse/Germany

Streak white. **Mohs' hardness** 4½–5. **Specific gravity** 2.8–2.9. **Characteristics:** colorless, white, grey, yellowish, greenish, reddish. Lustre: vitreous, on cleavage face mother-of-pearl, aggregates silky; translucent to transparent. Cleavage: complete. Fracture: fibrous and brittle; soluble in acid. Crystals: (triclinic) broad dendritic; fibrous, acicular, less often thick tabular; mostly surface growth; often twinning. **Aggregates:** sparlike, granular, radial, bladed, finely fibrous, rough; present in calc-silicate rocks, by-product of volcanic eruptions. **Accompanied by:** garnet, idocrase, diopside, epidote, graphite. **Found in:** Black Forest, Erzgebierge/Germany; Banat/Rumania; Finland; Vesuvius, Veltlin/Italy; Bretagne/France; Urals, eastern Siberia/USSR; Namibia; New York, California/USA; Mexico. **Similar to:** pectolite, tremolite, scolecite, zoisite.

Nepheline
KNa$_3$[AlSiO$_4$]$_4$

② Vesuvius/Italy

Streak white. **Mohs' hardness** 5–6. **Specific gravity** 2.6–2.7. **Characteristics:** colorless, white, grey, yellow to brownish, reddish and greenish. Lustre: vitreous, on cleavage face greasy; transparent or opaque–dull (eläolite). Cleavage: incomplete. Fracture: conchoidal to brittle. Flame test: yellow. Soluble in hydrochloric acid. Crystals: (hexagonal) prismatic, short columnar, less often thick tabular; intergrowth and surface growth. **Aggregates:** rough, granular to dense, present in basic magmatites and pegmatites; by-product of volcanic eruptions; seldom in metamorphic rocks. **Accompanied by:** feldspars, leucite, sodalite, melilite, cancrinite, augite, aegirine, hornblende, apatite. **Found in:** Odenwald, Kaiserstuhl, Saxony/Germany; Siebenbürgen/Rumania; Portugal; Kola, Urals/USSR; Transvaal/South Africa; Ontario/Canada; Montana/USA. **Similar to:** cancrinite, melilite, cordierite, apatite, quartz.

Carpholite
MnAl$_2$[(OH)$_4$ | Si$_2$O$_6$]

③ Schlaggenwald/Czechoslovakia 1:2

Streak white. **Mohs' hardness** 5–5½. **Specific gravity** 2.9–3.0. **Characteristics:** straw yellow, yellow-green, yellow-brown. Lustre: silky; translucent. Cleavage: complete. Fracture: fibrous, brittle; easily soluble in acid. Crystals: (rhombic) filamentary. **Aggregates:** finely fibrous, radial, bundle-like, matted; seldom rough; present in schist, lead-ore deposits. **Accompanied by:** fluorite, quartz, cassiterite. **Found in:** Harz mountains/Germany; Czechoslovakia; Macedonia/Yugoslavia; Ardennen/Belgium.

Melilite
(Ca,Na)$_2$(Mg,Al,Fe)[Si$_2$O$_7$]

④ with nepheline; Üdersdorf, Eifel/Germany 1:4
⑤ Capo di Bove/Italy

Streak white to grey. **Mohs' hardness** 5–6. **Specific gravity** 2.9–3.0. **Characteristics:** yellow, brown, grey, sometimes colorless. Lustre: vitreous, on fresh cleavage faces greasy; transparent to translucent. Cleavage: incomplete. Fracture: conchoidal, brittle; easily soluble in acid. Crystals: (tetragonal) thick tabular, short columnar, usually small, intergrowth and surface growth; sometimes crosslike twinning. **Aggregates:** rough, granular; present in basic volcanics. **Accompanied by:** perovskite, olivine, hornblende, augite, nepheline, leucite, apatite, calcite. **Found in:** Kaiserstuhl, Eifel/Germany; Czechoslovakia; Vesuvius/Italy; Kola/USSR; Madagascar; Quebec/Canada; Hawaii, Colorado/USA, Rurengo/Mexico. **Similar to:** nepheline.

90

arfvedsonite pg. 212, odontolite pg. 212

Turquoise

$CuAl_6[(OH)_2 | PO_4]_4 \cdot 4\, H_2O$

Streak white. **Mohs' hardness** 5–6. **Specific gravity** 2.6–2.9. **Characteristics:** azure blue to apple green. Lustre: vitreous, waxy, also dull; opaque. Cleavage: none. Fracture: conchoidal, brittle; distinct pleochroism; soluble in acid. Crystals: (triclinic) short prismatic; very small and very rare. **Aggregates:** rough, finely granular to dense, finely fibrous, botryoidal, crusty, accumulating in crevices, especially in ta-chytes, slate, sandstone. **Accompanied by:** limonite, chalcedony. **Found in:** Vogtland, Thüringen/Germany; Silesia/Poland; Iran; Turkestan/USSR; Manchuria; Zinai/Egypt; New Mexico, Arizona, Nevada/USA. **Similar to:** chrysocolla, variscite, vivianite, garnierite, odontolite, wardite.

Brazilianite

$NaAl_3[(OH)_2 | PO_4]_2$

Streak white. **Mohs' hardness** 5½. **Specific gravity** 2.98. **Characteristics:** yellow to greenish yellow. Lustre: vitreous; transparent to translucent. Cleavage: complete. Fracture: conchoidal, brittle. Flame test: yellow. Soluble in acid. Crystals: (mono-clinic) short prismatic, multifaceted. **Aggregates:** spheroidal, radial fibrous, rough; present in pegmatites. **Accompanied by:** apatite, amblygonite, tourmaline, wardite, lazulite, muscovite, albite. **Found in:** Minas Gerais, Paraiba/Brazil; New Hampshire/USA. **Similar to:** amblygonite, beryl, chrysoberyl, topaz, albite.

Milarite

$KCa_2AlBe_2[Si_{12}O_{30}] \cdot \frac{1}{2}\, H_2O$

Streak white. **Mohs' hardness** 5½–6. **Specific gravity** 2.5–2.6. **Characteristics:** colorless, light green, yellow-green. Lustre: vitreous, greasy; transparent to translu-cent. Cleavage: none. Fracture: conchoidal to uneven, brittle. Crystals: (hexagonal) prismatic, acicular, seldom thick tabular; usually surface growth. **Aggregates:** crystalline groups; present in alpine crevices; pegmatites; **Accompanied by:** anatase, brookite, chlorite, bertrandite, albite, adularia, quartz. **Found in:** Bavarian Forest, Thüringen/Germany; Graubuenden/Switzerland; Czechoslovakia; eastern Tyrol, Salzburg/Austria; Kola/USSR; Namibia; Mexico; Brazil. **Similar to:** beryl, apatite, phenakite.

Prehnite

$Ca_2Al_2[(OH)_2 | Si_3O_{10}]$

Streak white. **Mohs' hardness** 5½–6. **Specific gravity** 2.8–3.0. **Characteristics:** colorless, white, grey, greenish, yellowish, reddish. Lustre: vitreous, mother-of-pearl; transparent to translucent. Cleavage: incomplete. Fracture: uneven, brittle; only slowly soluble in hydrochloric acid. Crystals: (rhombic) tabular, short columnar; often distorted; single crystals rare; occasionally pseudomorphic. **Aggregates:** rough, fan-shaped, radial, spheroidal, reniform; present in basic magmatites, slate, alpine crevices. **Accompanied by:** stilbite, heulandite, pectolite, epidote, calcite, laumontite. **Found in:** Black Forest, Rhein-Pfalz, Thüringer Forest/Germany; Tyrol/Austria; Graubuenden/Switzerland; southern Tirol/Italy; Dauphiné/France; Bombay/India; Urals, Caucasus/USSR; Michigan, New Jersey/USA. **Similar to:** stilbite, wavelite, datolite.

Streak

white and
colorless

Mohs'
hardness 1
           2 ◄
           3 ◄
           4 ◄
          5 ◄
           6 ◄
           7 ◄
           8 ◄
           9 ◄
          10 ◄

Specific
gravity 1
           2 ◄
          3 ◄
           4 ◄
          5 ◄
          6 ◄
           7 ◄

Orthoclase Feldspars
K[AlSi$_3$O$_8$]

Streak white. **Mohs' hardness** 6. **Specific gravity** 2.53–2.56. **Characteristics**: colorless, white, yellow to brown, meat red to reddish brown, green. Lustre: vitreous, mother-of-pearl; transparent to translucent to opaque. Cleavage: complete, cleavage angle 90°. Fracture: conchoidal, uneven, splintery, brittle. Crystals: (monoclinic) orthoclase; (triclinic) microcline; prismatic, tabular, rhombohedral, often multifaceted; intergrowth and surface growth; often twinning and pseudomorphic. **Aggregates**: rough, sparlike, granular; intergrowth with quartz (graphic granite); combined with magmatites, metamorphic rocks; less often in sedimentary rocks; well-developed crystals in pegmatites, in crevices and veins. **Accompanied by**: quartz, plagioclase, mica, tourmaline, topaz, garnet.

Orthoclase   ② Saxony/Germany; ③ Arendal/Norway

Milky white, reddish white, light pink to meat red; usually cloudy, opaque, seldom clear yellow; often interpenetration twinning (among others: Carlsbad twinning); sometimes faint reddish-orange fluorescence under ultraviolet light. **Found in:** eastern Bavaria/Germany; Tauern/Austria; Tessin/Switzerland; Sweden; Norway; Canada; California/USA; Madagascar; Burma. **Similar to:** feldspars, barite, calcite.

Adularia   ⑥ Wallis/Switzerland

Variety of orthoclase; transparent, faintly cloudy to milky white; almost always surface growth in drusy cavities and alpine crevices; often sprinkled or intergrown with chlorite. **Found in:** Tessin, Graubünden/Switzerland; Tauern/Austria; Sri Lanka; South Africa.

Moonstone Variety of adularia or sanidine. Colorless, yellowish, milky, cloudy with bluish-white tint, and wavelike light reflections, particularly distinct when curved; weak bluish or orange fluorescence under ultraviolet light. **Found in:** Sri Lanka; India; Burma; western Australia; Tanzania; Madagascar; Virginia/USA; Brazil. **Similar to:** chalcedony, glass imitations.

Microcline   ① Setesdalen/Norway

Usually white, grey, yellowish, reddish; cloudy to opaque. **Found in:** eastern Bavaria/Germany; Scandinavia; Urals, Karelia/USSR; New Hampshire/USA; India. **Similar to:** feldspars, barite, dolomite.

Sanidine   ④ Vetralla, Latium/Italy

Colorless, transparent to opaque grey, grey brownish; large tabular and scattered crystals in young volcanic rocks. **Found in:** Siebengebirge/Germany; Vesuvius/Italy; Cacausus/USSR. **Similar to:** cancinite, tridymite.

Amazonite   ⑤ Pikes Peak, Colorado/USA

Variety of microcline. Green, bluish green, usually striped or spotted; opaque to translucent. **Found in:** Colorado/USA; Brazil; India; Madagascar; Urals/USSR. **Similar to:** jadeite, nephrite, turquoise.

Streak

white and
colorless

Mohs'
hardness

1 ◄
–
2 ◄
–
3 ◄
–
4 ◄
–
5 ◄
–
6 ◄
–
7 ◄
–
8 ◄
–
9 ◄
–
10 ◄

Specific
gravity

1 ◄
–
·
2 ◄
–
3 ◄
–
4 ◄
–
5 ◄
–
6 ◄
–
7 ◄

Plagioclase Feldspars   solid solution

(Albite) Na[AlSi$_3$O$_8$]
(Anorthite) Ca[Al$_2$Si$_2$O$_8$]

Streak white. **Mohs' hardness** 6–6½. **Specific gravity** 2.61–2.77. **Characteristics:** colorless, white, grey, green, reddish; occasionally colored labradorization. Lustre: vitreous, dull, mother-of-pearl on cleavage faces; transparent to opaque. Cleavage: complete, cleavage angle approximately 86°. Fracture: conchoidal to uneven, brittle; partially soluble in acid. Crystals: (triclinic) tabular, prismatic; intergrowth, and surficial growth; twinning sometimes, always striped. **Aggregates:** rough, granular, crusty; present as by-product in magmatites, metamorphic rocks, less often in sedimentary rocks. **Accompanied by:** quartz, orthoclase, mica, chlorite, calcite, zeolite, augite, hornblende.

Albite   ② Habachtal, Tyrol/Austria

Colorless, greyish white, seldom greenish, bluish, reddish; usually cloudy, transparent to opaque. Not easily soluble in acid. **Found in:** Tyrol/Austria; Switzerland; Elba, Trient/Italy; Czechoslovakia; Pyrenees; Maine/USA. **Similar to:** other plagioclase, orthoclase, barite.

Pericline   ③ with chlorite covering; Tauern/Austria

Variety of albite; white or greenish due to chlorite dusting; milky to cloudy. Particularly frequent in chlorite slate in alpine crevices.

Oligoclase Colorless, white, grey, greenish, yellowish, reddish; transparent, cloudy. Not easily soluble in acid; crystals mostly intergrown. **Similar to:** other feldspars.

Aventurine Feldspar   sunstone   ① polished; Norway

Variety of oligoclase; orange, reddish brown; opaque. Metallic sparkling due to intergrown hematite or goethite. **Found in:** USA; Canada; India; Norway; USSR. **Similar to:** aventurine quartz.

Andesine White, grey, yellowish, greenish; transparent to opaque. Not easily soluble in acid. **Found in:** eastern Bavaria/Germany; Czechoslovakia; Hungary; Caucasus/USSR; South America. **Similar to:** other feldspars.

Labradorite   ④ Spectrolite; Finland; ⑤ Antsirabé/Madagascar

White, grey, brown, bluish; transparent to opaque; sometimes blue, green, reddish labradorization. Crystals are rare. Soluble in acid. **Found in:** Labrador/Canada; Mexico; Madagascar; Ukraine/USSR. The finished variety from Finland is called spectrolite.

Bytownite White, grey, brownish, bluish; transparent to opaque. Occasionally colored iridescence; soluble in acid. **Found in:** Harz mountains/Germany; Sicily/Italy; Albania; Yugoslavia; Corsica/France; Canada. **Similar to:** labradorite.

Anorthite Colorless, white, grey, reddish; transparent, cloudy, opaque. Soluble in acid. **Found in:** Italy, India, Japan. **Similar to:** other feldspars.

96

Apatite
Ca₅[F,Cl,OH] | (PO₄)₃

① with quartz rock crystal; Mexico 1:2
② Krägerö, Norway

Streak white. **Mohs' hardness** 5. **Specific gravity** 3.16–3.22. **Characteristics:** colorless, white, also many other colors. Lustre: vitreous, on cleavage face greasy; transparent to opaque. Cleavage: incomplete. Fracture: conchoidal to uneven, brittle; sometimes bluish fluorescence under ultraviolet light. Easily soluble in acid. Crystals: (hexagonal) short and long columnar, thick tabular, dipyramidal, acicular, often multi-faceted; intergrown and surface growth. **Aggregates:** rough, granular to dense; fibrous, radial, reniform; present in alpine crevices, magmatites, and metamorphic rocks; on magnetite and cassiterite deposits, individual layers of sediments and concretions. **Accompanied by:** magnetite, cassiterite, sphere, rutile, wolframite, zircon, topaz. **Found in:** Eifel, Erzgebirge/Germany; Tyrol/Austria; Switzerland; Dauphné/France; Sweden; Norway; Kola, Urals/USSR; Mexico; Montana/USA. **Similar to:** pyromorphite, mimetite, nepheline, milarite, beryl, quartz.

Fassaite
Ca(Mg,Fe,Al)[(Si,Al)₂O₆]

③ with calcite; Fassatal, southern Tirol/Italy

Streak greenish white. **Mohs' hardness** 6. **Specific gravity** 2.9–3.3. **Characteristics:** light to dark green, black. Lustre: vitreous, transparent to opaque. Cleavage: incomplete. Fracture: uneven to conchoidal, brittle. Crystals: (monoclinic) short prisms, multifaceted; intergrowth and surficial growth. **Aggregates:** rough, granular to dense; present in marble, as by-product of volcanic eruptions. **Accompanied by:** grossular, idocrase, spinel, calcite, dolomite. **Found in:** southern Tirol, Vesuvius/Italy; Scotland; Sweden; Montana/USA; Sri Lanka. **Similar to:** diopside, grossular, idocrase.

Chondrodite
Mg₅[(OH,F)₂ | (SiO₄)₂]

④ New York/USA 1:2

Streak white. **Mohs' hardness** 6–6½. **Specific gravity** 3.1–3.2. **Characteristics:** yellow, brown, red, rarely green. Lustre: transparent to translucent. Cleavage: incomplete. Fracture: conchoidal to uneven, brittle. Crystals: (monoclinic) short columnar, usually small, multifaceted; often twinning. **Aggregates:** rough, granular, as impregnation; present in limestone, and dolomite marble, ore veins, as by-product of volcanic eruptions. **Accompanied by:** magnetite, sphalerite, galena, idocrase, spinel. **Found in:** Fichtelgebirge, Erzgebirge/Germany; Vogesen/France; Sweden; Finland; Ontario/Canada; New York/USA. **Similar to:** cancrinite, olivine.

Diaspore
AlOOH

⑤ Mineral Co., Nevada/USA

Streak white. **Mohs' hardness** 6½–7. **Specific gravity** 3.3–3.5. **Characteristics:** colorless, white, grey, yellow to brownish, green to blue. Lustre: vitreous, mother-of-pearl on cleavage faces; transparent to translucent. Cleavage: complete. Fracture: uneven, brittle; sometimes distinct pleochroism. Crystals: (rhombic) tabular, small, rare, often twinning. **Aggregates:** rough, bladed, radial; present in metamorphic rocks, rock-forming in lime-bauxites. **Accompanied by:** corundum, hematite, kyanite, spinel, dolomite, calcite. **Found in:** Switzerland; Tyrol/Austria; Greece; Norway; Urals/USSR; South Africa; Colorado/USA. **Similar to:** phlogopite, boehmite, tremolite.

---

98 | kyanite pg. 70, triphylite pg. 70, amblygonite pg. 86, tremolite pg. 86, eudialyte pg. 88, bronzite pg. 106, rhodonite pg. 106, sphene pg. 106

Streak

white and
colorless

Mohs'
hardness 1 ◄

2 ◄

3 ◄

4 ◄

5 ◄

6 ◄

7 ◄

8 ◄

9 ◄

10 ◄

Specific
gravity 1 ◄

2 ◄

3 ◄

4 ◄

5 ◄

6 ◄

7 ◄

Enstatite
Mg₂[Si₂O₆]

① Kragerö/Norway

Streak white. **Mohs' hardness** 5–6. **Specific gravity** 3.1–3.3. **Characteristics:** greyish white, yellowish to brown, greenish, seldom colorless or white. Lustre: vitreous; transparent to opaque. Cleavage: incomplete, cleavage angle 85°. Fracture: conchoidal to uneven, brittle. Crystals: (rhombic) short prismatic, thick tabular; rare. **Aggregates:** rough, sparlike, granular; present in silicic acid–poor magmatites, metamorphic rocks, sometimes rock-forming. **Accompanied by:** apatite, olivine, phlogopite, diopside, augite, hornblende. **Found in:** Harz mountains/Germany; Scotland; Ireland; Norway; Urals, Caucasus/USSR; Greenland; California/USA; South Africa. **Similar to:** hypersthene, diopside, andalusite.

Idocrase   vesuvianite
Ca₁₀(Mg,Fe)₂Al₄[(OH)₄ | (SiO₄)₅ | (Si₂O₇)₂]

② California/USA

Streak white. **Mohs' hardness** 6½. **Specific gravity** 3.27–3.45. **Characteristics:** grey, yellow, brown, green, black, seldom blue, red. Lustre: vitreous, on cleavage faces greasy; transparent to opaque. Cleavage: incomplete. Fracture: uneven to conchoidal, also splintery, brittle; partially soluble in acid. Crystals: (tetragonal) short and long columnar; dipyramidal, acicular, mostly vertically striped; intergrowth and surface growth. **Aggregates:** rough, granular to dense, radial; present in metamorphic rocks, as by-product of volcanic eruptions, rarely in magmatites. **Accompanied by:** garnet, diopside, wollastonite, epidote. **Found in:** Erzgebirge/Germany; Switzerland; Tyrol/Austria; Vesuvius, Piemonte/Italy; Czechoslovakia; eastern Siberia/USSR; California/USA; Mexico. **Similar to:** scapolite, epidote, grossular, zircon.

Humite
Mg₇[(OH,F)₂ | (SiO₄)₃]

③ Vesuvius/Italy 1:4

Streak white. **Mohs' hardness** 6–6½. **Specific gravity** 3.1–3.2. **Characteristics:** yellowish to brown, orange to red. Lustre: vitreous and resinous; transparent to translucent. Cleavage: incomplete. Fracture: uneven to conchoidal, brittle. Crystals: (rhombic) short columnar, multifaceted; very rare and usually small. **Aggregates:** rough, granular, as impregnation; present in metamorphosed limestones and dolomites, as by-product of volcanic eruptions, occasionally also in ore veins. **Accompanied by:** calcite, dolomite, spinel, magnetite, sphalerite, galena. **Found in:** Fichtelgebirge/Germany; Vesuvius/Italy; Andalusia/Spain; Sweden; Finland; New York/USA. **Similar to:** cancrinite.

Zoisite
Ca₂Al₃[O | OH | SiO₄ | Si₂O₇]

④ Baja California/Mexico
⑤ Zoisite-amphibolite with ruby; Tanzania
⑥ Thulite; Lexviken/Norway 1:2
⑦ Tanzanite; Tanzania

Streak white. **Mohs' hardness** 6–6½. **Specific gravity** 3.15–3.36. **Characteristics:** grey, brownish, green, red (thulite), blue (tanzanite). Lustre: vitreous, mother-of-pearl; transparent to opaque. Cleavage: complete. Fracture: uneven, brittle. Crystals: (rhombic) prismatic, acicular, vertically striped; mostly intergrowth. **Aggregates:** rough, sparlike, dendritic, fibrous; present in metamorphic rocks. **Accompanied by:** epidote, idocrase, quartz, feldspars, kyanite. **Found in:** Erzgebirge/Germany; Kärnten/Austria; Wallis/Switzerland; southern Tirol/Italy; Urals, Altai/USSR; Tanzania; Namibia; Wyoming/USA. **Similar to:** tremolite, sillimanite, clinozoisite.

andalusite pg. 122, jadeite pg. 122, axenite pg. 124, olivine pg. 128

Diopside
CaMg$[Si_2O_6]$

① Outokumpu/Finland; ② Diallag, Bad Harzburg/Germany

Streak white. **Mohs' hardness** 5–6½. **Specific gravity** 3.3–3.4. **Characteristics:** light to dark green, emerald green (chromediopside), grey, yellow, bronze-like (diallag), blue to violet (violane), rarely colorless, white. Lustre: vitreous; transparent to translucent. Cleavage: incomplete, cleavage angle approximately 90°. Fracture: uneven, brittle. Crystals: (monoclinic) short columnar, also tabular; intergrowth and surface growth; frequent twinning. **Aggregates:** rough, dendritic, radial, granular to dense; present in magmatites and metamorphic rocks, alpine crevices. **Accompanied by:** grossular, wollastonite, chlorite, calcite, magnetite, vesuvianite. **Found in:** Odenwald, Erzgebirge/Germany; Tyrol/Austria; Wallis/Switzerland; Sweden; Urals, Baikal Lake region/USSR; Madagascar; California, Montana/USA. **Similar to:** fassaite, hypersthene, bronzite, augite.

Clinozoisite
$Ca_2Al_3[O|OH|SiO_4|Si_2O_7]$

③ on scolecite; Tessin/Switzerland 1:3

Streak white to grey. **Mohs' hardness** 6–7. **Specific gravity** 3.2–3.5. **Characteristics:** grey, yellow, greenish, pink, less often blue and colorless. Lustre: vitreous; translucent to transparent. Cleavage: complete. Fracture: uneven, brittle. Crystals: (monoclinic) long and short prismatic, thick tabular, mostly vertically striped; often twinning. **Aggregates:** rough, dendritic, fibrous, granular; present in metamorphic rocks. **Accompanied by:** axinite, albite, actinolite, glaucophane, epidote, zoisite. **Found in:** Fichtelgebirge/Germany; Tyrol/Austria; Switzerland; Turin/Italy; Madagascar; Ontario/Canada; California, Nevada/USA; Sonora/Mexico; Brazil. **Similar to:** zoisite, epidote, tremolite.

Lazulite
$(Mg,Fe)Al_2[OH|PO_4]_2$

④ Yukon/Canada

Streak white. **Mohs' hardness** 5–6. **Specific gravity** 3.0–3.4. **Characteristics:** light to dark blue, white. Lustre: vitreous, greasy; opaque, transparent at the edges. Cleavage: incomplete. Fracture: uneven, brittle. Crystals: (monoclinic) long and short prismatic, thick tabular, mostly vertically striped; intergrowth and surface growth; rare, sometimes twinning. **Aggregates:** rough, granular to dense, as impregnation; present in quarztzite, quartz deposits. **Accompanied by:** corundum, rutile, garnet, kyanite, quartz. **Found in:** Thüringer Forest/Germany; Salzburg, Steiermark/Austria; Wallis/Switzerland; Sweden; Georgia, North Carolina/USA; Minas Gerais/Brazil. **Similar to:** sodalite, lapis lazuli, azurite, vivianite, charoite.

Sillimanite
$Al_2[O|SiO_4]$

⑤ New York/USA; ⑥ Pennsylvania/USA 1:3

Streak white. **Mohs' hardness** 6–7. **Specific gravity** 3.2–3.3. **Characteristics:** grey, yellow to brown, greenish, less often bluish, white, colorless. Lustre: vitreous, greasy, aggregates silky; transparent to translucent. Cleavage: complete. Fracture: uneven, brittle. Crystals: (rhombic) prismatic, acicular; intergrowth; very rare. **Aggregates:** dendritic, fibrous, radial, matted; present in metamorphic rocks. **Accompanied by:** quartz, feldspars, cordierite, andalusite, garnet, corundum, chrysoberyl, spinel. **Found in:** Bavarian Forest, Erzgebirge/Germany; Tyrol/Austria; Tient/Italy; South Africa; Idaho, New York/USA; Brazil; Assam/India; Sri Lanka; Burma. **Similar to:** kyanite, zoisite, andalusite, asbestos.

102

actinolite, pg. 148, augite pg. 142, hedenbergite pg. 142, hypersthene pg. 166

Hemimorphite
$Zn_4[(OH)_2 | Si_2O_7] \cdot H_2O$

① Chihuahua/Mexico

Streak white. **Mohs' hardness** 5. **Specific gravity** 3.3–3.5. **Characteristics:** colorless, white to grey, light green, bluish, yellowish to brown. Lustre: vitreous, silky; transparent to translucent. Cleavage: complete. Fracture: conchoidal to uneven, brittle; soluble in hydrochloric acid. Crystals: (rhombic) tabular, prismatic to acicular; usually small, surface growth; widely distributed twinning, pseudomorphic. **Aggregates:** radial, reniform, stalactitic, seldom granular, dense or crusty; present in oxidized zones of lead-zinc deposits. **Accompanied by:** smithsonite, sphalerite, hydrozincite, aurichalcite, galena, cerussite. **Found in:** Rheinland/Germany; Kärnten/Austria; Sardinia/Italy; England; Trans Baikal region/USSR; Algeria; Arizona, Colorado/USA; Mexico. **Similar to:** smithsonite, opal, topaz, chalcedony.

Kornerupine
$Mg_4Al_6[O,OH]_2 | BO_4 | (SiO_4)_4]$

② Waldheim, Saxony/Germany 1:2

Streak white. **Mohs' hardness** 6–7. **Specific gravity** 3.0. **Characteristics:** white, yellow, green, pink, sometimes colorless and red. Lustre: vitreous; transparent to translucent. Cleavage: incomplete. Fracture: conchoidal, brittle; strong pleochroism. Crystals: (rhombic) long prismatic, intergrowth. **Aggregates:** rough, thin dendritic, radial; present in gneissic rocks. **Accompanied by:** cordierite, tourmaline, zircon, spinel, kyanite, quartz, feldspars, biotite. **Found in:** Saxony/Germany; Finland; Ukraine, Kazakhstan/USSR; Madagascar; South Africa; Kenya; Tanzania; Sri Lanka; India; Burma; Greenland; Quebec/Canada. **Similar to:** enstatite, tourmaline.

Anthophyllite
$(Mg,Fe)_7[OH | Si_4O_{11}]_2$

③ Paaka/Finland 1:½

Streak white. **Mohs' hardness** 5½. **Specific gravity** 2.8–3.2. **Characteristics:** brownish, yellowish grey. Lustre: vitreous, seldom mother-of-pearl and silky; bronze-like glimmer; translucent. Cleavage: complete, cleavage angle approximately 125°. Fracture: uneven, fibrous, brittle; malleable in thin layers; lively pleochroism. Crystals: (rhombic) prismatic, rare. **Aggregates:** dendritic, fibrous (asbestiform), acicular, radial, dense, tough (nephrite); present in metamorphic rocks, sometimes rockforming. **Accompanied by:** cordierite, biotite, feldspars, quartz. **Found in:** Bavarian Forest/Germany; Czechoslovakia; southern Tirol/Italy; Norway; Finland; Urals/USSR; South Africa; California/USA. **Similar to:** bronzite, hypersthene, tremolite, actinolite, jadeite.

Spodumene
$LiAl[Si_2O_6]$

④ Hiddenite; Minas Gerais/Brazil 1:2
⑤ Kunzite; Minas Gerais/Brazil

Streak white. **Mohs' hardness** 6½–7. **Specific gravity** 3.1–3.2. **Characteristics:** colorless, white, grey, yellow to green (hiddenite), pink to violet (kunzite). Lustre: vitreous; on cleavage face mother-of-pearl; transparent to translucent. Cleavage: complete. Fracture: uneven, brittle. Flame test: intensively red. Sometimes distinct pleochroism. Crystals: (monoclinic) tabular, prismatic, horizontally striped; intergrowth and surface growth; twinning. **Aggregates:** rough, sparlike, wide dendritic; present in granite pegmatites, drusy cavities. **Accompanied by:** quartz, feldspars, beryl, tourmaline, amblygonite, triphyline, cassiterite. **Found in:** Sweden; Scotland; Zimbabwe; Namibia; Madagascar; South Dakota/USA; Brazil. **Similar to:** petalite, scapolite, amblygonite, feldspars.

arfvedsonite pg. 212, odontolite pg. 212

Streak

white and
colorless

Mohs'
hardness 1

— 2

3

—

4

5

6

7

—

8

9

—

10

Specific
gravity 1

2

3

4

5

—

6

7

Rhodonite
CaMn₄[Si₅O₁₅]

① New Jersey/USA

Streak white. **Mohs' hardness** 5½–6½. **Specific gravity** 3.4–3.7. **Characteristics:** light red, rose red, brownish red; often with black spots and veins. Lustre: vitreous, on cleavage faces mother-of-pearl; transparent to opaque. Cleavage: complete. Fracture: conchoidal to uneven, brittle; slowly soluble in hydrochloric acid. Crystals: (triclinic) tabular, columnar, often with rounded edges, rare. **Aggregates:** rough, sparlike, granular, dense; present in manganese- and iron-ore veins; in tungstenite. **Accompanied by:** magnetite, braunite, hausmannite, rhodochrosite, quartz, garnet. **Found in:** Harz mountains/Germany; Piemonte/Italy; Romania; Sweden; Urals/USSR; New Jersey/USA; Brazil; India; Japan; New South Wales/Australia. **Similar to:** rhodochrosite.

Sphene   titanite
CaTi[O|SiO₄]

② dusted with chlorite; Zillertal/Austria

Streak white. **Mohs' hardness** 5–6. **Specific gravity** 3.3–3.6. **Characteristics:** yellow, green, brown, red, black. Lustre: adamantine, vitreous, greasy; transparent to opaque. Cleavage: incomplete. Fracture: conchoidal, brittle; high double-refraction; soluble in sulfuric acid. Crystals: (monoclinic) envelope-shaped, tabular, prismatic; intergrowth and surface growth. **Aggregates:** rough, granular, scaly, present as by-product in magmatites and metamorphic rocks, in alpine crevices, sometimes on soapstone. **Accompanied by:** chlorite, hornblende, rutile, apatite, nepheline, feldspars, quartz, calcite. **Found in:** Eifel, Bavarian Forest, Saxony/Germany; Tyrol, Salzburg/Austria; Piemonte/Italy; St. Gotthard/Switzerland; Urals, Kola/USSR; Ontario/Canada; Maine, Massachusetts/USA: Mexico; Minas Gerais/Brazil. **Similar to:** axenite, cassiterite, monazite, zircon, anatase.

Periclase
MgO

③ Vesuvius/Italy 1:8

Streak white. **Mohs' hardness** 5½–6. **Specific gravity** 3.6–3.9. **Characteristics:** colorless, grey-green, yellowish. Lustre: transparent to translucent. Cleavage: complete. Fracture: conchoidal; soluble in acid as crystal is difficult, in powder form easy. Crystals: (cubic) cubes, octahedral; intergrowth and surface growth; usually small and rare, twinning. **Aggregates:** rough, granular; present in metamorphosed limestones and dolomites, by-product in volcanic eruptions. **Accompanied by:** calcite, hausmannite, magnesite, brucite. **Found in:** Vesuvius, Sardinia/Italy; Sweden; California/USA. **Similar to:** spinel.

Bronzite
(Mg,Fe)₂[Si₂O₆]

④ Kraubarth/Steiermark/Austria

Streak white, brownish. **Mohs' hardness** 5–6. **Specific gravity** 3.2–3.6. **Characteristics:** brown, green, bronze-colored. Lustre: metallic, silky; translucent to opaque. Cleavage: incomplete. Fracture: uneven, bladed, fibrous, brittle; weak pleochroism. Crystals: (rhombic) short columnar, seldom well-developed. **Aggregates:** rough, sparlike, granular; present in basic to intermediate magmatites and metamorphic rocks, rock-forming in bronzitite. **Accompanied by:** diopside, olivine, serpentine, ilmenite, magnetite, chromite. **Found in:** Harz mountains, Saxony/Germany; Steiermark/Austria; Norway; Urals/USSR; Transvaal/South Africa; Greenland; Colorado/USA. **Similar to:** hypersthene, anthophyllite, diopside, enstatite.

betaphite pg. 70, kyanite pg. 70, triphylite pg. 70, andradite pg. 126

Streak

white and
colorless

Mohs'
hardness 1 ◀
2 ◀
–
3 ◀
4 ◀
–
5 ◀
–
6 ◀
–
7 ◀
–
8 ◀
–
9 ◀
10 ◀

Specific
gravity 1 ◀
–
–
2 ◀
–
3 ◀
–
4 ◀
–
–
5 ◀
–
6 ◀
–
7 ◀

Willemite
$Zn_2[SiO_4]$

① Congo

Streak white. **Mohs' hardness** 5½. **Specific gravity** 4.0. **Characteristics:** colorless, white, yellow to green, less often pink, grey, brown. Lustre: vitreous, greasy; translucent to transparent. Cleavage: incomplete. Fracture: conchoidal, splintery, brittle. Sometimes greenish-yellow fluorescence in ultraviolet light; in powder form soluble in hydrochloric acid. Crystals: (trigonal) short and long columnar, usually small; sometimes pseudomorphic. **Aggregates:** rough, granular, crumbly; present in oxidized zones of lead, zinc, and zinc-manganese deposits. **Accompanied by:** franklinite, zincite, smithsonite, hydrozincite, hemimorphite, rhodonite, calcite. **Found in:** Rheinland/Germany; Zambia; Namibia; Kirghizia/USSR; New Jersey, New Mexico/ USA; southern Australia. **Similar to:** epidote, olivine.

Anatase
TiO_2

② red crystals; Val Vavona, Tessin/Switzerland 1:2

Streak white. **Mohs' hardness** 5½–6. **Specific gravity** 3.8–3.9. **Characteristics:** blue-black, yellow to brown, reddish, rarely colorless. Lustre: adamantine, metallic, greasy; translucent to transparent. Cleavage: complete. Fracture: conchoidal, uneven, brittle. Crystals: (tetragonal) pointed to flat pyramidal, tabular, small; often horizontally striped; usually surface growth. **Aggregates:** loose rounded grains, otherwise crystals; present in alpine crevices, in basic magmatites, also sedimentary rocks. **Accompanied by:** rutile, sphene, brookite, ilminite, quartz rock crystal, adularia, albite, calcite, chlorite. **Found in:** eastern Bavaria, Thüringer Forest/Germany; Wallis/ Switzerland; Salzburg, Tyrol/Austria; Norway; Urals/USSR; Colorado/USA; Minas Gerais/Brazil. **Similar to:** brookite, sphene.

Perovskite
$CaTiO_3$

③ Brennkogel, Hohe Tauern/Austria 1:3

Streak white to grey. **Mohs' hardness** 5½. **Specific gravity** 4.0–4.8. **Characteristics:** black, reddish brown, yellow. Lustre: adamantine, metallic, greasy; opaque to transparent. Cleavage: incomplete to complete. Fracture: conchoidal to uneven, brittle; soluble in boiling sulfuric acid. Crystals: (rhombic) cubes, often striped; intergrowth and surface growth, sometimes twinning. **Aggregates:** rough, granular, microcrystalline, reniform, rarely crystal skeletons; present in metamorphic rocks, basalt, magnetite and chromite deposits. **Accompanied by:** nepheline, leucite, melilite, magnetite, sphene, chlorite, talc, calcite. **Found in:** Eifel/Germany; Wallis/ Switzerland; Tyrol/Austria; Finland; Sweden; southern Tirol/Italy; Urals, Kola/USSR; Quebec/Canada; Colorado/USA; Sao Paulo/Brazil. **Similar to:** magnetite, melanite.

Benitoite
$BaTi[Si_3O_9]$

④ California/USA

Streak white. **Mohs' hardness** 6½. **Specific gravity** 3.7. **Characteristics:** light to deep blue, rarely pink or colorless. Lustre: vitreous; transparent to translucent, sometimes cloudy to speckled. Cleavage: none. Fracture: conchoidal, brittle; distinct pleochroism; lively blue fluorescence under ultraviolet light. Crystals: (trigonal) always dipyramidal; intergrowth; very rare. **Aggregates:** none; present in veins in glaucophane schist. **Accompanied by:** natrolite, neptunite, anatase, glaucophane. **Found in:** only Mt. Diablo, San Benito County, California/USA. **Similar to:** sapphire.

108 olivine pg. 128, augite pg. 142, hedenbergite pg. 142, hypersthene pg. 166

Streak

white and
colorless

Mohs'
hardness

Specific
gravity

Brookite
TiO$_2$

① Uri/Switzerland 1:10

Streak white, yellowish to brownish. **Mohs' hardness** 5½–6. **Specific gravity** 4.1–4.2. **Characteristics:** yellowish to brown, almost black (arkansite), seldom colorless. Lustre: adamantine, metallic; translucent to opaque. Cleavage: incomplete. Fracture: conchoidal, uneven, brittle. Crystals: (rhombic) thin tabular, prismatic, dipyramidal, often vertically striped, mostly small; individually occurring; pseudomorphic. **Aggregates:** scattered; present in alpine crevices, sandstones; **Accompanied by:** anatase, rutile, sphene, feldspars, quartz, hematite. **Found in:** Graubuenden/Switzerland; Tyrol/Austria; Wales; Urals/USSR; USA; Brazil. **Similar to:** anatase.

Scheelite
Ca[WO$_4$]

② on quartz, Erzgebirge/Germany

Streak white. **Mohs' hardness** 4½–5. **Specific gravity** 5.9–6.1. **Characteristics:** grey to white, yellow to brownish, rarely colorless. Lustre: greasy, adamantine; transparent. Cleavage: incomplete. Fracture: conchoidal, uneven, brittle; bluish to white fluorescence under ultraviolet light. Crystals: (tetragonal) dipyramidal, less often tabular, often striped along the edges; surface growth and intergrowth. **Aggregates:** rough, granular, crusty, as impregnation; present in pegmatites, alpine crevices, alluvial deposits. **Accompanied by:** cassiterite, wolframite, fluorite, quartz. **Found in:** Erzgebirge/Germany; Cornwall/England; Caucasus/USSR; Namibia; California/USA; Brazil; Tasmania/Australia. **Similar to:** stolzite, angelsite, betafite, powellite.

Monazite
Ce[PO$_4$]

③ Namibia

Streak white. **Mohs' hardness** 5–5½. **Specific gravity** 4.6–5.7. **Characteristics:** light yellow to dark brown, less often colorless, red, green. Lustre: vitreous, resinous, greasy; translucent to opaque. Cleavage: complete. Fracture: conchoidal, brittle; green fluorescence under ultraviolet light, often radioactive; easily soluble in sulfuric acid, in hydrochloric acid difficult. Crystals: (monoclinic) thick tabular, prismatic; intergrowth and surface growth, often twinning. **Aggregates:** rough, granular; present in basic magmatites and pegmatites, in gneiss, alpine crevices, sand, gravel. **Accompanied by:** ilminite, zircon, rutile, anatase, magnetite, garnet, quartz, feldspars. **Found in:** France; Norway; USSR; Madagascar; India; Sri Lanka; USA; Brazil. **Similar to:** euxenite, fergusonite, thortvietite, titanite.

Smithsonite
ZnCO$_3$

④ New Mexico/USA
⑤ Tsumed/Namibia

Streak white. **Mohs' hardness** 5. **Specific gravity** 4.3–4.5. **Characteristics:** yellowish, brown, grey, green, bluish, reddish, less often colorless, white. Lustre: vitreous, mother-of-pearl, greasy; transparent. Cleavage: complete. Fracture: uneven, conchoidal, brittle; easily soluble in warm acid. Crystals: (trigonal) rhombic, often pseudomorphic. **Aggregates:** rough, granular, dense, reniform, stalactitic, striped; present in oxidized zones of sulfure-rich lead-zinc deposits. **Accompanied by:** calcite, dolomite, sphalerite, hydrozincite, hemimorphite, malachite, galena, cerussite. **Found in:** Rheinland/Germany; Sardinia/Italy; Greece; Australia; Namibia; Oklahoma/USA. **Similar to:** hydrozincite, siderite, hemimorphite, chalcedony.

110

Beryl
$Al_2Be_3[Si_6O_{18}]$

① morganite; Kenya
② Utah/USA
③ emerald, chivor/Columbia
④ in quartz, Brazil

Streak white. **Mohs' hardness** 7½–8. **Specific gravity** 2.36–2.91. **Characteristics:** colorless, or in many different shades. Transparent beryl crystals that come in beautiful colors are used for jewelry and have their own names: goshenite (colorless), emerald (green), aquamarine (blue), gold-beryl (golden yellow), heliodore (yellow-green), morganite (pink to violet). Lustre: vitreous, dull; transparent to opaque. Cleavage: incomplete. Fracture: conchoidal to uneven, brittle. Crystals: (hexagonal) short or long prismatic; usually hexagonal, pyramidal, vertically striped, seldom tabular; intergrowth and surface growth; only occasional twinning. **Aggregates:** rough, dendritic; present in pegmatites, granites, mica schists, veins in limestone. **Accompanied by:** quartz, feldspars, calcite, chrysoberyl, topaz, apatite, phenakite, fluorite, wolframite, cassiterite. **Found in:** eastern Bavaria/Germany; Tyrol/Austria; Elba/Italy; Urals/USSR; Tanzania; Kenya; Zambia; Madagascar; Transvaal/South Africa; Namibia; California, Utah/USA; Columbia; Bahia/Brazil; India; Sri Lanka; Burma; South Korea; western Australia. **Similar to:** chrysoberyl, apatite, spinel, brazilianite, tourmaline.

Boracite
$Mg_3[Cl\,|\,B_7O_{13}]$

⑤ Lueneburg/Germany

Streak white, light grey. **Mohs' hardness** 7–7½. **Specific gravity** 2.9–3.0. **Characteristics:** colorless, white, grey, yellow to brown, light blue, greenish. Lustre: vitreous, adamantine; transparent to translucent. Cleavage: none. Fracture: conchoidal, brittle. Flame test: green. Slowly soluble in hydrochloric acid. Crystals: (cubic) cubes, tetrahedral, octahedral, dodecohedral, finely fibrous; always intergrowth; often twinning. **Aggregates:** rough, fibrous, tuberous, granular to dense; present in salt veins. **Accompanied by:** gypsum, anhydrite, halite, carnallite, sylvite, kieserite. **Found in:** Niedersachsen, Magdeburg/Germany; Yorkshire/England; Lorraine/France; Louisiana, California/USA; Namibia. **Similar to:** halite, fluorite, senarmontite.

Cordierite   dichroite, iolite
$Mg_2Al_3[AlSi_5O_{18}]$

⑥ Kisco/Finland

Streak white. **Mohs' hardness** 7–7½. **Specific gravity** 2.5–2.8. **Characteristics:** grey, blue to violet, yellow to brown, greenish, also colorless. Lustre: vitreous, on cleavage face greasy; transparent to translucent. Cleavage: incomplete. Fracture: conchoidal to uneven, brittle; very strong pleochroism, detectable with the naked eye. Crystals: (rhombic); short columnar with six or twelve sides and rounded edges; intergrowth and surface growth; rare; often twinning. **Aggregates:** rough, granular, dispersed; present in metamorphic rocks (rock-forming in cordierite gneiss), in magmatites, by-product of volcanic eruptions, as river gravel. **Accompanied by:** garnet, tourmaline, spinel, sillimanite, andalusite, quartz, feldspars, pyrrhotite, chalcopyrite. **Found in:** Eifel, Bavarian Forest, Saxony/Germany; Finland; Sweden; Norway; Urals/USSR; Madagascar; Sri Lanka; Madras/India; Burma; Connecticut/USA; northwest Canada; Minas Gerais/Brazil. **Similar to:** quartz, nepheline, sapphire.

tridymite pg. 84

Hambergite
$Be_2[(OH,F)|BO_3]$

① Gilgit/Pakistan 1:3

Streak white. **Mohs' hardness** 7½. **Specific gravity** 2.36. **Characteristics:** colorless, white, grey. Lustre: vitreous; transparent to translucent; Cleavage: complete. Fracture: conchoidal, brittle; high double refraction; soluble in hydrochloric acid. Crystals: (rhombic) prismatic, tabular, vertically striped, multifaceted; also twinning. **Aggregates:** none; only individual crystals; present in pegmatites, veins in sedimentary deposits. **Accompanied by:** feldspars. **Found in:** Norway; Madagascar; Kashmir/India; California/USA; Brazil. **Similar to:** quartz rock crystal and many other colorless minerals, glass.

Danburite
$Ca[Be_2Si_2O_8]$

② Sen Louis Potossi/Mexico

Streak white. **Mohs' hardness** 7–7½. **Specific gravity** 2.9–3.0. **Characteristics:** colorless, yellowish to dark brown, pink. Lustre: greasy; transparent to translucent. Cleavage: incomplete. Fracture: uneven to conchoidal, brittle. Flame test; green. Crystals: (rhombic) prismatic, pyramidal, sometimes vertically striped; usually surface growth. **Aggregates:** rough, granular; present in metamorphic rocks, marine salt deposits, alpine crevices, by-product of volcanic eruptions. **Accompanied by:** calcite, dolomite, quartz, datolite, prehnite, apophyllite, pyrite. **Found in:** Harz mountains/Germany; Graubuenden/Switzerland; Madagascar; eastern Siberia/USSR; Burma; Kyushu/Japan; Connecticut, New York/USA; Mexico; Bolivia. **Similar to:** datolite, topaz, citrine, colemanite.

Phenakite
$Be_2[SiO_4]$

③ Sao Miguel de Kiraciala/Brazil

Streak white. **Mohs' hardness** 7½–8. **Specific gravity** 2.96–3.0. **Characteristics:** colorless, yellowish, pink. Lustre: vitreous; transparent. Cleavage: incomplete. Fracture: conchoidal, brittle. Crystals: (trigonal) short columnar, tabular lens-shaped, often multifaceted, vertically striped; intergrowth and surface growth; often twinning. **Aggregates:** none; present in granite, pegmatites, mica schist, alpine crevices. **Accompanied by:** beryl, chrysoberyl, topaz, tourmaline, quartz, apatite, fluorite. **Found in:** Fichtelgebirge/Germany; Salzburg/Austria; Wallis/Switzerland; Norway; Vogesen/France; Urals, Trans Baikal region/USSR; Namibia; Colorado, California/USA; Minas Gerais/Brazil. **Similar to:** quartz, topaz, milarite.

Euclase
$AlBe[OH|SiO_4]$

④ Brazil
⑤ Brazil

Streak white. **Mohs' hardness** 7½. **Specific gravity** 3.0–3.1. **Characteristics:** colorless, light green, light blue. Lustre: vitreous; transparent to translucent. Cleavage: perfect. Fracture: conchoidal, brittle; weak pleochroism. Crystals: (monoclinic) long and short prisms, vertically striped, multifaceted; surface growth; rare. **Aggregates:** none; present in pegmatites, crevices and geodes, alliuvial deposits. **Accompanied by:** beryl, topaz, tourmaline, quartz, feldspars, muscovite. **Found in:** Fichtelgebirge/Germany; Tauern/Austria; Ireland; Norway; Urals/USSR; Zaire; Tanzania; India; Milas Gerais/Brazil; Colorado/USA. **Similar to:** quartz, aquamarine, hiddenite, albite.

114

bertrandite pg. 86, tourmaline pg. 120

Quartz macrocrystalline
SiO$_2$

Streak white. **Mohs' hardness** 7. **Specific gravity** 2.5–2.7. **Characteristics:** colorless, milky white, grey, and many other colors. Lustre: vitreous, on cleavage face greasy; transparent to opaque. Cleavage: none. Fracture: conchoidal, splintery, brittle; soluble in hydrofluoric acid; poor heat conductor. Crystals: (trigonal) hexagonal prisms, pyramidal with dipyramidal ends; on prism faces almost always horizontally striped; intergrowth and surficial growth; anomalies in development sometimes lead to peculiarities in crystal structure such as inclusions of liquid, gas, or small crystals. Twinning fairly common, pseudomorphs frequent. **Aggregates:** rough, granular, dense, dendritic, radial (star quartz), as crystal groups; present in basic magmatites, pegmatites, sand, gravel, particularly in drusy cavities, occasionally rock-forming. **Accompanied by:** feldspars, mica, calcite, tourmaline, garnet, wolframite, galena, sphalerite, pyrite, molybdenite.

Rock Crystal ⑥ with pyrite; Trebca/Yugoslavia
Colorless, transparent like water; crystal faces are well developed on all sides. **Found in:** Brazil; Madagascar; central Switzerland; Tyrol/Austria; Tuscany/Italy; New York/USA. **Similar to:** many of the colorless minerals, glass.

Smoky Quartz ③ Graubuenden/Switzerland
Smoky grey, brown to black (morion); transparent; often inclusion of rutile-needles. **Found in:** Brazil; Madagascar; central Switzerland. **Similar to:** andalusite, axinite, sanidine, vesuvianite.

Amethyst ⑤ Rio Grande do Sul/Brazil
Violet, often whitish, striped, spotted; transparent; prominently developed crystal points. **Found in:** Brazil, Uruguay, Madagascar. **Similar to:** beryl, fluorite, kunzite, spinel, topaz, tourmaline, strengite, glass.

Citrine ④ heat-treated, Brazil
Light yellow to golden brown; transparent; many citrine crystals are yellowish through burning of smoky quartz or amethyst. **Found in:** Brazil; Madagascar; Colorado/USA. **Similar to:** beryl, orthoclase, topaz, tourmaline, danburite.

Rose Quartz ① Minas Gerais/Brazil
Pink, usually cloudy because of small fissures; very rare crystal; usually rough. **Found in:** Madagascar; Brazil. **Similar to:** tourmaline.

Aventurine Green, golden brown due to inclusions of fuchsite crystals, or metallic lustre due to hematites particles; transparent to opaque. **Found in:** India; Brazil; USSR. **Similar to:** oligoclase (sunstone).

Prase Emerald quartz. Leek green due to inclusion of actinolite; transparent; rough. **Found in:** Scotland; North Carolina/USA; western Australia. **Similar to:** nephrite, jadeite.

Blue Quartz Siderite, sapphire quartz. Blue; translucent to opaque; rough. **Found in:** Brazil; South Africa; USA. **Similar to:** lapis lazuli, dumortierite.

Tiger's Eye ② Oranje/South Africa
Golden yellow; opaque; formed through pseudomorphism of crocidolite in quartz while maintaining its fibrous structure. **Found in:** South Africa; western Australia; Burma; India; USA.

1

2

3

4

5

6

Streak

white and
colorless

Mohs'
hardness

Specific
gravity

Quartz microcrystalline, chalcedony
SiO_2

Streak white. **Mohs' hardness** 6½–7. **Specific gravity** 2.57–2.64. **Characteristics:** milky white, grey, also all other shades; often spotted. Lustre: waxy or dull; translucent to opaque. Cleavage: none. Fracture: uneven and brittle, splintery; soluble in a potassium solution. Crystals: (trigonal) none, only microcrystalline aggregate with fine fibres or grains. **Aggregates:** dense, botryoidal, reniform; glass bead–shaped, stalactitic; present in nodules, veins, sedimentary rocks, as concretions and gravel. **Accompanied by:** macrocrystalline quartz, opal, calcite, chlorite, serpentine.

Chalcedony ② striped jasper; Brazil
White to grey, bluish; translucent. Natural chalcedony is never banded; blue-layered varieties are artificially colored agate. **Found in:** Brazil; Uruguay; Madagascar; India. **Similar to:** opal, smithsonite.

Cornelian Flesh-red to brownish red; dull, translucent. **Found in:** India; Brazil; Uruguay; Australia; Rumania. **Similar to:** opal.

Sard Reddish brown to dark brown; translucent. No clear distinction between sard and cornellian.

Chrysoprase ⑥ California/USA
Yellow-green to apple green; translucent to opaque; often cracked with irregular color distribution. **Found in:** Australia; Brazil; USA; Madagascar; South Africa; India. **Similar to:** jadeite, smithsonite, variscite.

Heliotrope bloodstone. Dark green with red spots; opaque. **Found in:** India; China; Australia; Brazil; USA.

Dendritic Agate ④ Rio Grande do Sul/Brazil
Whitish grey, with dark or reddish brown deposits (dendrites) of iron and manganese compounds; translucent. **Found in:** Brazil; India; USA.

Moss Agate ⑤ Kathivar/India
Colorless or milky white, with moss-like green, brown or red deposits of stem-like hornblende, or of iron and manganese oxides; translucent. **Found in:** India; China; USA; USSR.

Agate ① Idar-Oberstein, Rheinlandpfalz/Germany
Every conceivable color possible, band-like stripes; translucent to opaque; in the middle of the agate nodule often drusy development of quartz rock crystal, amethyst, smoke quartz, calcite, hematite, siderite, zeolite. **Found in:** Brazil; Uruguay; China; India; Madagascar; Mexico; USA.

Onyx Single-colored chalcedony, black, brown, red; double-layered agate with the base black and the top white is also called onyx.

Jasper ③ Idar-Oberstein, Rheinlandpfalz/Germany
All shades; striped, spotted or flamed; opaque, finely grained, dense; always in combination with foreign matierals. **Found in:** India; USSR; USA.

Fossilized Wood ⑦ Arizona/USA 1:½
Mostly brown, grey, red; opaque; petrification of wood by jasper in combination with chalcedony and, less frequently, opal; pseudomorphism after wood. **Found in:** Arizona/USA; Egypt; Argentina.

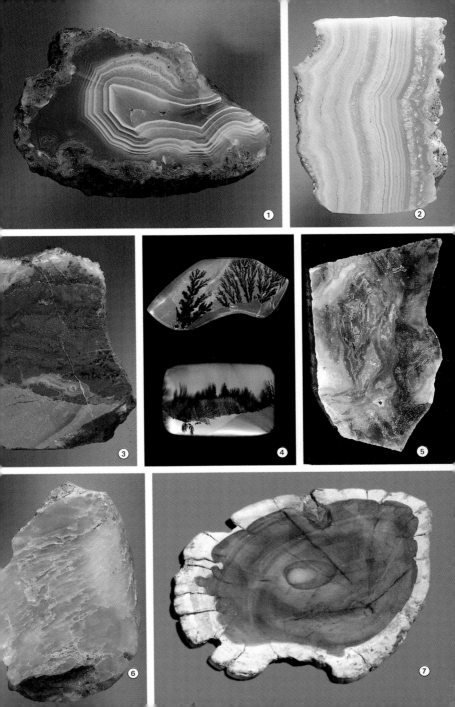

Corundum

Al_2O_3

① ruby in quartz; Norway
② sapphire; Sri Lanka 1:3

Streak white. **Mohs' hardness** 9. **Specific gravity** 3.9–4.1. **Characteristics:** colorless (leuco sapphire), blue (sapphire), red (ruby), grey, yellow to brown, greenish; often spotted and zoned shadings. Lustre: vitreous, dull; transparent to opaque. Cleavage: none. Fracture: conchoidal to splintery, brittle; occasional pleochroism more or less distinct; occasional asterism. Crystals: (trigonal) prismatic, dipyramidal, rhombohedral, tabular; often barrel-shaped and horizontally striped; usually intergrowth; frequent twinning. **Aggregates:** rough, sparlike, coarse and fine grained; a grainy mixture known as emery is a mixture of corundum and magnetite, quartz, hematite and ilmenite; present in plutonic rocks and pegmatites, metamorphic rocks, alluvial deposits. **Accompanied by:** spinel, garnet, zircon, rutile, tourmaline, topaz, calcite. **Found in:** Tessin/Switzerland; Norway; Turkey; Urals/USSR; Kenya; Tanzania; South Africa; Sri Lanka; Burma; Thailand; Australia; Ontario/Canada; Montana/USA. **Similar to:** chrysoberyl, spinel, menitoite, almandine, pyrope.

Chrysoberyl

Al_2BeO_4

③ Madagascar 1:3

Streak white. **Mohs' hardness** 8½. **Specific gravity** 3.7. **Characteristics:** yellow, yellow-green, brownish, light to emerald green. Lustre: vitreous, cleavage face greasy; transparent to translucent. Cleavage: incomplete. Fracture: conchoidal to brittle; sometimes strong pleochroism. Varieties: alexandrite is green in daylight and red in artificial light; cymophane occasionally has "wave-like" light ray (chrysoberyl cat's eye). Crystals: (rhombic) thick tabular, short columnar, often striped; usually intergrowth; frequent twinning, intergrowth triplings. **Aggregates:** collection of loose grains; present in granite pegmatites, gneiss, mica schist, alluvial deposits. **Accompanied by:** beryl, garnet, tourmaline, spinel, phenakite. **Found in:** Sweden; Urals/USSR; Zimbabwe; Sri Lanka; Burma; USA; Brazil; Tasmania/Australia. **Similar to:** brazilianite, beryl, corundum, olivine, spinel.

Tourmaline

$(Na,Li,Ca)(Fe,Mg,Mn,Al)_3$
$Al_6[(OH)_4 | (BO_3)_3 | Si_6O_{18}]$

④ schorl in quartz;
Minas Gerais/Brazil
⑤ California/USA 1:½

Streak white. **Mohs' hardness** 7–7½. **Specific gravity** 3.0–3.3. **Characteristics:** colorless (achroite), black (schorl), brown (dravite), green (verdelite), blue (indicolite), red (rubellite), violet (siberite); often in different zoned shades. Lustre: vitreous; transparent to opaque. Cleavage: none. Fracture: conchoidal to uneven, splintery, brittle; high double refraction; distinct to strong pleochroism. Crystals: (trigonal) prismatic, mostly elongated to acicular, with triangular cross sections and rounded sides, vertically striped; intergrowth and surface growth. **Aggregates:** dendritic, radial, seldom rough or dense; present in basic magmatites and pegmatites, metamorphic rocks, in alpine crevices, alluvial deposits. **Accompanied by:** quartz, beryl, topaz, apatite, fluorite, feldspars, mica. **Found in:** Harz mountains/Germany; Tyrol/Austria; Czechoslovakia; Elba/Italy; Cornwall/England; USSR; Tanzania; Madagascar; Mozambique; Namibia; Sri Lanka; New Hampshire/USA; Brazil; Tasmania/Australia. **Similar to:** epidote, neptunite, rutile, actinolite, emerald.

120 kyanite pg. 70, diaspore pg. 89, clinozoisite pg. 102, sillimanite pg. 102

Andalusite
$Al_2[O | SiO_4]$

① Chiastolite; Chile
② in quartz; Czechoslovakia

Streak white. **Mohs' hardness** 7½ (chiastolite 5½). **Specific gravity** 3.1–3.2. **Characteristics:** grey, yellow, brown, red, green, seldom colorless. Lustre: vitreous, dull; transparent to opaque. Cleavage: incomplete. Fracture: uneven, splintery, brittle; strong pleochroism. Crystals: (rhombic) thick columnar with almost square cross sections, seldom acicular; sometimes with carbonaceous inclusions that form a cross in cross section (chiastolite). **Aggregates:** rough, dendritic, radial; present in metamorphic rocks, as gravel in alluvial deposits, seldom in granitic rocks. **Accompanied by:** sillimanite, cordierite, tourmaline, garnet, quartz. **Found in:** Fichtelgebirge/Germany; Austria; Pyrenees/France; Elba/Italy; Sweden; California/USA; Brazil. **Similar to:** enstatite, tourmaline, augite, hornblende.

Dumortierite
$(Al,Fe)_7[O_3 | BO_3 | (SiO_4)_3]$

③ in quartz, California/USA

Streak white. **Mohs' hardness** 7–7. **Specific gravity** 3.3–3.4. **Characteristics:** blue to violet, grey, brownish red. Lustre: vitreous, silky; translucent to opaque. Cleavage: incomplete. Fracture: uneven, conchoidal, brittle; strong pleochroism. Crystals: (rhombic) thin columnar, acicular; rare. **Aggregates:** thinly fibrous, radial; present in pegmatites and metamorphic rocks. **Accompanied by:** tourmaline, cordierite, cyanite. **Found in:** Poland; Lyon/France; Urals, Uzbekistan/USSR; Madagascar; Namibia; Nevada/USA; Brazil. **Similar to:** kyante, lapis lazuli, azurite, sodalite.

Jadeite
$NaAl[Si_2O_6]$

④ partially cut; China

Streak white. **Mohs' hardness** 6–7. **Specific gravity** 3.2–3.4. **Characteristics:** green, white, yellowish, reddish, violet, green with black (chloromelanite); often spotted. Lustre: vitreous, dull; translucent to opaque. Cleavage: incomplete. Fracture: uneven, conchoidal, splintery and brittle. Flame test: yellow; sometimes whitish fluorescence under ultraviolet light. Crystals: (monoclinic) short prismatic; rare. **Aggregates:** dense, finely fibrous to granular, matted; very tough; in combination with nephrite known as jade; present in serpentinites, as river gravel. **Accompanied by:** quartz, feldspars, diopside. **Found in:** Burma; China; Guinea; Japan; California/USA; Mexico. **Similar to:** nephrite, serpentine, chalcedony.

Staurolite
$2\,FeO \cdot AlOOH \cdot 4Al_2[O | SiO_4]$

⑤ Bretagne/France
⑥ with kyanite; Tessin/Switzerland

Streak white. **Mohs' hardness** 7–7½. **Specific gravity** 3.7–3.8. **Characteristics:** reddish brown, black-brown, black. Lustre: vitreous, dull; on cleavage faces greasy; translucent to opaque. Cleavage: incomplete. Fracture: conchoidal, uneven, splintery, brittle. Crystals: (monoclinic) short and long columnar; always intergrown; interpenetration twinning at right angle or at 60°. **Aggregates:** often distinct intergrowth with kyanite; collections of individual crystals; present in metamorphic rocks, in sand. **Accompanied by:** kyanite, garnet, andalusite, quartz. **Found in:** Tessin/Switzerland; Steiermark/Austria; Czechoslovakia; Bretagne/France; Scotland; Namibia; Tennessee/USA. **Similar to:** tourmaline, garnet.

122

kornerupine pg. 104, spodumene pg. 104, euclase pg. 140

Diamond
C

① Namibia 1:3
② on kimberlite; South Africa

Streak white. **Mohs' hardness** 10. **Specific gravity** 4.47–5.55. **Characteristics:** yellowish, brown to black, less often colorless; occasionally green, blue, reddish. Lustre: adamantine, dull; transparent to opaque. Cleavage: complete. Fracture: conchoidal, splintery, brittle. Crystals: (cubic) octahedral, dodecahedral, cubes; always intergrowth. **Aggregates:** radial, spheroidal (bort, carbonado); present in ancient volcanic pipes with kimberlite as "mother stone," alluvial deposits. **Accompanied by:** chromite, pyrope, spinel, zircon, olivine. **Found in:** South Africa; Namibia; Botswana; Angola; Ghana; Zaire; USSR; India; Brazil; Venezuela; western Australia. **Similar to:** quartz, sapphire, topaz, zircon.

Topaz
$Al_2[F_2|SiO_4]$

③ Minas Gerais/Brazil

Streak white. **Mohs' hardness** 8. **Specific gravity** 3.5–3.6. **Characteristics:** colorless, yellow to brown, green, blue, violet, pink, red. Lustre: vitreous; transparent to translucent. Cleavage: complete. Fracture: conchoidal to uneven, brittle. Crystals: (rhombic) short or long columnar, pyramidal; often multifaceted and striped; usually surface growth. **Aggregates:** rough, radial, dendritic, as impregnation; present in basic magmatites and pegmatites, alluvial deposits. **Accompanied by:** tourmaline, beryl, fluorite, cassiterite, wolframite, quartz. **Found in:** Saxony/Germany; Urals, Trans-Baikal region/USSR; Namibia; Sri Lanka; Pakistan; Burma; Utah, Colorado/ USA; Mexico; Minas Gerais/Brazil. **Similar to:** quartz, chrysoberyl, cryolite, brazilianite, hemimorphite.

Axinite
$Ca_2(Fe,Mg,Mn)Al_2B[OH|O(Si_2O_7)_2]$

④ dusted with chlorite; Dauphine/France

Streak white. **Mohs' hardness** 6½–7. **Specific gravity** 3.26–3.36. **Characteristics:** brown, grey, blue, violet; greenish, less often yellow, red; more often dusted with green chlorite. Lustre: vitreous; transparent to translucent. Cleavage: incomplete. Fracture: conchoidal, brittle; strong pleochroism under ultraviolet light. Crystals: (triclinic) tabular, wedge-shaped, multifaceted, often striped; intergrowth and surface growth. **Aggregates:** rough, sparlike, dendritic, bladed, granular; present in drusy cavities in granitic rocks, calc-silicate rock, alpine crevices. **Accompanied by:** quartz, feldspars, calcite, chlorite, epidote, prehnite, tourmaline. **Found in:** Fichtelgebirge, Harz mountains, Erzgebirge/Germany; Switzerland; England; USSR; Nevada/USA; Australia. **Similar to:** titanite.

Spinel
$MgAl_2O_4$

⑤ Pleonaste in calcite; Madagascar
⑥ Hunza-Tal/Pakistan; 1:2

Streak white. **Mohs' hardness** 8. **Specific gravity** 3.6. **Characteristics:** yellow to brownish, blue to violet, red (ruby spinel), black (pleonaste, ceylonite), seldom colorless. Lustre: vitreous; transparent to opaque. Cleavage: incomplete. Fracture: conchoidal, brittle. Crystals: (cubic) octahedral, dodecahedral; frequent twinning. **Aggregates:** intergrown crystals, rounded grains; present in metamorphic rocks, magmatites, by-products of volcanic eruptions, in alluvial deposits. **Accompanied by:** zircon, garnet, corundum, magnetite, calcite. **Found in:** Odenwald/Germany; Vesuvius/Italy; Sweden; Urals/USSR; Sri Lanka; India; Thailand; Burma; New York/ USA; Brazil; Australia. **Similar to:** corundum, garnet, zircon, beryl.

124

olivine pg. 128, zircon pg. 128

Garnet

A group of differently colored minerals with similar crystal structures. **Streak** white. **Mohs' hardness** 6½–7½. **Specific gravity** 3.40–4.32. **Characteristics:** all colors except blue. Lustre: vitreous, greasy, resinous; translucent to opaque. Cleavage: incomplete. Fracture: conchoidal to splintery, brittle. Crystals: (cubic) rhombododecohedral, icositerahedron; intergrowth, and surficial growth; seldom twinning. **Aggregates:** rough, grainy to dense; present in metamorphic rocks, also as gravel and sand in alluvial deposits. **Accompanied by:** quartz, feldspars, mica, calcite, chlorite, idocrase, magnetite, chromite, wollastonite.

Pyrope
② Rodhaugen Sunnmore/Norway 1:½

$Mg_3Al_2[SiO_4]_3$ **Mohs' hardness** 7–7½. **Specific gravity** 3.58–3.91. Color: blood red with a brownish tint, reddish black, seldom light to dark red, rose red (rhodolite); always intergrowth. **Found in:** Czechoslovakia; India; Sri Lanka; Tanzania; South Africa; Australia. **Similar to:** almandine, ruby, spinel.

Almandine
⑧ Zillertal; Tyrol/Austria

$Fe_3Al_2[SiO_4]_3$ **Mohs' hardness** 7–7½. **Specific gravity** 3.95–4.32. Colored dark red with violet tint, reddish brown, brown, brownish black; always intergrowth. **Found in:** Oberpfalz/Germany; Tyrol/Austria; Sweden; Norway; Urals, Karelia/USSR; Sri Lanka; India; Afghanistan; Alaska/USA; Brazil. **Similar to:** pyrope, spessartite, ruby, spinel, glass imitations.

Spessartite
③ Madagascar

$Mn_3Al_2[SiO_4]_3$ **Mohs' hardness** 7–7½. **Specific gravity** 4.12–4.20. Color: orange to reddish brown, also pink. **Found in:** Spessart/Germany; Sweden; Madagascar; Sri Lanka; California/USA; Minas Gerais/Brazil. **Similar to:** almandine, hessonite.

Grossular
① hessonite; Italy

$Ca_3Al_2[SiO_4]_3$ **Mohs' hardness** 7–7½. **Specific gravity** 3.59–3.68. Colorless (leucogarnet), yellowish, green, emerald green (tsavorite), opaque green (hydrogrossular), brownish orange (hessonite); soluble in hot sulfuric acid. **Found in:** Piemonte, Elba/Italy; Tanzania; Kenya; South Africa; Sri Lanka; Pakistan; eastern Siberia/USSR; Canada; USA; Mexico. **Similar to:** demantoid, emerald, jadeite, idocrase, spessartite.

Andradite
④ Stanley Butte, Arizona/USA
⑤ Demantoide; Bernia/Italy
⑥ Topazolithe; California/USA

$Ca_3Fe_2[SiO_4]_3$ **Mohs' hardness** 6½–7½. **Specific gravity** 3.7–4.1. Color: usually brown, reddish brown to black (melanite), also colorless, green to emerald green (demantoid), yellow, yellow-green (topazolite); soluble in hot sulfuric acid. **Found in:** Fichtelgebirge/Germany; Austria; Switzerland; Piemonte/Italy; Urals/USSR; Namibia; British Columbia/Canada; Arkansas/USA. **Similar to:** grossular; olivine; emerald; idocrase; topaz.

Uvarovite
⑦ Urals/USSR 1:5

$Ca_3Cr_2[SiO_4]_3$ **Mohs' hardness** 7–7½. **Specific gravity** 3.40–3.77. Color: emerald green; soluble in hot sulfuric acid. **Found in:** Finland; Poland; Urals/USSR; Transvaal/South Africa; India; Tazmania/Australia; Quebec/Canada; Oregon/USA. **Similar to:** grossular, emerald, olivine. -

Streak

white and
colorless

Mohs'
hardness 1◄

2◄

3◄

4◄

5◄

6◄

7◄

8◄

9◄

10◄

Specific
gravity 1◄

2◄

3◄

4◄

5◄

6◄

7◄

YAG   yttrium aluminum garnet   ① polished 1:6
$Y_3Al_5O_{12}$

Streak white. **Mohs' hardness** 8–8½. **Specific gravity** 4.6. **Characteristics:** colorless, yellow, green, brown, red, violet. Lustre: transparent. Cleavage: none. Fracture: conchoidal, brittle. Crystals: (cubic) none; a synthetic product. **Similar to:** diamond, zircon, rock crystal, and synthetically produced "precious" stones.

Olivine   peridot, chrysolite   ② Dreiser Wether,
$(Mg,Fe)_2[SiO_4]$ Eifel/Germany

Streak white. **Mohs' hardness** 6½–7. **Specific gravity** 3.27–4.20. **Characteristics:** green, yellowish, brown to red-brown; seldom colorless. Lustre: on fractured surface greasy; transparent to translucent. Cleavage: incomplete. Fracture: conchoidal, brittle; in powder form soluble in sulfuric acid. Crystals: (rhombic) prismatic, thick tabular, usually intergrowth; twinning; pseudomorphic; olivine is the mineral series forsterite (Mg_2SiO_4) to fayalite (Fe_2SiO_4). **Aggregates:** rough, granular, tubular; present in basic magmatites, in metamorphic rocks. **Accompanied by:** augite, hornblende, feldspars, garnet, diopside, spinel. **Found in:** Eifel/Germany; Steiermark/Austria; Egypt; South Africa; Urals, Caucasus/USSR; Burma; Arizona/USA. **Similar to:** chrysoberyl, chondrodite, willemite.

Cassiterite   pewter stone   ③ Ehrenfriedersdorf,
SnO_2 Saxony/Germany

Streak white to yellowish. **Mohs' hardness** 7. **Specific gravity** 6.8–7.1. **Characteristics:** brown to black, seldom yellow, grey, reddish, colorless. Lustre: on fractured surface greasy; translucent, seldom transparent. Cleavage: incomplete. Fracture: conchoidal, brittle; occasionally distinct pleochroism. Crystals: (tetragonal) short columnar to acicular, sometimes with distinctly colored stripes; surface growth and intergrowth; twinning, pseudomorphic. **Aggregates:** rough, granular, radial glass bead–like (wood-tin), long acicular (needle-tin); present in pegmatites, veins, as impregnation (mountain-tin), alluvial deposits (placer-tin). **Accompanied by:** quartz, topaz, fluorite, wolframite, sphalerite, arsenopyrite, pyrrhotite, pyrite. **Found in:** Czechoslovakia; England; Nigeria; Malaysia; Indonesia; Mexico; Bolivia; Alaska/USA. **Similar to:** rutile, sphalerite, wolframite, sphene.

Zircon   ④ southern Tirol/Italy 1:6
$Zr[SiO_4]$

Streak white. **Mohs' hardness** 7–7½. **Specific gravity** 3.9–4.8. **Characteristics:** brown, yellowish red to reddish brown (hyacinth), straw yellow, red, green, blue (starlite), also colorless. Lustre: adamantine, fractured surface greasy; transparent to translucent. Cleavage: incomplete. Fracture: conchoidal, brittle; strong multiple refraction; sometimes weak pleochroism; occasionally yellowish fluorescence under ultraviolet light. Crystals: (tetragonal) short prismatic, dipyramidal; mostly intergrowth, seldom twinning. **Aggregates:** intergrown or loose grains; present in acidic magmatites and metamorphic rocks, sandstone, alluvial deposits. **Accompanied by:** spinel, corundum, garnet, feldspars, mica. **Found in:** Eifel/Germany; Austria; Florida/USA; Ontario/Canada; Brazil. **Similar to:** idocrase, rutile, cassiterite, spinel.

128 corundum pg. 120, almandine pg. 126, andradite pg. 126, spessartine pg. 126

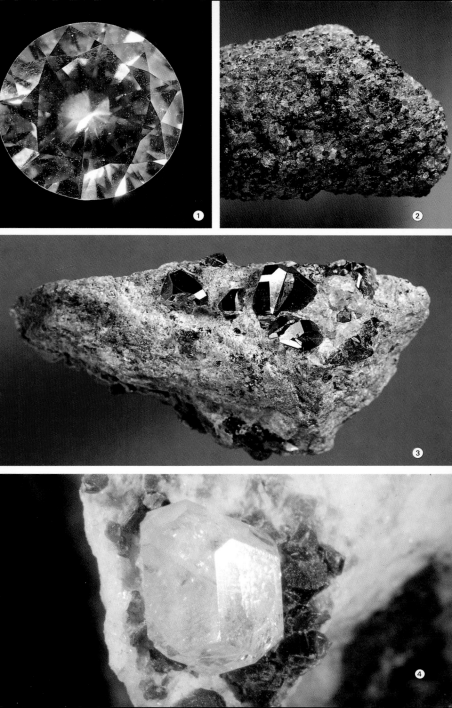

Streak

green

Mohs'
hardness 1 ◀

2 ◀

3 ◀
−
4 ◀
−
5 ◀
−
6 ◀
−
7 ◀

8 ◀
−
9 ◀

10 ◀

Specific
gravity 1 ◀

−

2 ◀

3 ◀

4 ◀

5 ◀

6 ◀

7 ◀

Garnierite
(Ni,Mg)$_6$[(OH)$_8$ | Si$_4$O$_{10}$]

① Riddle, Oregon/USA

Streak light green. **Mohs' hardness 2–4. Specific gravity 2.2–2.8. Characteristics:** apple green, blue-green. Lustre: greasy, waxy, dull; opaque. Cleavage: none. Fracture: conchoidal, brittle; soluble in warm hydrochloric acid. Crystals: (monoclinic) not known, amorphous. **Aggregates:** rough, stalactitic, botryoidal, bladed, granular, crumbly, dense; present as a product of weathering of ultrabasic magmatites and serpentinites. **Accompanied by:** serpentine, chlorite, magnesite, chalcedony, opal, limonite. **Found in:** Saxony; Urals/USSR; New Caledonia; Philippines; New Zealand; Borneo; Sulawesi/Indonesia; Oregon/USA; Cuba; Brazil. **Similar to:** serpentine, turquoise.

Chalcophyllite
Cu$_{18}$Al$_2$[(OH)$_9$ | SO$_4$ | AsO$_4$]$_3$ · 36 H$_2$O

② Redruth, Cornwall/England 1:3

Streak light green. **Mohs' hardness 2. Specific gravity 2.4–2.6. Characteristics:** bluish, light to emerald green. Lustre: vitreous, on cleavage surfaces mother-of-pearl or adamantine; transparent to translucent. Cleavage: complete. Fracture: bladed, thin blades malleable; high double-refraction; easily soluble in acid and ammonia. Crystals: (trigonal) thin tabular; usually with hexagonal contours; small. **Aggregates:** bladed, rosette-shaped, crusty, present in drusy cavities of oxidized zones of copper deposits. **Accompanied by:** cuprite, malachite, azurite, tyrolite, devilline. **Found in:** Erzgebirge/Germany; Tyrol/Austria; Cap Garonne/France; Rumania; England; Utah, Nevada/USA; Urals/USSR; Chile. **Similar to:** autunite, devilline.

Chrysocolla
Cu$_4$[(OH)$_8$ | Si$_4$O$_{10}$] · nH$_2$O

③ Zacatecas/Mexico

Streak greenish white. **Mohs' hardness 2–4. Specific gravity 1.0–2.3. Characteristics:** greenish, bluish. Lustre: vitreous, waxy, dull; transparent to opaque. Cleavage: none. Fracture: conchoidal, brittle; soluble in hydrochloric acid. Flame test: green. Crystals: (rhombic) seldom microcrystalline, usually amorphous. **Aggregates:** rough botryoidal, stalactitic, crusty, crumbly; dense, as surface covering; present in oxidized zones of copper deposits. **Accompanied by:** malachite, azurite, cuprite, dioptase. **Found in:** Baden, Erzgebirge/Germany; Cornwall/England; Urals, Altai/USSR; Zaire; Arizona, Idaho/USA; Mexico; Chile. **Similar to:** variscite, aurichalcite, turquoise, malachite.

Chlorite
(Fe,Mg,Al)$_6$[(OH)$_2$ | (Si,Al)$_4$O$_{10}$]

④ Zermatt/Switzerland
⑤ Bavarian Forest/Germany

Streak green to brown. **Mohs' hardness 2–3. Specific gravity 2.6–3.3. Characteristics:** green to greenish black, brown, seldom pink, violet, white. Lustre: vitreous, on cleavage face mother-of-pearl, also dull; translucent, in very thin blades transparent. Cleavage: complete. Fracture: foliated, mild, cleavage flakes nonelastic malleable. Crystals: (monoclinic) thin to thick tabular, columnar; mostly with hexagonal contours; twinning, pseudomorphic. **Aggregates:** rough, scaly, fibrous, granular, dense, botryoidal, as surface covering; present in metamorphic rocks, sedimentary rocks, in crevices. **Accompanied by:** garnet, rutile, titanite, diopside, idocrase, feldspars, quartz. **Found in:** Rheinpfalz; Saxony/Germany; Tauern/Austria; Wallis/Switzerland; Cornwall/England; Sweden; Urals/USSR; Pennsylvania, Massachusetts/USA; Transvaal/South Africa. **Similar to:** serpentine, talc, mica, brucite.

 annabergite pg. 44, tyrolite pg. 132, liroconite pg. 206

Torbernite
$Cu[UO_2|PO_4]_2 \cdot 8-12\ H_2O$

① Poppenreuth, Oberpfalz/Germany

Streak pale green. **Mohs' hardness** 2–2½. **Specific gravity** 3.3–3.7. **Characteristics**: grass to emerald green. Lustre: on cleavage face mother-of-pearl; translucent to transparent. Cleavage: complete. Fracture: uneven, brittle to mild; thin blades elastic; soluble in nitric acid; highly radioactive. Crystals: (tetragonal) thin and thick tabular, less often pyramidal; usually small; surface growth. **Aggregates**: scaly, crumbly, powdery, as crust, dusting; present in oxidized zones of uranium deposits, crevices. **Accompanied by**: autunite, zeunerite, uranocircite, uraninite, fluorite, barite, limonite, quartz. **Found in**: Black Forest, Oberpfalz, Erzgebirge/Germany; Czechoslovakia; Cornwall/England; central plateau/France; Portugal; Sardinia/Italy; Zaire; Utah, North Carolina/USA; Mexico; southern Australia. **Similar to**: autunite, zeunerite, uranocircite.

Zeunerite
$Cu[UO_2|AsO_4]_2 \cdot 8-12\ H_2O$

② Wheal Edward, Cornwall/England 1:2

Streak green. **Mohs' hardness** 2–2½. **Specific gravity** 3.4–3.8. **Characteristics**: emerald green to yellow-green. Lustre: vitreous, on cleavage face mother-of-pearl; transparent to translucent. Cleavage: complete. Fracture: uneven, brittle to mild; highly radioactive. Crystals: (tetragonal) tabular, less often pyramidal. **Aggregates**: bladed, crusty; present in oxidized zones of uranium and arsenic-rich deposits. **Accompanied by**: torbernite, uranocircite, uranophane, uraninite, sphalerite, galena, limonite, quartz, barite, fluorite, calcite. **Found in**: Black Forest, Rheinland Pfalz, Erzgebirge/Germany; Czechoslovakia; Cornwall/England; Utah, Colorado/USA. **Similar to**: torbernite.

Develline
$CaCu_4[(OH)_3|SO_4]_2 \cdot 3\ H_2O$

③ Richelsdorf/Germany 1:6

Streak light green. **Mohs' hardness** 2½. **Specific gravity** 3.13. **Characteristics**: emerald green to blue-green. Lustre: vitreous, mother-of-pearl; transparent to translucent. Cleavage: complete. Fracture: conchoidal, bladed; thin blades malleable. Crystals: (monoclinic) thin tabular with hexagonal contours, also bladed, acicular. **Aggregates**: rough, crusty, rosette-shaped, bladed, dendritic; present in oxidized zones of copper deposits. **Accompanied by**: malachite, azurite, tyrolite, calcite, gypsum, quartz. **Found in**: Czechoslovakia; Cornwall/England; Corsica/France; Kazakhstan/USSR; Pennsylvania/USA. **Similar to**: chalcophyllite.

Tyrolite
$Ca_2Cu_9\ [(OH)_{10}|(AsO_4)_4] \cdot 10\ H_2O$

④ Brixlegg, Tyrol/Austria 1:4

Streak light green to blue-green, also blue. **Mohs' hardness** 1½–2. **Specific gravity** 3.0–3.2. **Characteristics**: light green to blue-green, sky blue. Lustre: vitreous, cleavage face mother-of-pearl; translucent. Cleavage: perfect. Fracture: bladed, mild; in thin blades elastically malleable; soluble in acid. Crystals: (rhombic) thin bladed, pseudohexagonal; rare. **Aggregates**: rosette-shaped, scaly, radial, fibrous, rough, crusty, botryoidal, crumbly, dense, foamy; present in oxidized zones of copper deposits. **Accompanied by**: chalcophyllite, brochantite, malachite, azurite, schwazite, freibergite, tetrahedrite. **Found in**: Hesse, Erzgebirge, Thüringen/Germany; Tyrol/Austria; Czechoslovakia; Rumania; Nevada/USA. **Similar to**: azurite, brochantite.

132

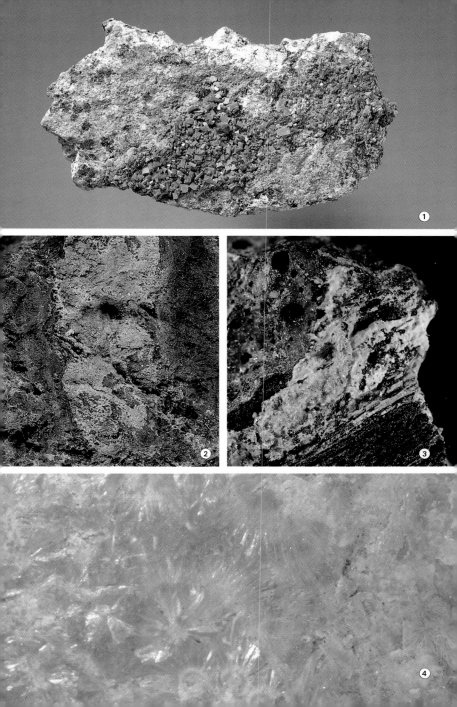

Streak

green

Mohs'
hardness 1

2

3

4

5

6

7

8

9

10

Specific
gravity 1

2

3

4

5

6

7

Brochantite
$Cu_4[(OH)_6 | SO_4]$

① Mina Raphaola/Chile 1:6

Streak light green. **Mohs' hardness** 3½–4. **Specific gravity** 3.97. **Characteristics:** emerald green to greenish black. Lustre: vitreous, cleavage faces mother-of-pearl; translucent to transparent. Cleavage: complete. Fracture: uneven, brittle; soluble in diluted acid. Crystals: (monoclinic) short prismatic, acicular, less often tabular, vertically striped; small; surface growth; occasional twinning. **Aggregates:** rough, radial, botryoidal, crusty, granular, dense, crumbly; present in oxidized zones of copper deposits. **Accompanied by:** malachite, azurite, atacamite. **Found in:** Lahn region/ Germany; Urals/USSR; Banat/Rumania; Sardinia/Italy; Spain; Attica/Greece; Algeria; Namibia; Arizona, New Mexico/USA; Chile. **Similar to:** malachite, atacamite, tyrolite.

Cronstedtite
$Fe_4Fe_2[(OH)_8 | Fe_2Si_2O_{10}]$

② on pyrite, Cornwall/England 1:3

Streak dark green. **Mohs' hardness** 3½. **Specific gravity** 3.3–3.4. **Characteristics:** deep black to greenish black, in thin blades deep green. Lustre: vitreous; transparent to translucent. Cleavage: complete. Fracture: cannot be determined, brittle; thin cleavage blades elastically malleable. Crystals: (monoclinic) narrow pyramidal with triangular or hexagonal contours; rare. **Aggregates:** radial, botryoidal; present in ore veins. **Accompanied by:** pyrite, sphalerite, limonite, calcite. **Found in:** Czechoslovakia; Cornwall/England; Minas Gerais/Brazil.

Euchroite
$Cu_2[OH | AsO_4] \cdot 3 H_2O$

③ Libethen/Czechoslovakia 1:5

Streak light green. **Mohs' hardness** 3½–4. **Specific gravity** 3.34–3.47. **Characteristics:** emerald green to leak green. Lustre: vitreous; transparent to translucent. Cleavage: incomplete. Fracture: conchoidal to uneven, brittle; soluble in hydrochloric and nitric acid. Crystals: (rhombic) short prismatic, less often thick tabular, vertically striped. **Aggregates:** crystal groups in drusy cavities and crusts; present in oxidized zones of copper deposits, mica schist. **Accompanied by:** olivenite, azurite, libethenite, cacoxenite. **Found in:** only Czechoslovakia. **Similar to:** dioptase, malachite, olivenite, libethenite.

Malachite
$Cu_2[(OH)_2 | CO_3]$

④ Shaba/Zaire

Streak green. **Mohs' hardness** 3½–4. **Specific gravity** 3.6–4.0. **Characteristics:** emerald green to greenish black. Lustre: vitreous, fibrous aggregates silky, also dull; transparent to translucent. Cleavage: complete. Fracture: conchoidal, brittle; strong pleochroism; easily soluble in hydrochloric acid (effervescence). Crystals: (monoclinic) long prismatic, acicular, filamentary; very rare; frequent twinning, pseudomorphic. **Aggregates:** clumps of acicular crystals, botryoidal, stalactitic, radially fibrous, crumbly, dense, glass bead–shaped, agate-like banding, dusting; present in oxidized zones of copper deposits, as impregnation in sandstone. **Accompanied by:** azurite, limonite, cuprite, chalcopyrite, chalcosite, bornite. **Found in:** Siegerland. Erzgebirge/Germany; Lyon/France; Cornwall/England; Urals/USSR; Zaire; Arizona, New Mexico/USA; New South Wales/Australia; Chile. **Similar to:** pseudomalachite, chrysocolla, atacamite, brochantite, dioptase.

134

Streak

green

Mohs'
hardness 1 ◀

2 ◀

3 ◀

4 ◀

5 ◀

6 ◀

7 ◀

8 ◀

9 ◀

10 ◀

Specific
gravity 1 ◀

2 ◀

3 ◀

4 ◀

5 ◀

6 ◀

7 ◀

Atacamite
$Cu_2(OH)_3Cl$

① Lafarola/Chile 1:4

Streak apple green. **Mohs' hardness** 3–3½. **Specific gravity** 3.76. **Characteristics:** grass green to greenish black. Lustre: vitreous, adamantine; translucent to transparent. Cleavage: complete. Fracture: conchoidal, brittle. Flame test: blue-green. Readily soluble in hydrochloric acid and ammonia. Crystals: (rhombic) prismatic, acicular, seldom tabular, often vertically striped. **Aggregates:** rough, radial, bladed, granular, dense, as dusting present in oxidized zones of copper deposits, seldom as a volcanic sublimation product. **Accompanied by:** malachite, cuprite, brochantite, hematite, limonite, gypsum. **Found in:** Sardinia, Vesuvius/Italy; Kazakhstan/USSR; Namibia; California, Arizona/USA; Baja California/Mexico; Peru; Bolivia; Atacama/Chile; southern Australia. **Similar to:** malachite, dioptase, brochantite, libethenite.

Scorodite
$Fe[AsO_4] \cdot 2\ H_2O$

② Black Forest/Germany 1:3

Streak greenish white. **Mohs' hardness** 3½–4. **Specific gravity** 3.1–3.3. **Characteristics:** light to dark green, seldom grey, violet, white, colorless. Lustre: vitreous to resinous, dull; transparent to translucent. Cleavage: incomplete. Fracture: splintery, conchoidal to uneven, brittle. Flame test: blue. Easily soluble in hydrochloric acid. Garlic odor when fractured. Crystals: (rhombic) dipyramidal, short columnar, tabular; usually small. **Aggregates:** botryoidal, crusty, fibrous, dense, granular, as dusting; present in oxidized zones of arsenic nonferrous metal deposits. **Accompanied by:** limonite, arsenopyrite, olivenite, adaminite, pyrite. **Found in:** Westerwald, Erzgebirge/Germany; England; Urals, Uzbekistan/USSR; Namibia; Ontario/Canada; Utah, South Dakota/USA; Mexico; Brazil. **Similar to:** strengite, dufrenite.

Libethenite
$Cu_2[OH \,|\, PO_4]$

③ Cornwall/England 1:4

Streak olive green. **Mohs' hardness** 4. **Specific gravity** 3.8–3.97. **Characteristics:** leak, olive green, greenish black, often black tarnish. Lustre: vitreous, greasy; transparent to translucent. Cleavage: none. Fracture: conchoidal to uneven, brittle. Crystals: (rhombic) short prismatic to octahedral; surface growth; usually small. **Aggregates:** radial, fibrous, spheroidal, reniform, crusty, dense; present in oxidized zones of copper deposits. **Accompanied by:** malachite, pseudomalachite, euchroite, limonite, quartz. **Found in:** Czechoslovakia; France; Cornwall/England; Urals/USSR; Shaba/Zaire; Nevada/USA. **Similar to:** malachite, pseudomalachite, olivenite, euchroite.

Dufrenite
$Fe_5(PO_4)_3(OH)_5 \cdot 2\ H_2O$

④ Cornwall/England 1:5

Streak yellow-green. **Mohs' hardness** 3½–4½. **Specific gravity** 3.1–3.5. **Characteristics:** leek-green, greenish black, sometimes brown covering. Lustre: greasy, vitreous, dull; transparent to opaque. Cleavage: complete. Fracture: uneven, brittle; soluble in hydrochloric acid. Crystals: (monoclinic) pseudocubic, also thick tabular; very rare and small. **Aggregates:** radially fibrous, botryoidal, glass bead–shaped, crusty and powdery; present in oxidized zones of iron ore deposits, in phosphate pegmatites. **Accompanied by:** limonite, wavellite, cacoxenite, strengite. **Found in:** Siegerland, Thüringen/Germany; England; Portugal; Alabama, Virginia/USA. **Similar to:** scorodite.

 beudantite pg. 138, pseudomalachite pg. 138

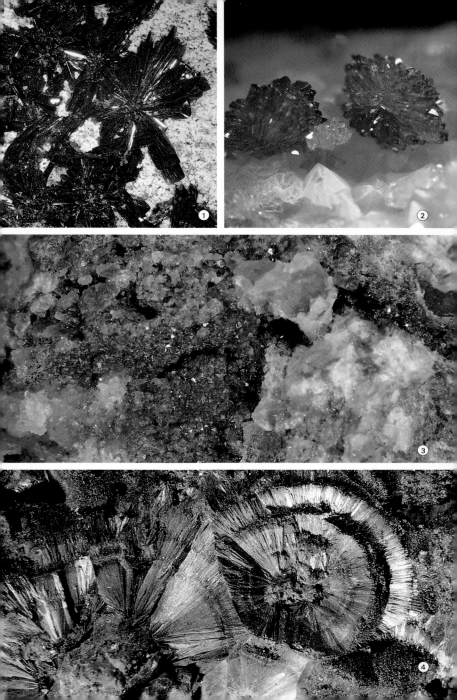

Olivenite
Cu$_2$[OH|AsO$_4$]

① Cornwall/England 1:4

Streak olive green, also brownish. **Mohs' hardness** 3. **Specific gravity** 4.3–4.5. **Characteristics:** greenish black, olive green to brown. Lustre: vitreous, silky, adamantine; translucent to opaque. Cleavage: incomplete. Fracture: conchoidal to uneven, brittle; soluble in acid and ammonia. Crystals: (rhombic) prismatic to acicular, tabular; small. **Aggregates:** radial, botryoidal, reniform, fibrous, granular, crumbly; present in oxidized zones of arsenic-rich copper deposits. **Accompanied by:** malachite, azurite, arsenopyrite, zeunerite. **Found in:** Black Forest/Germany; Czechoslovakia; Var/France; Cornwall, Cumberland/England; Attica/Greece; Urals/USSR; Namibia; Utah, Nevada/USA; Chile. **Similar to:** adaminite, euchroite, libethenite.

Pseudomalachite
Cu$_5$[(OH)$_2$|PO$_4$]$_2$

② Lichtenberg, Franken/Germany 1:3

Streak green. **Mohs' hardness** 4–5. **Specific gravity** 4.0–4.3. **Characteristics:** green to greenish black, often spotted. Lustre: greasy to vitreous; translucent. Cleavage: incomplete. Fracture: conchoidal, brittle. Crystals: (monoclinic) short prismatic, tabular; very small; single crystals rare. **Aggregates:** radial, fibrous, botryoidal, crusty, also rough and crumbly; present in oxidized zones of copper deposits. **Accompanied by:** malachite, azurite, chalcopyrite, cuprite, tenorite, chrysocolla, limonite, chalcedony. **Found in:** Rheinland, Vogtland/Germany; Czechoslovakia; Cornwall/England; Portugal; Urals/USSR; western Australia. **Similar to:** malachite, libethenite.

Mottramite
Pb(Cu,Zn)[OH|VO$_4$]

③ Tsumeb/Namibia 1:2

Streak green. **Mohs' hardness** 3½. **Specific gravity** 5.7–6.2. **Characteristics:** light green, olive green to greenish black. Lustre: vitreous, adamantine, resinous; transparent to opaque. Cleavage: none. Fracture: conchoidal to uneven, brittle. Crystals: (rhombic) pyramidal, prismatic, tabular; rare and small. **Aggregates:** radial, wartlike, dendritic, stalactitic, crusty; present in oxidized zones of ore deposits. **Accompanied by:** descloizite, vanadinite, pyromorphite, mimetite, cerussite, wulfenite, azurite, malachite, calcite. **Found in:** Kärnten/Austria; Cheshire/England; Namibia; Arizona, Montana, New Mexico/USA; Bolivia; Argentina. **Similar to:** descloizite, malachite.

Beudantite
PbFe$_3$[(OH)$_6$|SO$_4$|AsO$_4$]

④ Tsumeb, Namibia 1:5

Streak greenish, also yellowish. **Mohs' hardness** 3½–4½. **Specific gravity** 4.0–4.3. **Characteristics:** green, yellow to brown and black. Lustre: vitreous and resinous; transparent to opaque. Cleavage: incomplete. Fracture: conchoidal to uneven, brittle. Crystals: (trigonal) rhombohedral, pseudocubic, tabular. **Aggregates:** rough, crusty, crumbly; present in oxidized zones of ore deposits. **Accompanied by:** mimetite, jarosite, limonite. **Found in:** Westerwald/Germany; Haute Vienne/France; Attica/Greece; Namibia; Arizona/USA; Sonora/Mexico; western Australia. **Similar to:** jarosite.

138

chalcopyrite pg. 158, millerite pg. 160, uraninite pg. 174, carnotite pg. 194, powellite pg. 196, caledonite pg. 208, boleite pg. 210

Allanite

Ca(Ce,Th)(Fe,Mg)Al₂[O I OH I SiO₄ I Si₂O₇]

① Arriege/France 1:10

Streak greenish grey. **Mohs' hardness** 6–6½. **Specific gravity** 3.1–4.2. **Characteristics:** grey to black, brown, seldom yellow. Lustre: vitreous, greasy, resinous; opaque, thin splinters translucent. Cleavage: none. Fracture: conchoidal to uneven, brittle; strong pleochroism; soluble in hydrochloric acid. Crystals: (monoclinic) thick tabular, long prismatic; rare; twinning. **Aggregates:** rough, granular, dendritic; present in acidic plutonic rocks, metamorphic rocks, products of volcanic eruptions. **Accompanied by:** feldspars, epidote, biotite, monazite, gadolinite, quartz. **Found in:** Eifel, Saxony/Germany; Switzerland; Norway; Sweden; Urals/USSR; California/USA; Queensland/Australia. **Similar to:** fergusonite, gadolinite, columbite.

Gadolinite

Y₂FeBe₂[O I SiO₄]₂

② Birkeland/Norway 1:2

Streak greenish grey. **Mohs' hardness** 6½–7. **Specific gravity** 4.0–4.7. **Characteristics:** green, brown, black. Lustre: vitreous, resinous, greasy; translucent to opaque. Cleavage: none. Fracture: conchoidal, splintery, brittle; soluble in acid; mostly radioactive. Crystals: (monoclinic) short columnar, thick tabular; rare. **Aggregates:** rough, dense, granular, crumbly; present in granite pegmatites, in alpine crevices; **Accompanied by:** fluorite, epidote, titanite, feldspars, quartz. **Found in:** Harz mountains/Germany; Austria; central Switzerland; Norway; Sweden; Greenland; Texas, Arizona/USA. **Similar to:** fergusonite, allanite.

Ludwigite

(Mg,Fe)₂Fe[O₂ I BO₃]

③ Brosso, Piemonte/Italy 1:3

Streak greenish black, blue-green, black. **Mohs' hardness** 5. **Specific gravity** 3.6–4.2. **Characteristics:** black to greenish black. Lustre: vitreous, fibrous aggregates silky; opaque. Cleavage: complete. Fracture: fibrous, brittle; very strong pleochroism; easily soluble in hydrochloric acid. Crystals: (rhombic) prismatic, acicular, fibrous; very rare. **Aggregates:** rough to dense, radial, fine-grained, matted, tough; present in dolomite and limestone, in magnetite deposits. **Accompanied by:** magnetite, phlogopite, cassiterite, quartz. **Found in:** Erzgebirge/Germany; Rumania; Sweden; Norway; Nevada/USA; Korea. **Similar to:** tourmaline, hedenbergite, ilvaite.

Actinolite

Ca₂(Mg,Fe)₅[(OH,F) I Si₄O₁₁]₂

④ Tyrol/Austria

Streak greenish, white. **Mohs' hardness** 5½–6. **Specific gravity** 2.9–3.3. **Characteristics:** green, grey, also white, nearly colorless. Lustre: vitreous, silky; opaque, thin splinters translucent. Cleavage: complete. Fracture: uneven, splintery, brittle; thin blades malleable. Crystals: (monoclinic) linear prisms with a cleavage angle of approximately 120°, also acicular; frequent twinning. **Aggregates:** rough, dendritic, acicular, radial (amianthus), acicular matted (mountain leather), microcrystalline matted (nephrite); present in metamorphic rocks, alpine crevices, less often magmatites. **Accompanied by:** talc, serpentine, chlorite, epidote, mica. **Found in:** Erzgebirge, Thüringen/Germany; Tyrol/Austria; Graubuenden/Switzerland; Sondrio/Italy; Baikal Lake region, Turkestan/USSR; Wyoming/USA; New Zealand. **Similar to:** jadeite, epidote, tourmaline, augite, aegerine.

fassaite pg. 89, pseudomalachite pg. 138, thortveitite pg. 166, marcasite pg. 170, pyrite pg. 170

Augite

(Ca,Mg,Fe₂,Ti,Al)₂[(Si,Al)₂O₆]

$(Ca,Mg,Fe_2,Ti,Al)_2[(Si,Al)_2O_6]$

① Lochkov, Bohemia/Czechoslovakia 1:2
② in volcanic tuff; Vesuvius/Italy

Streak green, white. **Mohs' hardness** 5–6. **Specific gravity** 3.2–3.6. **Characteristics**: leak green to greenish black, pitch-black, brownish, rarely almost colorless. Lustre: vitreous; opaque, edges transparent. Cleavage: incomplete. Fracture: conchoidal to uneven, brittle; weak pleochroism, Crystals: (monoclinic) short prismatic with octahedral contours and a cleavage angle of approximately 90°; also thick tabular, acicular; frequent twinning, occasionally pseudomorphic. **Aggregates**: rough, radial, granular to dense; present as a component of magmatites, less often in metamorphic rocks. **Accompanied by:** hornblende, feldspars, biotite, olivine. **Found in:** Eifel/Germany; Czechoslovakia; Auvergne/France; Liparian Islands/Italy; Urals/USSR; Ontario/Canada; Colorado/USA. **Similar to:** hornblende, tourmaline, actinolite.

Dioptase

$Cu_6[Si_6O_{18}] \cdot 6\,H_2O$

③ Tsumeb/Namibia 1:3

Streak green. **Mohs' hardness** 5. **Specific gravity** 3.3. **Characteristics**: emerald green to dark green. Lustre: vitreous; transparent to translucent. Cleavage: incomplete. Fracture: conchoidal to uneven, brittle; soluble in hydrochloric and nitric acid, ammonia. Crystals: (trigonal) short prismatic. **Aggregates**: crystal groups as crusts; present in oxidized zones of copper deposits. **Accompanied by:** malachite, chrysocolla, azurite, limonite, calcite. **Found in:** Shaba/Zaire; Namibia; Kazakhstan/USSR; Arizona, California/USA; Chile; Peru. **Similar to:** atacamite, emerald, malachite, euchroite.

Hornblende

$(Ca,Na,K)_{2-3}(Mg,Fe,Al)_5\,[(OH,F)_2\,|\,(Si,Al)_2Si_6O_{22}]$

④ Schima, Bohemia/Czechoslovakia

Streak grey-green to grey-brown. **Mohs' hardness** 5–6. **Specific gravity** 2.9–3.4. **Characteristics**: green to black. Lustre: vitreous, silky; opaque, thin splinters transparent. Cleavage: complete. Fracture: uneven, brittle; strong pleochroism. Crystals: (monoclinic) prismatic, mostly short columnar with hexagonal contours, cleavage angle of approximately 120°; also long columnar and acicular; twinning, pseudomorphic. **Aggregates**: rough, dendritic, fibrous, less often granular; present as a constituent of magmatites, metamorphic rocks, magnetite deposits. **Accompanied by:** augite, garnet, biotite, feldspars, epidote. **Found in:** Eifel, Thüringer Forest/Germany; Czechoslovakia; Norway; Finland; Urals/USSR; Ontario/Canada; Idaho/USA; Japan. **Similar to:** augite, tourmaline, epidote, aegerine, idocrase.

Hedenbergite

$CaFe[Si_2O_6]$

⑤ Nordmark/Sweden 1:½

Streak greenish, brownish, grey, also colorless. **Mohs' hardness** 5–6. **Specific gravity** 3.5–3.6. **Characteristics**: dark green, greenish black, brownish black, black. Lustre: vitreous; transparent to translucent. Cleavage: incomplete. Fracture: conchoidal to uneven, brittle. Crystals: (monoclinic) short prismatic with almost rectangular cross sections, cleavage angle of approximately 90°; frequent twinning. **Aggregates**: rough, sparlike, radial, dendritic, granular; present in iron ore deposits, calc-silicate rocks. **Accompanied by:** magnetite, hematite, ilmenite, andradite, epidote, calcite, sphalerite. **Found in:** Erzgebirge/Germany; Elba, Tuscany/Italy; Sweden; Norway; Kazakhstan/USSR; Algeria; New Jersey/USA; Australia. **Similar to:** ludwigite.

142

thorianite pg. 147, uraninite pg. 174, aegerine pg. 189, fergusonite pg. 202

1

2

3

4

5

Streak

grey and
black

Mohs'
hardness 1

2

3

4

5

6

7

8

9

10

Specific
gravity 1

2

3

4

5

6

7

Molybdenite
MoS$_2$

① in quartz; Nevada/USA
② on quartz; Australia

Streak dark grey, finely pulverized dirty-green. **Mohs' hardness** 1–1½. **Specific gravity** 4.7–4.8. **Characteristics:** lead grey with violet tint. Lustre: metallic; opaque. Cleavage: perfect. Fracture: cannot be determined, soft; thin layers nonelastically malleable; greasy to the touch; will color paper; soluble in nitric acid and aqua regia. Flame test: greenish. Crystals: (hexagonal) flat tabular to bladed with hexagonal contours; rare. **Aggregates:** rough, bladed, scaly, as impregnation, granular, dense; present in quartz veins, pegmatites. **Accompanied by:** wolframite, scheelite, cassiterite, sphalerite, arsenopyrite, chalcopyrite, pyrite, magnetite, quartz. **Found in:** Erzgebirge, Kärnten/Austria; Sweden; Norway; Cornwall/USA; Caucasus/USSR; Quebec/Canada; Colorado, New Jersey/USA; Queensland/Australia. **Similar to:** graphite, galena, hematite, ilmenite, nagyagite, tetradymite.

Polybasite
(Ag,Cu)$_{16}$Sb$_2$S$_{11}$

③ Yukon Co./Canada 1:2

Streak black to deep red. **Mohs' hardness** 1½–2. **Specific gravity** 6.0–6.2. **Characteristics:** iron black. Lustre: metallic; thin splinters red translucent. Cleavage: complete. Fracture: uneven, soft. Crystals: (monoclinic) thin tabular, with hexagonal contours. **Aggregates:** rough, scaly, granular; present in silver ore veins. **Accompanied by:** stephanite, pyrargyrite, proustite, argentite. **Found in:** Harz mountains, Erzgebirge/Germany; Czechoslovakia; Nevada, Colorado/USA; Mexico; Bolivia; Chile. **Similar to:** stephanite, argentite, pyrargyrite, hematite, miagyrite.

Covellite
CuS

④ Bor/Yugoslavia

Streak blue-black. **Mohs' hardness** 1½–2. **Specific gravity** 4.68. **Characteristics:** blue-black. Lustre: metallic, greasy, dull, opaque, very thin blades translucent. Cleavage: perfect. Fracture: conchoidal, soft. Flame test: blue. Soluble in nitric acid. Color violet in water, red in oil. Crystals: (hexagonal) tabular to bladed; rare. **Aggregates:** rough, sparlike, bladed; fine-grained, dense, powdery, as covering or crust; present in weathered zones of copper-ore deposits; also as a volcanic sublimation product. **Accompanied by:** chalcopyrite, bornite, chalcosite, pyrite. **Found in:** Harz mountains/Germany; Sardinia/Italy; Serbia/Yugoslavia; Montana, Alaska/USA; Bolivia; Chile. **Similar to:** bornite.

Boulangerite
Pb$_5$Sb$_4$S$_{11}$

⑤ Ramsback, Sauerland/Germany 1:4
⑥ Müsen, Westfalia/Germany

Streak black. **Mohs' hardness** 2½–3. **Specific gravity** 5.8–6.2. **Characteristics:** lead grey to grey-black. Lustre: metallic; opaque. Cleavage: complete. Fracture: uneven, brittle; thin fibres malleable; soluble in warm nitric or hydrochloric acid. Crystals: (monoclinic) long prismatic to acicular; very rare. **Aggregates:** rough, fine-grained, dense, fibrous, radial; present in lead-ore deposits. **Accompanied by:** galena, sphalerite, stibnite, arsenopyrite, pyrite, quartz. **Found in:** Sauerland/Germany; Urals/USSR; Czechoslovakia; Serbia/Yugoslavia; South Dakota/USA. **Similar to:** stibnite, jamesonite, bournonite, tetrahedrite, galena.

144

chalcosite pg. 160, pyrolusite pg. 172, berthierite pg. 190

Jamesonite
$Pb_4FeSb_6S_{14}$

① in quartz; Neumühle, Thüringen/Germany
② with pyrite, Zacatecas/Mexico

Streak black to grey. **Mohs' hardness** 2½. **Specific gravity** 5.63. **Characteristics:** lead grey, often colored tarnish. Lustre: metallic, silky; opaque. Cleavage: complete. Fracture: cannot be detected, brittle. Crystals: (monoclinic) acicular to filamentary. **Aggregates:** rough, radial, fibrous, dense; present in veins. **Accompanied by:** galena, bournonite, sphalerite, arsenopyrite. **Found in:** Harz mountains, Erzgebirge/Germany; Czechoslovakia; Rumania; Cornwall/England; Utah/USA; Bolivia. **Similar to:** boulangerite, stibnite.

Bournonite
$PbCuSbS_3$

③ with siderite; Horhausen/Germany

Streak grey. **Mohs' hardness** 2½–3. **Specific gravity** 5.7–5.9. **Characteristics:** steel grey to iron black. Lustre: metallic, dull; opaque. Cleavage: incomplete. Fracture: conchoidal, brittle; soluble in nitric acid. Crystals: (rhombic) thick tabular, short columnar; rare; twinning. **Aggregates:** rough, sparlike, granular, dense; present in lead and zinc deposits. **Accompanied by:** stibnite, tetrahedrite, galena, sphalerite, chalcopyrite, quartz. **Found in:** Siegerland, Harz mountains/Germany; Kärnten/Austria; Slowenia/Yugoslavia; Czechoslovakia; Cornwall/England; Ukraine, trans-Baikal region/USSR; Arkansas, Colorado/USA; Mexico; Bolivia; Chile. **Similar to:** boulangerite, tennantite, freibergite, schwazite, tetrahedrite.

Graphite
C

④ Trieben, Steiermark/Austria

Streak grey to black. **Mohs' hardness** 1. **Specific gravity** 2.1–2.3. **Characteristics:** steel grey, dark grey to black. Lustre: metallic, dull; opaque, very thin blades translucent. Cleavage: perfect. Fracture: bladed, uneven; nonelastically malleable; good heat conductor; greasy to the touch, color brushes off when touched. Crystals: (hexagonal) tabular with hexagonal contours. **Aggregates:** bladed, scaly, dendritic, fine-grained to dense; present in pegmatites, metamorphic rocks, by-product in magmatites. **Accompanied by:** wollastonite, garnet, spinel, calcite. **Found in:** Bavarian Forest/Germany; Steiermark/Austria; Finland; Ukraine, middle Siberia/USSR; Quebec/Canada; New York/USA; Mexico; Madagascar; Sri Lanka. **Similar to:** molybdenite, nagyagite, tetradymite.

Stibnite   antimonite
Sb_2S_3

⑤ Pribram/Czechoslovakia

Streak grey. **Mohs' hardness** 2. **Specific gravity** 4.6–4.7. **Characteristics:** blue-grey to black, often colorful tarnish. Lustre: metallic, dull; opaque. Cleavage: perfect. Fracture: conchoidal, soft; very thin blades nonelastically malleable; soluble in hydrochloric and nitric acid, potassium leach; will melt in the flame of a candle with a pale blue-green color. Crystals: (rhombic) columnar, sparlike, acicular; usually surface growth. **Aggregates:** radial, acicular, spheroidal, also rough, densely matted; present in quartz veins, in lead, silver, and cinnabar deposits. **Accompanied by:** gold, cinnabar, realgar, auripigment, galena, barite, quartz. **Found in:** Westphalen, Harz mountains/Germany; Czechoslovakia; Kärnten/Austria; Auvergne/France; Ukraine/USSR; China; Japan; South Africa; Nevada/USA; Bolivia. **Similar to:** bismuthinite, galena, pyrolusite, manganite, boulangerite.

146

Streak

grey and
black

**Mohs'
hardness** 1

2

3

4

5

6

7

8

9

10

**Specific
gravity** 1

2

3

4

5

6

7

Argentite
Ag$_2$S

① Oberschlema/Germany
② with calcite; Pribram/Czechoslovakia

Streak lead grey to black, usually shiny. **Mohs' hardness** 2–2½. **Specific gravity** 7.2–7.4. **Characteristics**: lead grey, usually black tarnish. Lustre: on fresh surfaces metallic, otherwise dull; opaque. Cleavage: complete. Fracture: conchoidal to uneven; elastic, can be cut and shaped; soluble in acid. Crystals: (cubic: argentite; monoclinic: acanthite) cubes, octahedral, prismatic, tabular, acicular; frequently pseudomorphic, also twinning. **Aggregates**: rough, granular, scattered, skeletal, dendritic, filamentary, powdery; present in silver-ore veins. **Accompanied by**: pyrargyrite, proustite, chlorargyrite, polybasite, stephanite, pure silver, galena, cerussite, sphalerite, fluorite, barite, calcite. **Found in**: Erzgebirge/Germany; Czechoslovakia; Norway; Sieben-bürgen/Rumania; Altai/USSR; Nevada, Utah/USA; Mexico; Bolivia; Peru. **Similar to**: polybasite, silver, argyrodite, stephanite, chalcosite, galena.

Krennerite
AuTe$_2$

③ Sacaramb, Rumania 1:4

Streak yellowish grey. **Mohs' hardness** 2–3. **Specific gravity** 8.6. **Characteristics**: silver-white to brass yellow. Lustre: metallic; opaque. Cleavage: complete. Fracture: uneven. Crystals: (rhombic) short prismatic, horizontally striped; small and very rare. **Aggregates**: rough, coarse, sparlike, granular and scattered; present in gold deposits. **Accompanied by**: sylvanite, calaverite, nagyagite, quartz. **Found in**: Transylvania/Rumania; Quebec/Canada; Colorado/USA; western Australia. **Similar to**: sylvanite, pure tellurium, calaverite, pyrite.

Bismuthinite
Bi$_2$S$_3$

④ with pyrite; Vogtland/Germany

Streak lead grey, shiny. **Mohs' hardness** 2. **Specific gravity** 6.8–7.2. **Characteristics**: lead grey to pewter white, often multicolored or yellowish tarnish. Lustre: metallic; opaque. Cleavage: perfect. Fracture: splintery, soft; thin blades nonelastically malleable; will melt in flame of a candle; easily soluble in warm hydrochloric acid. Crystals: (rhombic) columnar, acicular; seldom well-developed. **Aggregates**: rough, radial, dendritic, bladed, granular, scattered; present in veins, pegmatites, as volcanic exhalation products. **Accompanied by**: pure bismuth, chalcopyrite, arsenopyrite, cassiterite, wolframite, quartz. **Found in**: Erzgebirge/Germany; Rumania; Cornwall/England; South Dakota/USA; Mexico; Bolivia; Peru; New South Wales; Queensland/Australia. **Similar to**: stibnite, emplectite.

Meneghinite
Pb$_{13}$CuSb$_7$S$_{24}$

⑤ Bottino/Italy 1:2

Streak black. **Mohs' hardness** 2½. **Specific gravity** 6.3–6.4. **Characteristics**: lead grey to black. Lustre: metallic; opaque. Cleavage: complete. Fracture: conchoidal, brittle; soluble in nitric acid. Crystals: (rhombic) long acicular, vertically striped; rare. **Aggregates**: rough, granular to dense, fibrous; present in zinc-bearing deposits. **Accompanied by**: sphalerite, galena, jamesonite, boulangerite, stannite. **Found in**: northern Bavaria, Erzgebirge/Germany; Tuscany/Italy; Sweden; California/USA; Ontario/Canada; New South Wales/Australia. **Similar to**: stibnite, jamesonite.

148
boulangerite pg. 144, polybasite pg. 144, galena; 162

Streak

grey and
black

Mohs'
hardness 1

2

3

4

5

6

7

8

9

10

Specific
gravity 1

2

3

4

5

6

7

Sylvanite
AuAgTe₄

① Siebenbürgen/Rumania 1:8
② yellowish crystals, USA 1:2

Streak grey. **Mohs' hardness** 1½–2. **Specific gravity** 8.0–8.3. **Characteristics:** steel grey to silver-white, also brass yellow, occasionally yellow tarnish. Lustre: metallic; opaque. Cleavage: complete. Fracture: uneven, soft; soluble in nitric acid and aqua regia. Crystals: (monoclinic) tabular, prismatic, often vertically striped; usually small and rare; occasionally pseudomorphic; frequent twinning. **Aggregates:** skeletal crystals mimic closely spaced written characters; also occurs scattered, as dust, less often rough, granular; present in gold-ore veins. **Accompanied by:** argentite, nagyagite, calaverite, crennerite, pure gold, sphalerite, pyrite, tetrahedrite, quartz, calcite, fluorite. **Found in:** Siebenbürgen/Rumania; California, Colorado/USA; Sumatra, Java/Indonesia; western Australia. **Similar to:** krennerite, calaverite, nagyagite, tetrahedrite, tellurium.

Emplectite
CuBiS₂

③ Mackenheim/Germany 1:2

Streak black. **Mohs' hardness** 2. **Specific gravity** 6.38. **Characteristics:** pewter white to steel grey, often yellow tarnish. Lustre: metallic; opaque. Cleavage: complete. Fracture: uneven to conchoidal, brittle; soluble in acid. Crystals: (rhombic) prismatic to acicular, vertically striped; usually surface growth; rare. **Aggregates:** rough, dendritic, granular, scattered; present in bismuth-bearing veins. **Accompanied by:** pure bismuth, scutterudite, chalcopyrite, fluorite, quartz, barite. **Found in:** Black Forest, Erzgebirge/Germany; Czechoslovakia; Norway; Peru; Chile. **Similar to:** stibnite, bismuthite.

Argyrodite
Ag₈GeS₆

④ Colquechara/Bolivia 1:5

Streak grey to black. **Mohs' hardness** 2½. **Specific gravity** 6.1–6.3. **Characteristics:** steel grey with a reddish tint, often black tarnish. Lustre: metallic; opaque. Cleavage: none. Fracture: conchoidal to uneven, brittle. Crystals: (cubic) octahedral, rhombododecahedral; usually very small; sometimes twinning. **Aggregates:** rough, reniform, botryoidal, dense; present in silver-ore veins. **Accompanied by:** argentite, pyrargyrite, proustite, galena, sphalerite, pyrite, siderite. **Found in:** Erzgebirge/Germany; Bolivia; Argentina. **Similar to:** argentite, germanite.

Bismuth, pure
Bi

⑤ Hartenstein, Saxony/Germany
⑥ Mackenheim, Odenwald/Germany 1:5

Streak grey. **Mohs' hardness** 2–2½. **Specific gravity** 9.7–9.8. **Characteristics:** silver-white with reddish tint, often colorful or brass-yellow tarnish. Lustre: metallic; opaque. Cleavage: complete. Fracture: hook-shaped, uneven, brittle; can be cut; soluble in nitric acid. Crystals: (trigonal) cubes, rare; twinning with characteristic stripes. **Aggregates:** knitted, dendritic, bladed, granular, scattered; present in ore veins, pegmatites. **Accompanied by:** bismuthinite, niccolite, chloanthite, cassiterite, stannite, molybdenite, wolframite, galena, arsenopyrite, pyrite, quartz. **Found in:** Black Forest, Erzgebirge/Germany; Czechoslovakia; Cornwall/England; Spain; California, South Dakota/USA; Ontario/Canada; Bolivia; New South Wales, Queensland/Australia. **Similar to:** linneite, niccolite, breithauptite.

150

bismuthite pg. 164, calaverite pg. 164

Tellurium, pure
Te

① Hope Mine/USA 1:2

Streak grey. **Mohs' hardness** 2–2½. **Specific gravity** 6.1–6.3. **Characteristics:** pewter white. Lustre: metallic; opaque. Cleavage: complete. Fracture: uneven, brittle. Flame test: green. Soluble in concentrated sulfuric acid. Crystals: (trigonal) prismatic; rare, usually small. **Aggregates:** rough, scattered, dendritic, fine-grained; present in gold-ore veins. **Accompanied by:** pure gold, nagyagite, sylvanite, galena, pyrite, quartz. **Found in:** Siebenbürgen/Rumania; Cornwall/England; Colorado, California/ USA; Sonora/Mexico; Hokkaido/Japan; western Australia. **Similar to:** krennerite, sylvanite.

Tetradymite
Bi$_2$Te$_2$S

② Schemnitz/Czechoslovakia 1:3

Streak grey, shiny. **Mohs' hardness** 1½–2. **Specific gravity** 7.1–7.9. **Characteristics:** lead grey, steel grey to pewter white, often dark tarnish. Lustre: on fresh cleavage face metallic, otherwise dull; opaque. Cleavage: complete. Fracture: uneven, soft; nonelastically malleable; leaves color on paper. Crystals: (trigonal) narrow pyramidal, tabular; very rare; quadrupling is characteristic. **Aggregates:** rough, bladed, also granular; present in gold deposits. **Accompanied by:** gold, pure bismuth, bismuthinite, tetrahedrite, molybdenite, galena, chalcopyrite, arsenopyrite, pyrite, quartz. **Found in:** Carpaten/Rumania; Czechoslovakia; Sweden; Urals/USSR; Colorado, Montana/USA; Canada; Japan; western Australia. **Similar to:** molybdenite, graphite.

Nagyagite
Au(Pb,Sb,Fe)$_8$(Te,S)$_{11}$

③ with rhodochrosite; Nagyag/ Rumania 1:4

Streak grey, black. **Mohs' hardness** 1–1½. **Specific gravity** 7.4–7.5. **Characteristics:** dark lead-grey and iron black. Lustre: metallic; opaque. Cleavage: complete. Fracture: hook-shaped, soft; thin blades malleable; soluble in nitric acid and aqua regia. Crystals: (tetragonal) thin tabular; rare. **Aggregates:** rough, bladed, granular; present in gold-ore veins. **Accompanied by:** pure gold, sylvanite, calaverite, argentite, tellurium, pyrite, calcite, rhodochrosite, quartz. **Found in:** Siebenbürgen/Rumania; Colorado, North Carolina/USA; Canada; western Australia; New Zealand; Japan. **Similar to:** sylvanite, molybdenite, graphite.

Stephanite
5Ag$_2$S·Sb$_2$S$_3$

④ Freiberg, Saxony/Germany 1:3
⑤ with silver; Aue, Saxony/Germany

Streak black, shiny. **Mohs' hardness** 2–2½. **Specific gravity** 6.2–6.4. **Characteristics:** lead grey to black, often black tarnish. Lustre: metallic, dull; opaque. Cleavage: incomplete. Fracture: conchoidal to uneven, brittle; soluble in nitric acid. Crystals: (rhombic) short prismatic, thick tabular; frequent twinning. **Aggregates:** rosette-shaped, scattered, seldom rough and as dusting; present in silver-ore veins. **Accompanied by:** argentite, pyrargyrite, polybasite, pure silver, galena, pyrite, barite, fluorite, calcite. **Found in:** Erzgebirge/Germany; Czechoslovakia; Sardinia/Italy; Cornwall/ England; Ontario/Canada; Nevada, Virginia/USA; Mexico; Peru; Chile. **Similar to:** argentite, polybasite, miargyrite, pyrargyrite, chalcosite.

152

Streak

grey and
black

Mohs'
hardness

1

2

3

4

5

6

7

8

9

10

Specific
gravity

1

2

3

4

5

6

7

Tetrahedrite series with tennantite ① Pasto Bueno/Peru
$Cu_{12}Sb_4S_{13}$

Streak black, gives off brown color when rubbed vigorously. **Mohs' hardness** 3–4½.
Specific gravity 4.6–5.2. **Characteristics:** steel grey to black with olive-colored tint.
Lustre: on cleavage face metallic, otherwise dull; opaque. Cleavage: none. Fracture:
conchoidal to uneven, brittle; soluble in nitric acid and aqua regia. Crystals: (cubic)
tetrahedral, seldom dodecahedral, cubes, often edge-parallel striped; frequent twinning. **Aggregates:** rough, scattered, granular to dense; present in lead and copper
deposits. **Accompanied by:** chalcopyrite, bournonite, galena, pyrargyrite, sphalerite,
arsenopyrite, pyrite. **Found in:** Harz mountains, Siegerland, Erzgebirge/Germany;
Czechoslovakia; England; Sweden; Montana/USA; Peru; Bolivia; Namibia. **Similar to:**
tennantite, bournonite, galena, sphalerite, sylvanite.

Germanite ② with blue-grey chalcosite;
$Cu_3 (Ge,Fe)S_4$ Kolaazi/Zaire

Streak black. **Mohs' hardness** 3–4. **Specific gravity** 4.4–4.6. **Characteristics:**
violet to pink, usually dark violet tarnish. Lustre: metallic; opaque. Cleavage: none.
Fracture: not determined, brittle; soluble in nitric acid. Crystals: (cubic) microscopically small. **Aggregates:** rough, granular, scattered; present in ore veins. **Accompanied by:** tennantite, tetrahedrite, sphalerite, pyrite, enargite, chalcosite, galena,
azurite, malachite. **Found in:** only Tsumeb/Namibia. **Similar to:** argyrodite.

Tennantite series with tetrahedrite ③ Mandeln, Hesse/Germany
$Cu_{12}As_4S_{13}$

Streak black, in powder form red-brown. **Mohs' hardness** 3–4½. **Specific gravity**
4.6–5.2. **Characteristics:** steel grey, lead grey with olive-colored tint. Lustre: on
fresh surface metallic, otherwise dull; opaque; thin layers red, translucent. Cleavage:
none. Fracture: conchoidal to uneven, brittle; soluble in sulfuric acid. Crystals: (cubic) tetrahedral, seldom dodecahedral, cubes, often edge-parallel striped; frequent
twinning. **Aggregates:** rough, scattered, granular to dense; present in lead and copper deposits. **Accompanied by:** chalcopyrite, enargite, bournonite, galena, sphalerite,
arsenopyrite, pyrite. **Found in:** Harz mountains, Erzgebirge/Germany; Czechoslovakia; Sweden; Montana/USA; Peru; Bolivia; Namibia; Japan; Queensland/
Australia. **Similar to:** tetrahedrite, freibergite, enargite, bournonite, galena,
arsenopyrite.

Schwazite ④ Schwaz, Tyrol/Austria
$(CuHg)_3SbS_4$ ⑤ Rudnany/Czechoslovakia

Streak grey to black. **Mohs' hardness** 3–4½. **Specific gravity** 4.6–5.2. **Characteristics:** dark steel-grey to black. Lustre: on fresh surfaces metallic, otherwise dull;
opaque. Cleavage: none. Fracture: conchoidal to uneven, brittle; soluble in nitric acid.
Crystals: (cubic) tetrahedral, seldom dodecahedral, cubic; frequent twinning. **Aggregates:** rough, scattered, granular to dense; present in lead and copper deposits. **Accompanied by:** cinnabar, mercury, chalcopyrite, bournonite, galena, sphalerite, arsenopyrite, pyrite, barite. **Found in:** Rheinpfalz/Germany; Tyrol/Austria; Czechoslovakia; Cornwall/England; Sweden; Idaho, Montana/USA; Namibia. **Similar to:**
tennantite, tetrahedrite, sphalerite, bournonite.

154 | ankerite pg. 64, dolomite pg. 64, betafite pg. 70, triphylite pg. 70

Streak

grey and
black

Mohs'
hardness

1

2

3

4

5

6

7

8

9

10

Specific
gravity

1

2

3

4

5

6

7

Arsenic, pure

As

① St. Andreasberg/Germany

Streak black. **Mohs' hardness** 3–4. **Specific gravity** 5.4–5.9. **Characteristics:** pale lead-grey to pewter white, copper to black tarnish. Lustre: on fresh surfaces metallic, otherwise dull; opaque. Cleavage: complete. Lustre: uneven, brittle; garlic odor when fractured. Crystals: (trigonal) rhombohedral, cubic, acicular; rare and small. **Aggregates:** rough, fine-grained, botryoidal, glass bead–like; present in arsenic-rich ore veins. **Accompanied by:** dyscrasite, proustite, antimony, galena, calcite. **Found in:** Harz mountains, Erzgebirge/Germany; Czechoslovakia; Vogesen/France; Norway; New Jersey/USA; Chile; West Australia; Japan. **Similar to:** antimony, silver.

Tenorite

CuO

② Nickenich, Eifel/Germany 1:4

Streak black. **Mohs' hardness** 3–4. **Specific gravity** 5.8–6.4. **Characteristics:** steel grey to black. Lustre: metallic, dull; opaque; very fine blades brown, translucent. Cleavage: indeterminable. Fracture: conchoidal to uneven, brittle; elastically malleable when very thin; easily soluble in acid. Crystals: (monoclinic) tabular with hexagonal contours, paper thin; rare. **Aggregates:** rough, crumbly, fine-grained, crusty; present in oxidized zones of copper deposits, occasionally as a volcanic exhalation product. **Accompanied by:** chalcosite, cuprite, malachite, limonite. **Found in:** northern Bavaria, Erzgebirge/Germany; Vesuvius/Italy; Shaba/Zaire; Namibia; Tennessee, Michigan/USA; Chile. **Similar to:** pyrolusite.

Pentlandite

(Ni,Fe)$_9$S$_8$

③ Ontario/Canada

Streak black. **Mohs' hardness** 3½–4½. **Specific gravity** 4.5–5.0. **Characteristics:** bronze yellow. Lustre: metallic; opaque. Cleavage: complete. Fracture: conchoidal, brittle; soluble in nitric acid. Crystals: (cubic) rare, usually with irregularly shaped contours. **Aggregates:** rough, scattered, usually intergrowth with pyrrhotite; present in basic magmatites. **Accompanied by:** pyrrhotite, chalcopyrite, pyrite, magnetite, ilmenite. **Found in:** Black Forest/Germany; Norway; Finland; Kola, Siberia/USSR; South Africa; Ontario/Canada; California/USA. **Similar to:** pyrrhotite, cubanite.

Pyrrhotite

FeS

④ with siderite; Trepca/Yugoslavia

Streak grey to black. **Mohs' hardness** 3½–4½. **Specific gravity** 4.6–4.7. **Characteristics:** bronze-colored with brownish tint, often dark-brown tarnish. Lustre: metallic, dull; opaque. Cleavage: incomplete. Fractured: conchoidal to uneven, brittle; strongly magnetic; solubility in acid difficult. Crystals: (hexagonal) usually tabular with hexagonal contours, isolated prismatic; rare. **Aggregates:** rough scattered, granular to dense, rosette-shaped; present as a by-product in magmatites, less often in metamorphic rocks, sedimentary rocks, in sulfide deposits. **Accompanied by:** chalcopyrite, chalcosite, pyrite, arsenopyrite, pentlandite, sphalerite, galena. **Found in:** Siegerland, northern Bavaria, Erzgebirge/Germany; Serbia/Yugoslavia; Sweden; Norway; Urals/USSR; Namibia; Tennessee/USA; Mexico; Brazil. **Similar to:** niccolite, bornite, cubanite, chalcopyrite, pyrite.

156

Streak

grey and
black

**Mohs'
hardness** 1

2

3

4

5

6

7

8

9

10

**Specific
gravity** 1

2

3

4

5

6

7

Cubanite
CuFe₂S₃

① Marro Velho/Brazil 1:4

Streak black. **Mohs' hardness** 3½–4. **Specific gravity** 4.0–4.2. **Characteristics:** bronze yellow. Lustre: metallic; opaque. Cleavage: incomplete. Fracture: conchoidal, brittle; strongly magnetic. Crystals (rhombic) columnar, acicular, vertically striped; rare; frequent twinning. **Aggregates:** rough; present in copper deposits. **Accompanied by:** chalcopyrite, pyrrhotite, pyrite, siderite, magnetite. **Found in:** Erzgebirge/ Germany; Czechoslovakia; Sweden; Transvaal/South Africa; Ontario/Canada; Alaska/ USA; Cuba; Minas Gerais/Brazil. **Similar to:** purrhotite, chalcopyrite, pentlandite.

Chalcopyrite
CuFeS₂

② Siegen, Westfalen/Germany

Streak greenish black to black. **Mohs' hardness** 3½–4. **Specific gravity** 4.1–4.3. **Characteristics:** brass yellow with greenish tint, often colorful or black tarnish. Lustre: metallic; opaque. Cleavage: incomplete. Fracture: conchoidal to uneven, brittle; soluble in nitric acid. Crystals: (tetragonal) pseudo-octahedral, pseudododecahedral, often distorted with rough faces; usually surface growth, twinning. **Aggregates:** rough, fine-grained, crystalline crusts, botryoidal; present in magmatites, pegmatites, copper deposits. **Accompanied by:** pyrrhotite, pyrite, sphalerite, galena, tetrahedrite, pentlandite. **Found in:** Harz mountains, Thüringen/Germany; Alsace/ France; Cornwall, Devonshire/England; Urals, Kazakhstan/USSR; Ontario/Canada; New York/USA; Transvaal/South Africa; Namibia; Japan. **Similar to:** gold, bornite, marcasite, pyrrhotite.

Enargite
Cu₃AsS₄

③ Pasto Bueno/Peru 1:2

Streak black. **Mohs' hardness** 3–3½. **Specific gravity** 4.4–4.5. **Characteristics:** steel grey to iron black with violet tint. Lustre: metallic; opaque. Cleavage: complete. Fracture: uneven, brittle; soluble in nitric acid and aqua regia. Crystals: (rhombic) prismatic; often vertically striped, also tabular; frequent twinning. **Aggregates:** rough, sparlike, radial, fine-grained, scattered; present in arsenic-rich copper deposits. **Accompanied by:** chalcosite, covellite, bornite, pyrite, tennantite. **Found in:** Baden/Germany; Hungary; Tyrol/Austria; Serbia/Yugoslavia; Namibia; Montana, Utah/USA; Chile; Luzon/Philippines. **Similar to:** tennantite, freibergite, sphalerite, manganite, arsenopyrite.

Stannite
Cu₂FeSnS₄

④ in Zinwaldite, Erzgebirge/Germany
⑤ San José Mine/Bolivia

Streak black. **Mohs' hardness** 3–4. **Specific gravity** 4.3–4.5. **Characteristics:** steel grey with olive tint. Lustre: metallic; opaque. Cleavage: incomplete. Fracture: uneven, brittle; soluble in nitric acid. Crystals: (tetragonal) pseudo-octahedral; pseudocubic, tabular, rare, usually small; twinning. **Aggregates:** rough, fine-grained to dense; scattered, often intergrowth with chalcopyrite, sphalerite, fahlerz; present in zinc-ore deposits. **Accompanied by:** sphalerite, chalcopyrite, cassiterite, wolframite, arsenopyrite, tetrahedrite, galena, quartz. **Found in:** Erzgebirge/Germany; Czechoslovakia; England; eastern Siberia/USSR; South Dakota/USA; Bolivia; Tasmania/Australia. **Similar to:** chalcopyrite, arsenopyrite.

158 berthierite pg. 190, manganite pg. 196

Streak

grey and
black

Mohs'
hardness

Specific
gravity

Millerite
NiS

① Belmunt, Tarragona/Spain 1:3

Streak greenish black. **Mohs' hardness** 3½. **Specific gravity** 5.3–5.6. **Characteristics:** brass yellow, greenish grey, brownish to blackish. Lustre: metallic, silky, dull; opaque. Cleavage: complete. Fracture: uneven, brittle; soluble in nitric acid and aqua regia. Crystals: (trigonal) acicular, filamentary, often striped; twinning. **Aggregates:** radial, filamentary tuffs, matted, seldom rough or granular; present in niccolite deposits, as volcanic exhalation products. **Accompanied by:** linneite, gersdorffite, pentlandite, galena, sphalerite, pyrrhotite, calcite. **Found in:** Siegerland, Erzgebirge/Germany; Czechoslovakia; Quebec/Canada; New York, Pennsylvania/USA. **Similar to:** marcasite, pyrite.

Freibergite
(Ag,Cu)$_{12}$(Sb,As)$_4$S$_{13}$

② Cavnic/Rumania 1:3

Streak grey to black. **Mohs' hardness** 3–4½. **Specific gravity** 4.6–5. **Characteristics:** lead grey to steel grey. Lustre: on fresh surfaces metallic, otherwise dull; opaque. Cleavage: none. Fracture: conchoidal to uneven, brittle; soluble in nitric acid. Crystals: (cubic) tetrahedral; seldom dodecahedral, cubic. **Aggregates:** rough, scattered, granular to dense; present in lead and copper deposits. **Accompanied by:** argentite, pure silver, polybasite; argyrodite, stephanite. **Found in:** Erzgebirge/Germany; Czechoslovakia; Idaho/USA. **Similar to:** bournonite, enargite, sphalerite.

Bornite
Cu$_5$FeS$_4$

③ Neue Hart Mines, Siegerland/Germany

Streak grey-black. **Mohs' hardness** 3. **Specific gravity** 4.9–5.3. **Characteristics:** on fresh surfaces reddish to bronze-brown, often multicolored tarnish. Lustre: metallic; opaque. Cleavage: incomplete. Fracture: conchoidal, soft; soluble in nitric acid and concentrated hydrochloric acid. Crystals: (cubic) cubes, also pseudo-octahedral; very rare. **Aggregates:** rough, scattered, granular to dense, as covering and dusting; present in magmatites, veins, pegmatites, alpine crevices and as impregnation. **Accompanied by:** chalcosite, chalcopyrite, enargite, pyrite, malachite, magnetite, galena. **Found in:** Siegerland, Thüringen, Saxony/Germany; Silesia/Poland; Cornwall/England; Transvaal/South Africa; Namibia; Connecticut/USA; Chile. **Similar to:** Covellite, pyrrhotite, niccolite, chalcopyrite.

Chalcocite
Cu$_2$S

④ Camborne, Cornwall/England 1:3

Streak grey to black. **Mohs' hardness** 2½–3. **Specific gravity** 5.5–5.8. **Characteristics:** dark lead-grey, usually black tarnish. Lustre: on fresh surfaces metallic, otherwise dull; opaque. Cleavage: incomplete. Fracture: conchoidal, soft; soluble in nitric acid. Crystals: (rhombic or hexagonal) thick tabular, short columnar, also pyramidal; rare; twinning, pseudomorphic. **Aggregates:** rough, crumbly, scattered, as dusting; present in copper-ore veins, as impregnation. **Accompanied by:** chalcopyrite, enargite, bornite, covellite, malachite, tetrahedrite, magnetite. **Found in:** Siegerland, Thüringen/Germany; Czechoslovakia; Selesia/Poland; Cornwall/England; Siberia/USSR; Zaire; Transvaal/South Africa; Namibia; Montana, Arizona/USA. **Similar to:** argenite, stephanite, bournonite, fahlerz.

Streak

grey and
black

Mohs'
hardness 1

2

3

4

5

6

7

8

9

10

Specific
gravity 1

2

3

4

5

6

7

Dyscrasite
Ag$_3$Sb

① St. Andreasberg/Germany

Streak grey. **Mohs' hardness** 3½–4. **Specific gravity** 9.4–10. **Characteristics:** silver-white, cream-white, often grey or with yellow-brown tarnish. Lustre: metallic; opaque. Cleavage: complete. Fracture: uneven, soft; can be cut; soluble in nitric acid. Crystals: (rhombic) pyramidal, prismatic, often vertically striped; frequent twinning. **Aggregates:** rough, sparlike, granular, bladed, scattered, as dusting; present in ore deposits, particularly silver-ore veins. **Accompanied by:** pure arsenic, pure silver, pyrargyrite, galena, calcite. **Found in:** Harz mountains, Black Forest/Germany; Vogesen/France; Sweden; Ontario/Canada; Colorado, Nevada/USA; Chile; New South Wales/Australia. **Similar to:** antimony, silver.

Antimony, pure
Sb

② Torrington, New South Wales/Australia

Streak lead grey. **Mohs' hardness** 3–3½. **Specific gravity** 6.6–6.7. **Characteristics:** pewter white, often grey tarnish. Lustre: metallic; opaque. Cleavage: complete. Fracture: uneven, brittle. Flame test: bluish green. Soluble in aqua regia. Crystals: (trigonal) thick tabular, cubes; rare, usually small. **Aggregates:** rough, sparlike, bladed, granular, scattered, botryoidal; present in ore veins. **Accompanied by:** stibnite, arsenic, sphalerite, galena, pyrite, calcite. **Found in:** Harz mountains/Germany; Czechoslovakia; Portugal; Sardinia/Italy; Sweden; Quebec/Canada; California/USA; Borneo/Indonesia; Australia. **Similar to:** arsenic, silver, dyscrasite.

Jordanite
Pb$_4$As$_2$S$_7$

③ Binntal/Switzerland 1:2

Streak black. **Mohs' hardness** 3. **Specific gravity** 6.4 **Characteristics:** lead grey, sometimes multicolored tarnish. Lustre: metallic; opaque. Cleavage: complete. Fracture: uneven to conchoidal, brittle. Crystals: (monoclinic) tabular, often with rounded edges and striped, multifaceted, usually small; twinning, pseudomorphic. **Aggregates:** rough, botryoidal, spheroidal, scaly; present in lead-zinc deposits, dolomite marble. **Accompanied by:** sphalerite, realgar, galena, pyrite, barite. **Found in:** Baden/Germany; Selesia/Poland; Wallis/Switzerland; Rumania; Japan. **Similar to:** galena, bournonite.

Galena
PbS

④ Siegen, Westfalen/Germany

Streak grey-black. **Mohs' hardness** 2½–3. **Specific gravity** 7.2–7.6. **Characteristics:** reddish grey with reddish tint, often dark grey and bluish tarnish. Lustre: on fresh surfaces strongly metallic, otherwise dull; opaque. Cleavage: perfect. Fracture: conchoidal, soft; soluble in nitric acid. Crystals: (cubic) cubic, octahedral, rhombododecahedral; occasionally edge-parallel striped; usually surface growth; often twinning, pseudomorphic. **Aggregates:** rough, coarsely sparlike, granular, less often botryoidal, fibrous, dendritic; present in veins and as replacement. **Accompanied by:** sphalerite, wurtzite, chalcopyrite, tetrahedrite, bournonite, proustite, pyrite, marcasite, barite, quartz, calcite. **Found in:** Harz mountains, Erzgebirge, Siegerland/Germany; Serbia/Yugoslavia; Kärnten/Austria; Zambia; Caucasus, eastern Siberia/USSR; Ontario/Canada; Idaho, Colorado/USA. **Similar to:** antimonite, boulangerite, molybdenite, tetrahedrite, argentite, sphalerite.

162

boulangerite pg. 144, krennerite pg. 148, tenorite pg. 156

Streak

grey and
black

Mohs'
hardness
1

2

3

4

5

6

7

8

9

10

Specific
gravity
1

2

3

4

5

6

7

Bismutite

① Namibia 1:3

$Bi_2[O_2 | CO_3]$

Streak grey to whitish. **Mohs' hardness** $2\frac{1}{2}$–$3\frac{1}{2}$. **Specific gravity** 6.1–7.7. **Characteristics:** straw yellow to brown, greenish, also grey to black, seldom blue. Lustre: vitreous, mother-of-pearl, dull; transparent to opaque. Cleavage: indeterminable. Fracture: conchoidal to uneven. Crystals: (tetragonal) microscopically small. **Aggregates:** rough, crumbly, botryoidal, radial, crusty, powdery; present in oxidized zones of bismuth-ore deposits. **Accompanied by:** bismuthinite, pure bismuth, wolframite. **Found in:** Erzgebirge/Germany; Cornwall/England; Madagascar; Colorado, Arizona/USA; Mexico; Peru; Bolivia; Australia. **Similar to:** greenockite, all ochre types such as hematite.

Calaverite

② Cripple Creek, Colorado/USA 1:5

$AuTe_2$

Streak yellowish grey. **Mohs' hardness** $2\frac{1}{2}$–3. **Specific gravity** 9.3. **Characteristics:** light brass yellow. Lustre: metallic; opaque. Cleavage: none. Fracture: conchoidal to uneven, brittle. Flame test: blue-green. Crystals: (monoclinic) columnar, vertically striped, multifaceted; rare; frequent twinning. **Aggregates:** rough, granular, scattered, bladed, dense; present in old ore mines. **Accompanied by:** sylvanite, gold, nagyagite, krennerite, pyrite, quartz. **Found in:** Siebenbürgen/Rumania; California, Colorado/USA; Ontario/Canada; Mexico; western Australia. **Similar to:** sylvanite, krennerite, pyrite.

Platinum, pure

③ Urals/USSR

Pt

Streak steel grey to silver-white. **Mohs' hardness** 4–$4\frac{1}{2}$. **Specific gravity** 14.0–21.4. **Characteristics:** steel grey to silver-white, often dark tarnish. Lustre: metallic; opaque. Cleavage: none. Fracture: hook-shaped, elastically malleable, ductile, can be formed with a hammer; soluble in hot aqua regia; sometimes magnetic. Crystals: (cubic) cubes, mostly distorted; very rare. **Aggregates:** irregular or rounded nuggets, blades and leaves; present in basic rocks and alluvial deposits. **Accompanied by:** sperrylite, gold, chromite, magnetite, ilmenite, pyrrhotite. **Found in:** Urals, middle Siberia/USSR; Bushveld/South Africa; Ontario/Canada; Alaska/USA; Columbia; Peru; New Zealand. **Similar to:** silver, iron, sperrylite.

Iron, pure

④ Meteoric iron; Arizona/USA
⑤ Widmanstett figures; Toluca/Mexico
⑥ Iron meteorite; Arizona/USA

Fe

Streak steel grey, shiny. **Mohs' hardness** 4–5. **Specific gravity** 7.3–7.9. **Characteristics:** steel grey to iron black. Lustre: metallic; opaque. Cleavage: none. Fracture: hook-shaped, elastic. Crystals: (cubic) unknown. **Aggregates:** terrestrial: rough, scattered, granular, clumps, nuggets; meteoric: rough and granular, nuggets, usually with black, melted crusts; if polished often take on "beam" structures (widmannstett figures); always combined with niccolite; terrestrial iron occurs in many formations; meteoric iron occurs in some matter from the solar system that reaches the surface of the earth. **Accompanied by:** pyrrhotite, pentlandite, graphite. **Found in:** terrestrial iron in Hesse/Germany; Ireland; Auvergne/France; Greenland; Missouri/USA; Meteoric iron in Arizona/USA; Mexico; Namibia; Siberia/USSR. **Similar to:** platinum.

164

uranite pg. 174, safflorite pg. 178

Epidote

① Baja California/Mexico
② Valle Magia, Tessin/Switzerland

$Ca_2(Fe,Al)Al_2[O\,|\,OH\,|\,SiO_4\,|\,Si_2O_7]$

Streak grey. **Mohs' hardness** 6–7. **Specific gravity** 3.3–3.5. **Characteristics**: green, less often yellow, grey. Lustre: vitreous; transparent to opaque. Cleavage: complete. Fracture: conchoidal, uneven, splintery, brittle; strong pleochroism. Crystals: (monoclinic) long columnar, broadly dendritic to acicular, often striped, multifaceted; frequent twinning, pseudomorphic. **Aggregates**: rough, radial, bunched, acicular, as dusting; present in metamorphic rocks, magmatites, pegmatites, alpine crevices. **Accompanied by**: actinolite, idocrase, augite, hornblende, apatite, quartz, garnet, feldspars. **Found in**: Salzburg, Tyrol/Austria; Dauphené/France; Alba, Piemonte/Italy; Norway; Urals/USSR; Michigan, California/USA; Mexico. **Similar to**: actinolite, hornblende, idocrase, tourmaline, willemite.

Thortveitite

③ Hiltvert/Norway 1:2

$(Sc,Y)_2[Si_2O_7]$

Streak light grey, grey-green. **Mohs' hardness** 6½. **Specific gravity** 3.6–3.8. **Characteristics**: dirty green to almost black. Lustre: vitreous; transparent to opaque. Cleavage: incomplete. Fracture: conchoidal to uneven, brittle. Crystals: (monoclinic) long columnar; always intergrowth; frequent twinning. **Aggregates**: radial, rosette-shaped; present in granite pegmatites. **Accompanied by**: monazite, zircon, beryl, euxenite, fergusonite, magnetite, ilmenite, quartz, feldspars. **Found in**: Norway; Urals, Kazakhstan/USSR; Madagascar; Japan. **Similar to**: monazite.

Riebeckite

④ Rosswald, Wallis/Switzerland 1:2

$Na_2Fe_4[OH\,|\,Si_4O_{11}]_2$

Streak blue-grey. **Mohs' hardness** 5–6. **Specific gravity** 3.0–3.4. **Characteristics**: blue to blue-black. Lustre: vitreous, silky; translucent to opaque. Cleavage: complete. Fracture: uneven to brittle. Flame test: yellow. Crystals: (monoclinic) long prismatic, vertically striped; rare. **Aggregates**: radial, fibrous (asbestos form crocidolite), dendritic, bladed, granular; present in acidic magmatites, schist. **Accompanied by**: quartz, orthoclase, albite, epidote, hematite, magnetite. **Found in**: Corsica/France; Shetland Island/Scotland; Ukraine/USSR; Madagascar; South Africa; Rhode Island, Massachusetts/USA; western Australia. **Similar to**: tourmaline, amianthus.

Hypersthene

⑤ Quebec/Canada

$(Fe,Mg)_2[Si_2O_6]$

Streak grey, brownish, whitish. **Mohs' hardness** 5–6. **Specific gravity** 3.3–3.8. **Characteristics**: dark green, dark brown, black, often metallized, sometimes with copper-red lustre. Lustre: vitreous; transparent to opaque. Cleavage: incomplete. Fracture: uneven to brittle; distinct pleochroism. Crystals: (rhombic) short prismatic, tabular, mostly small, multifaceted. **Aggregates**: rough, granular, bladed; present in basic magmatites, as a volcanic exhalation product. **Accompanied by**: olivine, augite, hornblende, feldspars, diopside, pyrrohotite. **Found in**: Eifel, Harz mountains/Germany; Rumania; Central Range/France; Baikal Lake region/USSR; Labrador/Canada; Colorado/USA. **Similar to**: enstatite, bronzite, diallag.

betafite pg. 70, triphyline pg. 70, millerite pg. 90, clinozoisite pg. 102, perovskite pg. 108, boracite pg. 112, allanite pg. 140, ludwigite pg. 140, hedenbergite pg. 142, hornblende pg. 142, ilvaite pg. 172

Streak
grey and black

Mohs' hardness	
1	
2	◄
3	◄
4	◄
5	◄
6	◄
7	◄
8	◄
9	◄
10	◄

Specific gravity	
1	
2	◄
3	◄
4	◄
5	◄
6	◄
7	◄

Bixbyite sitaparite
(Mn,Fe)₂O₃

① Thomas Range, Utah/USA 1:4

Streak black. **Mohs' hardness** 6–6½. **Specific gravity** 4.9–5.0. **Characteristics:** black with bronze-colored tint. Lustre: metallic; opaque. Cleavage: incomplete. Fracture: uneven, brittle. Crystals: (cubic) cubes. **Aggregates:** rough, fine-grained; present in rhyolite, manganese deposits. **Accompanied by:** topaz, garnet, manganite, psilomelane, hausmannite, braunite, hollandite. **Found in:** Sweden, Gerona/Spain; South Africa; India; Utah, New Mexico/USA; Argentina. **Similar to:** braunite, magnetite.

Magnetite
Fe₃O₄

② in chlorite-slate; Tyrol/Austria 1:4

Streak black. **Mohs' hardness** 5½–6½. **Specific gravity** 5.2. **Characteristics:** iron-black. Lustre: metallic; opaque. Cleavage: incomplete. Fracture: conchoidal, brittle; highly magnetic; as powder soluble in hydrochloric acid. Crystals: (cubic) octahedral, rhombododecahedral; rarely hexahedral, often striped; intergrowth and surface growth; frequent twinning, pseudomorphic. **Aggregates:** rough, scattered, granular to dense, sometimes scoriaceous, individual rounded grains; present in magmatites, alpine crevices, as isolated deposits, in sand and alluvial deposits. **Accompanied by:** ilmenite, hematite, hedenbergite, spinel, garnet, chalcopyrite, pyrite, apatite, olivine, calcite. **Found in:** Siegerland, Erzgebirge, Thüringen/Germany; Sweden; Norway; Finland; Lothringen/France; Ukraine, Urals, Altai/USSR; India; Transvaal/South Africa; Michigan, Utah/USA. **Similar to:** chromite, hematite, hausmannite, ilmenite, betafite, descloizite.

Arsenopyrite
FeAsS

③ with calcite; Trepca/Yugoslavia

Streak grey to black. **Mohs' hardness** 5–6. **Specific gravity** 5.9–6.2. **Characteristics:** pewter white to steel grey; often yellowish or dark grey tarnish. Lustre: metallic; opaque. Cleavage: incomplete. Fracture: uneven, brittle; garlic odor when fractured; soluble in nitric acid. Crystals: (rhombic) columnar, dendritic, often striped; frequent twinning. **Aggregates:** rough, radial, fibrous, botryoidal, granular; present in ore veins. **Accompanied by:** gold, chalcopyrite, pyrite, pyrrhotite, magnetite, sphalerite, apatite, rutile, tourmaline, quartz. **Found in:** Harz mountains, northern Bavaria, Erzgebirge/Germany; Czechoslovakia; Cornwall/England; Sweden; Urals, eastern Siberia/USSR; Transvaal/South Africa; California/USA; Tasmania/Australia. **Similar to:** tennanite, loellingite, pyrite, marcasite, chloanthite, skutterudite.

Linneite
Co₃S₄

④ Stahlberg, Siegerland/Germany 1:4
⑤ Littfeld, Siegerland/Germany

Streak grey to black. **Mohs' hardness** 4½–5½. **Specific gravity** 4.8–5.8. **Characteristics:** silver-white with reddish or yellowish tint, sometimes steel-grey, copper-red or violet-blue tarnish. Lustre: metallic; opaque. Cleavage: incomplete. Fracture: uneven, brittle; soluble in nitric acid. Crystals: (cubic) octahedral; sometimes twinning. **Aggregates:** rough, granular, scattered; present in ore deposits. **Accompanied by:** siderite, tetrahedrite, pyrite, cobaltite, galena, barite. **Found in:** Siegerland/Germany; Sweden; Shaba/Zaire; Zambia; Missouri/USA. **Similar to:** cobaltite, niccolite, pure bismuth, skutterudite, gersdorffite, ullmannite.

168 | betafite pg. 70, perovskite pg. 108, allanite pg. 140, ludwigite pg. 140

Streak
grey and black

Pyrite
FeS$_2$

① Calais/France
② Elba/Italy

Streak greenish black. **Mohs' hardness** 6–6½. **Specific gravity** 5.0–5.2. **Characteristics:** brass yellow, golden yellow, frequent multicolored tarnish, sometimes rust-colored, weathered crust. Lustre: metallic; opaque. Cleavage: none. Fracture: conchoidal, brittle. Flame test: bluish; soluble in nitric acid. On fracturing sulfuric odor and sparkling. Crystals: (cubic) cubes with striped faces, octahedral, pentagondodecahedral; intergrowth and surface growth; frequent twinning, pseudomorphic. **Aggregates:** rough, granular to dense, scattered; radial, tuberous, botryoidal, oolitic; present in isolated deposits, sulphur-ore mines, as by-product in magmatites. **Accompanied by:** pyrrhotite, chalcopyrite, arsenopyrite, sphalerite, galena, quartz, calcite. **Found in:** Westfalen, Harz mountains, Erzgebirge/Germany; Piemonte, Elba/Italy; Huelva/Spain; Norway; Sweden; Chalkidike/Greece; Urals/USSR; Transvaal/South Africa; Colorado, Tennessee/USA; Tasmania/Australia. **Similar to:** marcasite, pyrrhotite, chalcopyrite, arsenopyrite, gold, millerite.

Marcasite
FeS$_2$

③ Indiana/USA
④ Brüx/Czechoslovakia

Streak greenish black. **Mohs' hardness** 6–6½. **Specific gravity** 4.8–4.9. **Characteristics:** brass yellow with greenish tint; often multicolored tarnish, sometimes with rust-colored, weathered crust. Lustre: metallic. Cleavage: incomplete. Fracture: uneven, brittle; when fracturing sulfuric odor and sparkling; soluble in hydrochloric acid. Crystals: (rhombic) tabular, columnar, acicular, intergrowth and surface growth, sometimes striped; twinning very frequent; dimorph of pyrite; speer-like and cockscomb-like; also pseudomorphic. **Aggregates:** as crystal groups, rough, coarse-radial to fine-fibrous, dense, botryoidal, tuberous, crusty, as dusting; present in veins in limestone, as concretion in argillaceous and carbonaceous rocks, as weathering product. **Accompanied by:** pyrite, pyrrhotite, sphalerite, galena. **Found in:** Westfalen, Erzgebirge/Germany; Czechoslovakia; Champagne/France; Urals/USSR; Missouri/USA; Bolivia. **Similar to:** pyrite, chalcopyrite, arsenopyrite, pyrrhotite, gold.

Ilmenite
FeTiO$_3$

⑤ Norway

Streak black with brownish tint, in powder form dark brown. **Mohs' hardness** 5–6. **Specific gravity** 4.5–5.0. **Characteristics:** black with violet tint. Lustre: metallic, often dull tarnish; opaque, very thin blades translucent. Cleavage: none. Fracture: conchoidal to uneven, brittle; sometimes slightly magnetic; lively pleochroism; in powder form soluble in concentrated hydrochloric acid. Crystals: (trigonal) tabular, rhombohedral; intergrowth and surface growth; frequent twinning. **Aggregates:** rough, granular, scattered, individual grains; rosette-shaped (rose iron); present in magmatites, their pegmatites, sand and alluvial deposits, alpine crevices. **Accompanied by:** magnetite, hematite, rutile, monazite, apatite, feldspars, quartz. **Found in:** Norway; Sweden; St. Gotthard/Switzerland; Urals/USSR; India; Natal/South Africa; Quebec/Canada; Wyoming, New York/USA; Queensland/Australia. **Similar to:** chromite, rutile, hematite, magnetite, columbite.

Mohs' hardness	Specific gravity
1	1
2 ◄	2 ◄
3 ◄	3 ◄
4 ◄	4 ◄
5 ◄	5 ◄
6	6
7 ◄	7
8 ◄	
9	
10 ◄	

170

Streak

grey and
black

Mohs'
hardness

1

2

3

4

5

6

7

8

9

10

Specific
gravity

1

2

3

4

5

6

7

Ilvaite
CaFe$_2$Fe[OH | O | Si$_2$O$_7$]

① Elba/Italy 1:3

Streak black with greenish or brownish tint. **Mohs' hardness** 5½–6. **Specific gravity** 3.8–4.1. **Characteristics:** black with brownish or greenish tint. Lustre: on fresh cleavage face vitreous, otherwise metallic or greasy; opaque. Cleavage: incomplete. Fracture: uneven to conchoidal, brittle; distinct pleochroism; easily soluble in hydrochloric acid. Crystals: (rhombic) long columnar to acicular, vertically striped. **Aggregates:** rough, radial, dendritic, granular; present in metamorphic rocks, ore deposits. **Accompanied by:** hedenbergite, garnet, magnetite, arsenopyrite, pyrite. **Found in:** Harz mountains/Germany; Elba/Italy; Serbia/Yugoslavia; Serifos/Greece; Urals/USSR; Idaho/USA. **Similar to:** ludwigite, tourmaline, actinolite.

Pyrolusite
MnO$_2$

② California/USA

Streak black. **Mohs' hardness** in crystals 6–7, in rough form 2–6. **Specific gravity** 4.5–5.0. **Characteristics:** grey to black. Lustre: metallic, dull; opaque. Cleavage: complete. Fracture: uneven, fibrous, crumbly; brittle; color rubs off when touched; soluble in hydrochloric acid. Crystals: (tetragonal) columnar, acicular; rare; twinning; pseudomorphic. **Aggregates:** rough, radial, glass bead–like; crusty, fine-grained to dense, crumbly (wad); present in oxidized zones of manganese deposits, as separate deposits, as tubers on deep ocean floor. **Accompanied by:** magnetite, psilomelane, hausmannite. **Found in:** Siegerland, Harz mountains/Germany; Ukraine/USSR; South Africa; Arkansas/USA; Brazil. **Similar to:** manganite, stibnite, psilomelane.

Gersdorffite
NiAsS

③ Montana/USA
④ Heimberg, Harz mountains/Germany 1:3

Streak grey-black. **Mohs' hardness** 5–5½. **Specific gravity** 5.6–6.2. **Characteristics:** silver-white to steel grey, usually dark grey tint. Lustre: metallic, dull; opaque. Cleavage: complete. Fracture: uneven, brittle; soluble in nitric acid. Crystals: (cubic) cubes, octahedral; intergrowth or on drusen; rare and small. **Aggregates:** rough, sparlike, granular, scattered; present in siderite veins and silver-cobalt-nickel deposits. **Accompanied by:** siderite, niccolite, chalcopyrite, galena, quartz, calcite. **Found in:** Siegerland/Germany; Vogtland/France; Steiermark, Salzburg/Austria; Ontario/Canada; Colorado/USA; Bolivia; Tasmania/Australia. **Similar to:** ullmannite, cobaltite, skutterudite, linneite.

Psilomelane   wad, romanechite
(Ba,Mn)$_3$(O,OH)$_6$Mn$_8$O$_{16}$

⑤ Raubach, Westerwald/Germany

Streak brownish black. **Mohs' hardness** 5–6. **Specific gravity** 4.4–4.7. **Characteristics:** black, brownish black, grey. Lustre: metallic, dull; opaque. Cleavage: none. Fracture: conchoidal to uneven, brittle; soluble in hydrochloric acid. Crystals: (monoclinic) unknown; microcrystalline to amorphous. **Aggregates:** rough, fine-grained to dense; radial, dendritic, botryoidal, glass bead–like, crumbly; present in oxidized zones of manganese deposits, as concretions in sedimentary rocks. **Accompanied by:** pyrolusite, manganite, hausmannite, calcite, barite. **Found in:** Black Forest, Siegerland, Erzgebirge/Germany; Sweden; Belgium; Saone/France; Ukraine/USSR; India; Virginia/USA. **Similar to:** pyrolusite, hausmannite.

172

Ullmannite
NiSbS

series with
Willyamite

① Ramsbeck,
Sauerland/Germany 1:5

Streak black. **Mohs' hardness** 5–5½. **Specific gravity** 6.6–6.7. **Characteristics:** silver-white to steel grey, sometimes multicolored tarnish. Lustre: metallic; opaque. Cleavage: complete. Fracture: uneven, brittle. Crystals: (cubic) cubes with striped faces, octahedral, pentagondodecahedral; rare. **Aggregates:** rough, granular, scattered; present in ore deposits. **Accompanied by:** gersdorffite, linneite, sphalerite, galena, siderite, calcite. **Found in:** Siegerland, Harz mountains/Germany; Kärnten/Austria; Sardinia/Italy; Colorado/USA. **Similar to:** gersdorffite, chloanthite, linneite.

Sperrylite
PtAs₂

② Talnakh, Siberia/USSR 1:5

Streak dark grey to black. **Mohs' hardness** 6–7. **Specific gravity** 10.4–10.6. **Characteristics:** pewter white. Lustre: strongly metallic. Cleavage: incomplete. Fracture: conchoidal, brittle. Crystals: (cubic) cubes, octahedral; usually small and intergrown, sometimes multifaceted. **Aggregates:** individual grains; present in sulphide and alluvial deposits. **Accompanied by:** chalcopyrite, pyrrhotite, pentlandite, niccolite, pure platinum, pure gold. **Found in:** Transvaal/South Africa; eastern Siberia/USSR; Ontario/Canada; North Carolina, Wyoming/USA. **Similar to:** cobaltite, platinum.

Thorianite
(Th,U)O₂

③ Madagascar 1:2

Streak grey, grey-green to black. **Mohs' hardness** 6½–7. **Specific gravity** 9.7–10.0. **Characteristics:** dark grey, brownish black to black. Lustre: metallic, resinous; often dull tarnish; opaque; very thin blades translucent. Cleavage: incomplete. Fracture: conchoidal to uneven, brittle; usually radioactive; soluble in nitric acid. Crystals: (cubic) cubes, intergrowth, twinning. **Aggregates:** rounded grains; present in pegmatites, marble, alluvial deposits. **Accompanied by:** monazite, diopside, scapolite, pitchblende. **Found in:** South Africa; Madagascar; Transbaikal region/USSR; Ontario/Canada; Pennsylvania/USA. **Similar to:** pitchblende.

Uraninite
UO₂

④ St. Joachimsthal/Czechoslovakia

Streak black, brownish black, greenish. **Mohs' hardness** 4–6. **Specific gravity** 7.5–10.6. **Characteristics:** pitch black to grey, sometimes wih brownish or greenish tint; weathered yellowish to reddish. Lustre: on fresh surfaces pitch black and greasy, otherwise dull, opaque; only occasionally in very thin splinters reddish brown, translucent. Cleavage: none. Fracture: conchoidal, brittle; highly radioactive; easily soluble in warm nitric and sulfuric acid. Crystals: (cubic) octahedral, less often dodecahedral; occasional twinning, pseudomorphic. **Aggregates:** rough (pitchblende), granular to dense, scattered, botryoidal, spheroidal; present in acidic magmatites, pegmatites, and ore veins, in ancient placer deposits and sandstone. **Accompanied by:** fluorite, apatite, barite, monazite, zircon, feldspars, quartz, pyrite. **Found in:** Black Forest, eastern Bavaria, Erzgebirge/Germany; Czechoslovakia; Vendée/France; Shaba/Zaire; Transvaal/South Africa; Ontario/Canada; Northern Territory/Australia; Turkestan/USSR. **Similar to:** betafite, thorianite, psilomelane.

174

iron pg. 164, arsenopyrite pg. 168, gersdorffite pg. 172

Streak

grey and
black

Mohs'
hardness 1

2

3

4

5

6

7

8

9

10

Specific
gravity 1

2

3

4

5

6

7

Rammelsbergite
NiAs₂

① Bou Azzar/Morocco 1:3

Streak grey to black. **Mohs' hardness** 5½–6. **Specific gravity** 7.0–7.1. **Characteristics:** pewter white with reddish tint, usually dark tarnish; occasional green covering (annabergite). Lustre: metallic, opaque. Cleavage: incomplete. Fracture: uneven, brittle; garlic odor when fractured. Crystals: (rhombic) short prismatic, tabular; small, rare; occasional twinning. **Aggregates:** rough, radial, granular; occasionally intergrown with skutterudite; present on nickel- and cobalt-rich ore deposits. **Accompanied by:** niccolite, chloanthite, skutterudite, maucherite, loellingite. **Found in:** Harz mountains/Germany; Wallis/Switzerland; Ontario/Canada; Michigan/USA. **Similar to:** chloanthite, safflorite, skutterudite, loellingite, maucherite.

Cobaltite   cobaltine
CoAsS

② Tunaberg/Sweden 1:3

Streak grey to black. **Mohs' hardness** 5½. **Specific gravity** 6.0–6.4. **Characteristics:** silver-white with reddish or steel-grey tint, often reddish-grey tarnish, sometimes reddish covering (erythrite). Lustre: metallic; opaque. Cleavage: incomplete. Fracture: conchoidal to uneven, brittle; soluble in hot nitric acid. Crystals: (cubic) cubes with striped faces, octahedral, dodecahedral; always intergrowth. **Aggregates:** rough, granular, scattered; present in ore veins, in metamorphic rocks. **Accompanied by:** pyrrhotite, chalcopyrite, pyrite, cubanite, skutterudite, linneite, erythrine. **Found in:** Siegerland, Erzgebirge/Germany; Sweden; Caucasus/USSR; Ontario/Canada; Colorado, Idaho/USA; Mexico; New South Wales/Australia. **Similar to:** arsenopyrite, gersdorffite, linneite, ullmannite.

Columbite   combination of
niobite and tantalite
(niobite)   (Mn,Fe)Nb₂O₆
(tantalite) (Mn,Fe)Ta₂O₆

③ black crystals; Oberpfalz,
Bavaria/Germany

Streak brown to black. **Mohs' hardness** 6–6½. **Specific gravity** 5.1–8.2. **Characteristics:** black to brown. Lustre: pitch and metallic; transparent to opaque. Cleavage: incomplete. Fracture: conchoidal, brittle. Crystals: (rhombic) tabular, columnar, occasionally striped, usually intergrown; frequent twinning. **Aggregates:** rough, scattered, rounded grains; present in granite and granite pegmatites, alluvial deposits. **Accompanied by:** cassiterite, spodumene, beryl, tourmaline, lepidolite, quartz. **Found in:** eastern Bavaria/Germany; Sweden; Norway; Urals/USSR; Nigeria; Namibia; South Dakota/USA; Brazil; western Australia. **Similar to:** wolframite, ilmenite, allanite, euxenite.

Loellingite
FeAs₂

④ in rondonite; Australia
⑤ Reichenstein, Silesia/Poland

Streak grey to black. **Mohs' hardness** 5–5½. **Specific gravity** 7.1–7.5. **Characteristics:** silver-white, often grey tarnish. Lustre: metallic; opaque. Cleavage: incomplete. Fracture: uneven, brittle; soluble in nitric acid. Crystals: (rhombic) prismatic, acicular, mostly small; usually intergrown. **Aggregates:** rough, scattered, granular, dendritic; present in veins, pegmatites, as impregnation. **Accompanied by:** arsenopyrite, chloanthite, magnetite, siderite, galena, sphalerite, pyrite. **Found in:** Harz mountains, Erzgebirge/Germany; Kärnten/Austria; Sweden; Siberia/USSR; Ontario/Canada; South Dakota/USA. **Similar to:** arsenopyrite, chloanthite, safflorite.

176

Streak

grey and black

Mohs' hardness

1
2
3
4
5
6
7
8
9
10

Specific gravity

1
2
3
4
5
6
7

Chloanthite
(Ni,Co)As₃

① Schneeberg, Saxony/Germany

Streak grey to black. **Mohs' hardness** 5½–6. **Specific gravity** 6.4–6.6. **Characteristics:** pewter white to steel grey, often dark-grey tarnish; reddish or green surface covering. Lustre: metallic; opaque. Cleavage: none. Fracture: uneven, brittle; arsenic odor when fractured; soluble in nitric acid. Crystals: (cubic) cubes with warped faces, also octahedral, dodecahedral; usually surface growth; frequent twinning. **Aggregates:** rough, scattered, granular, dense, botryoidal; present in cobalt deposits. **Accompanied by:** niccolite, safflorite, skutterudite, maucherite, fluorite, quartz. **Found in:** Black Forest, Erzgebirge, Thüringen/Germany; Czechoslovakia; Alsace/France; Morocco; Ontario/Canada; New Jersey/USA. **Similar to:** arsenopyrite, skutterudite, loellingite, rammelsbergite.

Maucherite
Ni₁₁As₈

② Zinkwald, Salzburg/Austria 1:3

Streak brownish to grey-black. **Mohs' hardness** 5. **Specific gravity** 8.0. **Characteristics:** silver-grey with reddish tint, often reddish-grey tarnish. Lustre: metallic; opaque. Cleavage: none. Fracture: uneven, brittle; soluble in concentrated nitric acid. Crystals: (tetragonal) thin tabular, narrow pyramidal; small and rare. **Aggregates:** rough, bladed, radial, granular; present in ore veins. **Accompanied by:** niccolite, chloanthite, cobaltite, calcite. **Found in:** Thüringen/Germany; Steiermark/Austria; Spain; Morocco; Ontario/Canada. **Similar to:** niccolite, breithauptite, rammelsbergite.

Safflorite
CoAs₂

③ Niederschlemma, Saxonia/Germany 1:4

Streak grey to black. **Mohs' hardness** 4½–5½. **Specific gravity** 6.9–7.3. **Characteristics:** pewter white, usually dark-grey tarnish. Lustre: metallic; opaque. Cleavage: none. Fracture: uneven to conchoidal, brittle; emits garlic odor when fractured. Crystals: (monoclinic): prismatic, tabular; very small, rare; often star-shaped tripling. **Aggregates:** rough, radial, fibrous, botryoidal, crusty, fine-grained to dense; present in cobalt-rich veins. **Accompanied by:** skutterudite, erythrite, niccolite, choanthite, rammelsbergite, pure bismuth, silver, arsenic. **Found in:** Black Forest, Erzgebirge/Germany; Czechoslovakia; Ontario/Canada; Mexico. **Similar to:** skutterudite, chloanthite, rammelsbergite, arsenopyrite.

Skutterudite
(Co,Ni)As₃

④ Schneeberg, Saxony/Germany

Streak black. **Mohs' hardness** 6. **Specific gravity** 6.8. **Characteristics:** pewter white to steel grey, occasionally red-tinted tarnish, also greenish (annabergite) or pinkish-red (erytherite) surface crusts. Lustre: metallic; opaque. Cleavage: none. Fracture: conchoidal to uneven, brittle; soluble in nitric acid. Crystals: (cubic) octahedral, often with curved faces. **Aggregates:** rough, scattered, granular to dense, also reniform and knitted; present in cobalt-nickel deposits. **Accompanied by:** cobaltite, safflorite, chloanthite, rammelsbergite, niccolite, bismuthite, silver. **Found in:** Harz mountains, Black Forest, Erzgebirge/Germany; Czechoslovakia; Steiermark/Austria; Norway; Morocco; Ontario/Canada; Colorado/USA. **Similar to:** arsenopyrite, gersdorffite, chloanthite, rammelsbergite, safflorite.

Copper, pure
Cu

① Santa Vita/Mexico 1:2

Streak copper red, metallic. **Mohs' hardness** 2½–3. **Specific gravity** 8.93. **Characteristics**: copper red, darkly tarnished to brown, black, or green crust. Lustre: metallic; opaque; very thin layers green, translucent. Cleavage: none. Fracture: hook-like, soft, very elastic; excellent heat conductor; easily soluble in nitric acid. Crystals: (cubic) cubic, octahedral, severely distorted; twinning, pseudomorphic. **Aggregates**: rough, as grains, nuggets, foliated, skeletal, dendritic; present in oxidized zones of copper deposits, pore space of magmatites, alluvial deposits. **Accompanied by**: cuprite, cobaltite, malachite, azurite, calcite. **Found in**: Siegerland, Saxonia, Germany; Corsica/France; Sweden; Zambia; Michigan, Arizona/USA; Urals/USSR. **Similar to**: silver.

Erythrite
$CO_3[AsO_4]_2 \cdot 8\ H_2O$

② Bou Azzer/Morocco

Streak pink. **Mohs' hardness** 2. **Specific gravity** 3.07. **Characteristics**: peach-blossom red. Lustre: vitreous, adamantine, on cleavage faces mother-of-pearl; transparent to translucent. Cleavage: perfect. Fracture: uneven, soft; thin blades elastic; strong pleochroism; soluble in hydrochloric acid. Crystals: (monoclinic) prismatic, acicular, tabular. **Aggregates**: acicular, dendritic, bladed, spheroidal, reniform, crumbly, as dusting, also rough; present in oxidized zones of cobalt-rich deposits. **Accompanied by**: skutterudite, cobaltite, annabergite, malachite, azurite. **Found in**: Black Forest, Erzgebirge/Germany; Cornwall/England; Azerbaijan/USSR; Morocco; Ontario/Canada; Idaho/USA; Mexico. **Similar to**: cinnabar.

Proustite
Ag_3AsS_3

③ Erzgebirge, Saxony/Germany 1:3

Streak scarlet-red. **Mohs' hardness** 2½. **Specific gravity** 5.5–5.7. **Characteristics**: cinnabar- to scarlet-red, quickly darkens when exposed to light. Lustre: adamantine; translucent. Cleavage: complete. Fracture: conchoidal, brittle; soluble in nitric acid. Crystals: (trigonal) prismatic, pyramidal; multifaceted, mostly surface growth. **Aggregates**: rough, dendritic, as dusting; present in ore veins. **Accompanied by**: pyrargyrite, algenite, polybasite, stephanite, galena, rhodochrosite, pyrite, calcite, quartz. **Found in**: Black Forest, Erzgebirge, Harz mountains/Germany; Vogesen/France; Czechoslovakia; Sardinia/Italy; Ontario/Canada; Colorado, Nevada/USA; Mexico; Chile. **Similar to**: pyrargyrite, miargyrite, cuprite, cinnabar, hematite.

Kermesite
Sb_2S_2O

④ Pribram, Bohemia/Czechoslovakia 1:10

Streak red, brownish red, in powder form yellow-orange. **Mohs' hardness** 1–1½. **Specific gravity** 4.7. **Characteristics**: dark red to violet. Lustre: vitreous to adamantine; translucent to opaque. Cleavage: complete. Fracture: fibrous, soft; can be cut; thin splinters elastic. Crystals: (monoclinic) acicular, filamentary; surface growth; rare, scattered. **Aggregates**: radial, tangled-fibrous, as surface covering; present in oxidized zones of antimony (stibnite) deposits. **Accompanied by**: stibnite, valentinite, senarmontite, berthierite. **Found in**: Erzgebirge/Germany; Hungary; Czechoslovakia; Tuscany/Italy; Algeria; Quebec/Canada; California, Idaho/USA; Sonora/Mexico.

180

polybasite pg. 144, realgar pg. 190

Streak

red and
orange

Mohs'
hardness 1 ◄

         2 ◄
          –
         3 ◄
          –
         4 ◄
          –
         5 ◄
          –
         6 ◄
          –
         7 ◄
          –
         8 ◄
          –
         9 ◄

        10 ◄

Specific
gravity 1 ◄

         2 ◄
          –
         3 ◄
          –
         4 ◄
          –
         5 ◄

         6 ◄

      ⬇ 7 ◄

Pyrargite
Ag₃SbS₃

① Quiruvilca/Peru 1:2
② Sonora/Mexico 1:2

Streak cherry red. **Mohs' hardness** 2½–3. **Specific gravity** 5.8. **Characteristics:** dark red to grey-black. Lustre: metallic; transparent. Cleavage: incomplete. Fracture: conchoidal to splintery, brittle; soluble in nitric acid. Crystals: (trigonal) prismatic, pyramidal, rhombohedral, multifaceted; usually surface growth; twinning, pseudomorphic. **Aggregates:** rough, dendritic, as surface covering; present in ore veins. **Accompanied by:** proustite, argentite, stephanite, galena, rhodochrosite, calcite, quartz. **Found in:** Harz mountains, Erzgebirge/Germany; Czechoslovakia; Sardinia/Italy; Spain; Ontario/Canada; Colorado, Nevada/USA; Mexico; Bolivia; Peru; Chile. **Similar to:** proustite, miargyrite, cuprite, cinnabar, hematite.

Crocoite
PbCrO₄

③ Tasmania/Australia

Streak orange. **Mohs' hardness** 2½–3. **Specific gravity** 5.9–6.1. **Characteristics:** yellowish red, orange. Lustre: adamantine; translucent. Cleavage: complete. Fracture: conchoidal to uneven, soft; strong double refraction; soluble in hydrochloric acid. Crystals: (monoclinic) long prismatic with parallel stripes, often hollow; also acicular, speer-like; multifaceted, many shapes; surface growth or dispersed. **Aggregates:** rough, surface covering; present in oxidized zones of lead deposits. **Accompanied by:** galena, cerussite, mimetesite. **Found in:** Erzgebirge/Germany; Urals/USSR; California, Arizona/USA; Brazil; Tasmania/Australia. **Similar to:** realgar, cinnabar, cuprite, vanadenite.

Miargyrite
AgSbS₂

④ St. Andreasberg/Germany 1:10

Streak cherry red. **Mohs' hardness** 2–2½. **Specific gravity** 5.2. **Characteristics:** steel grey, lead grey to black. Lustre: metallic, adamantine; opaque; red, translucent in thin layers. Cleavage: incomplete. Fracture: small conchoidal to uneven, brittle. Crystals: (monoclinic) thick tabular, speer-like, multifaceted; mostly small; surface growth or dispersed. **Aggregates:** rough; present in silver-ore veins. **Accompanied by:** pyrargyrite, proustite, stephanite, polybasite, galena. **Found in:** Harz mountains, Erzgebirge/Germany; Czechoslovakia; Spain; Rumania; Idaho, Colorado/USA; Mexico; Bolivia; Chile. **Similar to:** pyrargyrite, proustite, stephanite, polybasite, freibergite, tennantite.

Cinnabar
HgS

⑤ with mercury; Almaden/Spain

Streak scarlet red. **Mohs' hardness** 2–2½. **Specific gravity** 8.0–8.2. **Characteristics:** scarlet red, brownish red, often bluish tarnish. Lustre: adamantine, dull; transparent to translucent. Cleavage: complete. Fracture: splintery, brittle; strong double-refraction; soluble in aqua regia. Crystals: (trigonal) prismatic, thick tabular, rhombohedral, dipyramidal, multifaceted; rare, small; twinning. **Aggregates:** rough, granular, crumbly, powdery, as impregnation; present in veins and pore space of sedementary rocks, volcanic hot springs, less often in alluvial deposits. **Accompanied by:** pyrite, marcasite, stibnite, realgar, galena, hematite, fluorite, chalcedony. **Found in:** Rheinland Pfalz/Germany; Sierra Morena/Spain; Serbia/Yugoslavia; Tuscany/Italy; Ukraine/USSR; China; Japan; California, Texas/USA; Mexico; Peru. **Similar to:** crocoite, proustite, realgar, cuprite, hematite.

Purpurite

(Mn,Fe)[PO₄]

① Sandamab/Namibia

Streak purple. **Mohs' hardness** 4–4½. **Specific gravity** 3.2–3.4. **Characteristics:** pink to purplish red, often black or brown tarnish. Lustre: vitreous, metallic, on fresh surfaces silky, also dull; translucent to opaque. Cleavage: complete. Fracture: uneven, brittle; strong pleochroism. Crystals: (rhombic) very small; always intergrowth. **Aggregates:** rough, coarse-grained to dense, crusty; present in pegmatites. **Accompanied by:** heterosite. **Found in:** Sweden; France; Portugal; Namibia; California/USA; western Australia. **Similar to:** heterosite.

Heterosite

(Fe,Mn)[PO₄]

② Namibia

Streak brownish red. **Mohs' hardness** 4–4½. **Specific gravity** 3.2–3.4. **Characteristics:** pink to purplish red, often brown or black tarnish. Lustre: vitreous, on fresh surfaces silky, also dull; translucent to opaque. Cleavage: complete. Fracture: sparlike, uneven, brittle; strong pleochroism. Crystals: (rhombic): always pseudomorphic after triphylite; intergrowth. **Aggregates:** rough, speer-like, spar-like, coarse-grained, crusty; present in pegmatites. **Accompanied by:** purpurite, triphylite, vivianite. **Found in:** Bavarian Forest/Germany; Limoges/France; Portugal; Sweden; Namibia; South Dakota/USA; Australia. **Similar to:** purpurite.

Cuprite

Cu₂O

③ on cerussite, Tsumeb/Namibia

Streak brownish red. **Mohs' hardness** 3½–4. **Specific gravity** 5.8–6.2. **Characteristics:** deep red, carmine red, red-brown, often grey-black tarnish. Lustre: metallic on crystal and fresh cleavage faces, aggregates are dull; opaque, in thin splinters translucent. Cleavage: complete. Fracture: conchoidal to uneven, brittle; soluble in hydrochloric acid (effervescence). Flame test: green. Crystals: (cubic) octahedral, dedocahedral, less often cubed, acicular; usually surface growth; frequently pseudomorphic. **Aggregates:** rough, granular, scattered, powdery, filamentary (chalcotrichite); sometimes mixed with powdery limonite, also in a thick mixture with limonite and silica (copper pitch ore); present in oxidized zones of copper deposits, rarely as a volcanic exhalation product. **Accompanied by:** copper, malachite, azurite, chrysocolla, timonite, limonite. **Found in:** Siegerland/Germany; Vesuvius, Etna/Italy; Lyon/France; Cornwall/England; Urals/USSR; Arizona/USA; Peru; Chile; Namibia. **Similar to:** proustite, pyrargyrite, cinnabar, crocoite, realgar, hematite.

Roselite

Ca₂(Co,Mg)[AsO₄]₂·2 H₂O

④ Bou Azzer/Mexico 1:5

Streak reddish. **Mohs' hardness** 3½. **Specific gravity** 3.5–3.7. **Characteristics:** pink to rose-red, dark red. Lustre: vitreous; transparent to translucent. Cleavage: complete. Fracture: uneven to brittle. Crystals: (monoclinic) short prismatic, thick tabular, usually small; frequent twinning. **Aggregates:** crystal groups speroidal or in drusy cavities; also rough and crusty; present in oxidized zones of cobalt-rich deposits. **Accompanied by:** erythrite. **Found in:** Black Forest, Saxony/Germany; Morocco.

Hematite
Fe₂O₃

① iron glass; Elba/Italy
② red iron ore; Hunsrück/Germany
③ red glass bead; Cumberland/England
④ iron-rose; Tessin/Switzerland

Streak red, red-brown, seldom black. **Mohs' hardness** 5½–6½. **Specific gravity** 5.2–5.3. **Characteristics:** color of coarse-crystalline types are steel gray to iron black, often with bluish tint; crystal faces sometimes colorfully tarnished; fine-grained types are red to red-brown. Lustre: on fresh surfaces metallic, otherwise dull; opaque; thin layers red, translucent. Cleavage: none. Fracture: conchoidal, brittle; slowly soluble in hydrochloric acid. Crystals: (trigonal) dipyramidal, cubelike-rhombohedral, thick and thin tabular, often striped; intergrowth and surface growth; frequent twinning, pseudomorphic. **Aggregates:** coarse-crystalline, granular or scaly (iron glass, specularite); rough, fine-grained, dense, and usable for jewelry (blood stone); radial-fibrous with smooth surface (red glass bead); thin-bladed (iron glass); rosette-like scaly (iron rose); crumbly-powdery (red iron ochre); crumbly-powdery with color rubbing off (red chalk); present as a by-product in many rocks, also as isolated deposits, and in alpine crevices, rarely as a sublimation product. **Accompanied by:** magnatite, pyrite, siderite, limonite, calcite, quartz. **Found in:** eastern upper Bavaria, Siegerland, Lahn-Dill region, Thüringen, Erzgebirge/Germany; Elba/Italy; Auvergne/France; Rumania; Sweden; Ukraine, Urals/USSR; Newfoundland/Canada; upper Great Lakes region/USA; Minas Gerais/Brazil; India; southern Australia. **Similar to:** magnetite, ilmenite, pyrargyrite, cinnabar, cuprite.

Lepidocrocite
FeOOH

⑤ Erzgebirge/Germany 1:3

Streak reddish, brownish. **Mohs' hardness** 5. **Specific gravity** 4.0. **Characteristics:** ruby red, dark red, yellow to red. Lustre: adamantine; translucent, thin layers transparent. Cleavage: complete. Fracture: uneven, brittle; strong double refraction; soluble in hydrochloric acid. Crystals: (rhombic) tabular, acicular; usually surface growth; rare. **Aggregates:** rosette-shaped crystals, rough, fibrous, scaly, glass bead–like, crumbly, powdery; present as a formation on many rock surfaces, in oxidized zones of sulfur-ore deposits, and combined with limonite. **Accompanied by:** goethite, hematite, pyrolusite, calcite, quartz. **Found in:** Siegerland/Germany; Kärnten/Austria; Lothringen/France; Luxemburg; Attika/Greece; Crimea/USSR; Pennslyvania, California/USA; Mexico; India; Japan. **Similar to:** goethite, hematite, limonite.

Piemontite
Ca₂(Mn,Fe)Al₂[O | OH | SiO₄ | Si₂O₇]

⑥ Aostatal/Italy

Streak cherry red. **Mohs' hardness** 6–6½. **Specific gravity** 3.4–3.5. **Characteristics:** red, brownish red, reddish black to black. Lustre: vitreous; translucent to opaque. Cleavage: complete. Fracture: uneven, brittle; strong pleochroism. Crystals: (monoclinic) prismatic, acicular. **Aggregates:** rough, radial, granular, dense; present in manganese deposits, schist, seldom in pegmatites and volcanic rocks. **Accompanied by:** quartz, glaucophane, braunite, rhodonite, rhodochrosite. **Found in:** Piemonte/Italy; Graubünden/Switzerland; Bretagne/France; Sweden; Scotland; Egypt; California, Arizona/USA; Japan; New Zealand.

Mohs' hardness
1 ◄
–
2 ◄
–
3 ◄
–
4 ◄
–
5 ◄
–
6 ◄
–
7 ◄
–
8 ◄
–
9 ◄
–
10 ◄

Specific gravity
1 ◄
–
2 ◄
–
–
3 ◄
–
4 ◄
–
5 ◄
–
6 ◄
7

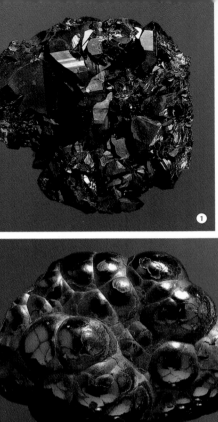

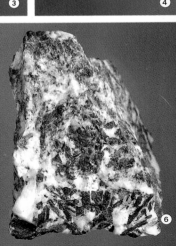

Uranocircite
Ba[UO_2|PO_4]$_2$·8 H_2O

① Menzenschwand, Black Forest/
Germany

Streak yellowish. **Mohs' hardness** 2½. **Specific gravity** 3.5. **Characteristics:** yellowish green to yellow. Lustre: vitreous, mother-of-pearl; translucent. Cleavage: complete. Fracture: uneven, brittle to soft; thin blades malleable; blue-green fluorescence under ultraviolet light. Crystals: (tetragonal) thin tabular with rectangular contours, acicular, pyramidal. **Aggregates:** bladed, dusting; present in oxidized zones of uranium deposits, quartz veins. **Accompanied by:** autunite, torbernite, quartz. **Found in:** Black Forest, eastern Bavaria, Vogtland/Germany; France. **Similar to:** autunite, torbernite, carnotite.

Autunite
Ca[UO_2|PO_4]$_2$·8-12 H_2O

② on quartz, Erzgebirge/Germany

Streak yellowish, colorless. **Mohs' hardness** 2–2½. **Specific gravity** 3.2. **Characteristics:** yellow with greenish tint. Lustre: vitreous, on cleavage surfaces mother-of-pearl; translucent. Cleavage: complete. Fracture: uneven, brittle; thin blades malleable; soluble in hydrochloric acid; yellow-green fluorescence under ultraviolet light. Highly radioactive. Crystals: (tetragonal) tabular; usually surface growth. **Aggregates:** clusters, crusty, dense, as dusting; present in oxidized zones of uranium deposits. **Accompanied by:** torbernite, uranocircite, fluorite, barite, quartz. **Found in:** eastern Bavaria, Erzgebirge/Germany; France; England; Czechoslovakia; Zaire; Washington/USA; southern Australia. **Similar to:** torbernite, uranocircite, carnotite, chalcophyllite, auripigment.

Uranophane
CaH$_2$[UO_2|SiO_4]$_2$·5 H_2O

③ New Mexico/USA

Streak pale yellow. **Mohs' hardness** 2½. **Specific gravity** 3.8–3.9. **Characteristics:** yellow. Lustre: vitreous, mother-of-pearl on cleavage faces; transparent to translucent. Cleavage: complete. Fracture: conchoidal, brittle; soluble in acid. Crystals: (monoclinic) prismatic, acicular. **Aggregates:** radial, crumbly; botryoidal, as dusting; present in oxidized zones of uranium deposits, in pegmatites. **Accompanied by:** torbernite, autunite, uranocircite, uraninite, fluorite. **Found in:** E. Bavaria/Germany; Czechoslovakia; Zaire; New Mexico/USA; Canada; Australia. **Similar to:** sulfur.

Gold, pure
Au

① Nugget; Tipuani/Bolivia 1:3
② on quartz; California/USA

Streak yellow. **Mohs' hardness** 2½–3. **Specific gravity** 15.5–19.3. **Characteristics:** gold-yellow to brass yellow, in powder form brown (mustard gold). Lustre: metallic; opaque, very thin layers green translucent. Cleavage: none. Fracture: hook-like, soft; can be cut with a knife and flattened to the very thinnest of sheets; soluble in aqua regia and mercury. Crystals: (cubic) octahedral, cubes, dodecahedral; frequent twinning. **Aggregates:** rough, springy; wire- and moss-shaped, dendritic; as grains, nuggets, dusting; often with high silver content (electrum); present in veins (mountain gold) or alluvial deposits (placer gold). **Accompanied by:** pyrite, pyrrhotite, chalcopyrite, sphalerite, magnetite, quartz, tourmaline. **Found in:** Hohe Tauern/Austria; Rumania; Altai, Siberia/USSR; India; western Australia; Transvaal/South Africa; British Columbia/Canada; California/USA. **Similar to:** pyrite, chalcopyrite, biotite, markasite.

**Mohs'
hardness** 1 ◀

2 ◀

3 ◀
–
4 ◀
–
5 ◀
–
6 ◀
–
7 ◀

8 ◀

9 ◀

10 ◀

**Specific
gravity** 1 ◀

2 ◀

3 ◀
–
4 ◀
–
5 ◀

6 ◀
–
⇩ 7 ◀

188

ozocerite pg. 28, krennerite pg. 148, calaverite pg. 164

Realgar

As_4S_4

① on limestone; Washington/USA 1:2

Streak yellow-orange. **Mohs' hardness** 1½–2. **Specific gravity** 3.5–3.6. **Characteristics:** red, red-orange; Lustre: adamantine, on cleavage face greasy; translucent. Cleavage: incomplete. Fracture: conchoidal, soft to brittle; can be cut; thin blades malleable; soluble in aqua regia. Flame test: bluish white. Crystals: (monoclinic) short prismatic, vertically striped. **Aggregates:** rough, bladed, fine-grained, as dusting; present as volcanic sublimation product. **Accompanied by:** orpiment, stibnite, pyrite, sphalerite, barite, calcite. **Found in:** Wallis/Switzerland; Macedonia/Yugoslavia; Siebenbürgen/Rumania; Czechoslovakia; Caucasus/USSR; Utah, Wyoming/USA; Mexico. **Similar to:** crocoite, cinnabar, orpiment, proustite, sulfur, cuprite.

Berthierite

$FeSb_2S_4$

② Herja/Rumania

Streak brownish, also grey. **Mohs' hardness** 2–3. **Specific gravity** 4.6. **Characteristics:** dark steel-grey, often colorful tarnish. Lustre: metallic; opaque. Cleavage: incomplete. Fracture: uneven, brittle. Crystals: (rhombic) prismatic; dendritic, acicular, filamentary, vertically striped. **Aggregates:** radial, fibrous, granular to dense; present in antimony-ore deposits. **Accompanied by:** stibnite, quartz, arsenopyrite, pyrite. **Found in:** Saxony/Germany; Auvergne/France; Czechoslovakia; England; Rumania; South Africa; Ontario/Canada; Colorado/USA; Mexico; Bolivia. **Similar to:** stibnite.

Calomel

Hg_2Cl_2

③ with cinnabar; Nevada/USA

Streak light yellow, white. **Mohs' hardness** 1–2. **Specific gravity** 6.4–7.1. **Characteristics:** grey, yellowish brown, colorless. Lustre: adamantine; transparent to translucent. Cleavage: incomplete. Fracture: conchoidal, soft, can be cut; strong double refraction; soluble in aqua regia; dark red fluorescence under ultraviolet light. Crystals: (tetragonal) prismatic, tabular, acicular, pyramidal; very small. **Aggregates:** crusty; rough, crumbly; hornlike; present in oxidized zones of mercury deposits. **Accompanied by:** cinnabar, mercury, schwazite, barite, quartz. **Found in:** Rheinpfalz/Germany; Spain; Yugoslavia; Texas, California/USA; Mexico. **Similar to:** chlorargyrite.

Orpiment

As_2S_3

④ Khorassan/Iran
⑤ Goyaz/Brazil

Streak light yellow to orange. **Mohs' hardness** 1½–2. **Specific gravity** 3.48. **Characteristics:** lemon yellow to orangish yellow. Lustre: adamantine, greasy, on cleavage faces mother-of-pearl; transparent to translucent. Cleavage: perfect. Fracture: bladed, soft; can be cut; thin cleavage blades inelastically malleable; soluble in nitric acid, aqua regia, potassium leach. Crystals: (monoclinic) short prismatic; tabular; very rare. **Aggregates:** rough, dendritic, reniform, crusty, as dusting; present in deposits of arsenic-rich ore, in clay and marl stone, as volcanic sublimation product. **Accompanied by:** realgar, stibnite, pyrite, sphalerite, calcite. **Found in:** Harz mountains/Germany; Macedonia/Yugoslavia; eastern Anatolia/Turkey; Hungary; Rumania; Tuscany/Italy; Wallis/Switzerland; Caucasus/USSR; Utah, Nevada/USA. **Similar to:** realgar, sulfur, greenockite, autunite.

190

kermesite pg. 180, vivianite pg. 206

Streak

gold and
brown

| Mohs'
hardness	1 ◄
	2 ◄
	3 ◄
	4 ◄
	5 ◄
	6 ◄
	7 ◄
	8 ◄
	9 ◄
	10 ◄

| Specific
gravity	1 ◄
	2 ◄
	3 ◄
	4 ◄
	5 ◄
	6 ◄
	7 ◄

Cacoxenite
$Fe_4[OH | PO_4]_3 \cdot 12\ H_2O$

① Svappavara/Sweden 1:4

Streak straw yellow. **Mohs' hardness** 3–4. **Specific gravity** 2.2–2.4. **Characteristics:** yellow to brownish, seldom greenish. Lustre: silky, waxy; translucent. Cleavage: indeterminable. Fracture: fibrous, brittle; soluble in hydrochloric acid. Flame test: bluish green. Crystals: (hexagonal) prismatic, acicular, filamentary, occasionally with hexagonal contours, small. **Aggregates:** fibrous, clusters, reniform, as dusting; present in limonite deposits, pegmatites. **Accompanied by:** hematite, limonite, siderite, strengite. **Found in:** Hesse, northern Bavaria, Thüringen/Germany; Czechoslovakia; France; Sweden; Arkansas, Alabama/USA. **Similar to:** all types of ochre, such as hematite.

Jarosite
$KFe_3[(OH)_6 | (SO_4)_2]$

② Laurion/Greece

Streak yellow. **Mohs' hardness** 3–4. **Specific gravity** 2.9–3.3. **Characteristics:** ochre-yellow, brown to blackish brown. Lustre: vitreous, adamantine, dull; translucent. Cleavage: incomplete. Fracture: conchoidal to uneven, brittle; greasy to the touch when rubbed; soluble in acid. Crystals: (trigonal) tabular, rhombohedral, very small; occasionally pseudomorphic. **Aggregates:** rough, scaly, fibrous, botryoidal, crusty, granular, crumbly; present in oxidized zones of sulphide deposits. **Accompanied by:** limonite, hematite, alunite, quartz. **Found in:** Erzgebirge/Germany; Spain; Greece; Urals/USSR; South Dakota/USA; Chile. **Similar to:** limonite, beudantite, all types of ochre such as hematite.

Wurtzite
ZnS

③ Pribram/Czechoslovakia 1:½
④ Wiesloch, Baden/Germany

Streak light brown. **Mohs' hardness** 3½–4. **Specific gravity** 4.0. **Characteristics:** light to dark brown. Lustre: vitreous, resinous; translucent. Cleavage: complete. Fracture: uneven, brittle; soluble in hydrochloric acid; occasionally orange fluorescence under ultraviolet light. Crystals: (hexagonal) prismatic to pyramidal, also tabular, mostly horizontally striped; rare and small; twinning; quadrupling. **Aggregates:** rough, crusty, finely fibrous to dense; polymorph of sphalerite often combined in banded intergrowth with protruding surfaces; present in veins, in sedimentary rocks. **Accompanied by:** sphalerite, galena; pyrite; siderite; marcasite; quartz. **Found in:** Erzgebirge/Germany; Czechoslovakia; Upper Silesia/Poland; Yugoslavia; Montana, Missouri/USA; Bolivia; Peru. **Similar to:** sphalerite.

Hauerite
MnS_2

⑤ Sicily/Italy

Streak reddish brown. **Mohs' hardness** 4. **Specific gravity** 3.5. **Characteristics:** brownish red to brownish black. Lustre: metallic, adamantine, dull; opaque, thin layers transparent. Cleavage: complete. Fracture: conchoidal to uneven, brittle; soluble in hydrochloric acid. Crystals: (cubic) octahedral or cubo-octahedral; usually intergrowth. **Aggregates:** dendritic, spheroidal; crusty, granular to dense; present in clay and gypsum stone, on salt and sulfur deposits, also in schist. **Accompanied by:** gypsum, calcite, sulfur, pyrite. **Found in:** Czechoslovakia; Sicily/Italy; Louisiana/USA; New Zealand.

ankerite pg. 64, astophyllite pg. 68, betafite pg. 70, chlorite pg. 130, dufreni
pg. 136, beudanite pg. 138, heterosite pg. 184, sphalerite pg. 194, limonite
pg. 198

Sphalerite   zincblende   ① Trepca/Yugoslavia
ZnS

Streak brown, white. **Mohs' hardness** 3½–4. **Specific gravity** 3.9–4.2. **Characteristics:** yellow, brown to black, seldom red, green. Lustre: adamantine, greasy, metallic; transparent to translucent. Cleavage: complete. Fracture: conchoidal, brittle; soluble in nitric acid; foul-smelling odor when rubbed on streak plate. Crystals: (cubic) tetrahedral, dodecahedral, hexahedral, often distorted and striped; twinning, pseudomorphic. **Aggregates:** rough, sparlike, granular, dense, radial; partially intergrown with wurtzite; present in plutonic rocks, in ore veins, schist, as petrification medium. **Accompanied by:** galena, chalcopyrite, pyrrhotite, arsenopyrite, pyrite, marcasite, barite, fluorite. **Found in:** western Westfalia, Erzgebirge/Germany; Czechoslovakia; Upper Silesia/Poland; Serbia/Yugoslavia; eastern Siberia/USSR; Idaho/USA. **Similar to:** galena, sulfur, tennantite, tetrahedrite, wolframite, garnet.

Zincite   ② New Jersey/USA 1:3
ZnO

Streak orange to yellow. **Mohs' hardness** 4–5. **Specific gravity** 5.4–5.7. **Characteristics:** red to reddish brown. Lustre: adamantine, greasy; transparent to translucent. Cleavage: complete. Fracture: conchoidal, brittle; soluble in acid. Crystals: (hexagonal) pyramidal; very rare. **Aggregates:** rough, sparlike, granular, scattered; present in marble. **Accompanied by:** franklinite, willemite, calcite, garnet. **Found in:** Tuscany/Italy; Poland; Spain; New Jersey, Colorado/USA; Tasmania/Australia. **Similar to:** rutile, cinnabar.

Carnotite   ③ Arizona/USA
$K_2[(UO_2)_2 | V_2O_8] \cdot 3 H_2O$

Streak yellow, greenish. **Mohs' hardness** approximately 4. **Specific gravity** 4.5–4.7. **Characteristics:** canary yellow to greenish yellow, seldom red, green. Lustre: adamantine, greasy; transparent to translucent. Cleavage: complete. Fracture: bladed, brittle; powder exposed to hydrochloric acid will turn blood-red; not readily soluble in acid. Highly radioactive. Crystals: (monoclinic) tabular, bladed; small and rare. **Aggregates:** crusty, reniform, granular, crumbly, as impregnation; present in sedimentary rocks, in uranium deposits. **Accompanied by:** pitchblende; pyrite, chalcopyrite, bornite. **Found in:** England; Morocco; Zaire; Uzbekistan/USSR; south Australia; Colorado/USA. **Similar to:** uranocircite, autunite.

Vanadinite   ④ Mibladen/Morocco
$Pb_5[Cl | (VO_4)_3]$

Streak yellowish, white. **Mohs' hardness** 3. **Specific gravity** 6.5–7.1. **Characteristics:** yellow, brown, orangish red. Lustre: adamantine, greasy; translucent to opaque. Cleavage: none. Fracture: conchoidal, brittle; readily soluble in nitric acid. Crystals: (hexagonal) short columnar, tabular, pyramidal, sometimes barrel-shaped; pseudomorphic. **Aggregates:** rough, radial, fibrous, reniform, spheroidal; present in oxidized zones of lead deposits. **Accompanied by:** descloicite, pyromorphyte, wulfnite, mottramite, calcite. **Found in:** Kärnten/Austria; Karawanken/Yugoslavia; Morocco; Zambia; Kazakhstan/USSR; Arizona/USA; Argentina; Chihuahua/Mexico. **Similar to:** pyromorphyte, mimetite, apatite, cocroite, descloicite.

betafite pg. 70, beudantite pg. 138, olivinite pg. 138, krennerite pg. 148, tennantite pg. 154, tetrahedrite pg. 154, calaverite pg. 164, uraninite pg. 174

Powellite
Ca[MoO₄]

① Poona, India

Streak yellowish to white, greenish. **Mohs' hardness** 3½–4. **Specific gravity** 4.2–4.3. **Characteristics:** greenish yellow, grey, brown, blue to blue-black. Lustre: adamantine, vitreous, greasy; transparent. Cleavage: incomplete. Fracture: uneven, brittle; soluble in hydrochloric acid; yellow to orange fluorescence under ultraviolet light. Crystals: (tetragonal) dipyramidal, flat tabular; small; pseudomorphic. **Aggregates:** rough, scaly, dendritic, crusty, crumbly, as dusting; present in oxidized zones of ore deposits. **Accompanied by:** molybdenite, scheelite, laumontite, calcite, quartz. **Found in:** Turkey; Morocco; Caucasus/USSR; Michigan/USA. **Similar to:** scheelite, wulfenite.

Greenockite
CdS

② Mittenwald/Germany 1:3

Streak yellow. **Mohs' hardness** 3–3½. **Specific gravity** 4.8–5.0. **Characteristics:** yellow to orange, brown. Lustre: greasy-adamantine, resinous; translucent. Cleavage: complete. Fracture: conchoidal, brittle; soluble in hydrochloric acid; sometimes orange fluorescence under ultraviolet light. Crystals: (hexagonal) pyramidal, prismatic, thick tabular, often horizontally striped; rare and small; twinning. **Aggregates:** powdery covering; present in oxidized zones of sphalerite-bearing deposits. **Accompanied by:** sphalerite, smithsonite, natrolite, quartz, calcite. **Found in:** Erzgebirge/Germany; Czechoslovakia; Scotland; Urals/USSR; Bolivia; Missouri, Arkansas/USA. **Similar to:** orpiment, realgar, wulfenite, and all types of ochre.

Manganite
MnOOH

③ Ilfeld/Germany

Streak dark brown, black. **Mohs' hardness** 4. **Specific gravity** 4.3–4.4. **Characteristics:** brownish black, weathered steel grey, Lustre: metallic; opaque, very thin splinters red, translucent. Cleavage: complete. Fracture: uneven, brittle; soluble in hydrochloric acid. Crystals: (monoclinic) prismatic, vertically striped, rarely tabular; twinning, pseudomorphic. **Aggregates:** rough, radial tangles, crumbly, granular, oolitic; present in magmatite veins, also as weathering on sedimentary deposits. **Accompanied by:** barite, pyrolusite, psilomelane, braunite, hausmannite, limonite, calcite. **Found in:** Harz mountains, Thüringer Forest/Germany; Cornwall/England; Ukraine/USSR; Sardinia/Italy; Vogesen/France; Nova Scotia/Canada; California, Arizona/USA; India. **Similar to:** stibnite, pyrolusite, goethite, enargite.

Descloizite
Pb(Zn,Cu)[OH|VO₄]

④ Ankas/Namibia 1:2

Streak light brown. **Mohs' hardness** 3½. **Specific gravity** 5.5–6.2. **Characteristics:** brown, brownish red, brownish black. Lustre: resinous, adamantine, on cleavage face greasy; transparent to opaque. Cleavage: none. Fracture: conchoidal, brittle; soluble in acid. Crystals: (rhombic) prismatic, dipyramidal, tabular. **Aggregates:** rough, radial, botryoidal, crusty; present in oxidized zones of nonferrous metal deposits. **Accompanied by:** vandanite, pyromorphite, cerussite, wulfenite, limonite, quartz. **Found in:** Rheinpfalz/Germany; Kärnten/Austria; Algeria; Zaire; Zambia; Arizona, New Mexico/USA; Argentina. **Similar to:** mottramite, magnetite, wulfenite, vandanite.

cuprite pg. 184, gold pg. 188, berthierite pg. 190, limonite pg. 198, huebnerite pg. 204

Aegirine   acmite   ① Eker/Norway

$NaFe[Si_2O_6]$

Streak yellow to brownish, greenish. **Mohs' hardness** 6–6½. **Specific gravity** 3.5–3.6. **Characteristics:** dark green, greenish black, brownish. Lustre: vitreous, resinous; opaque, on edges greasy, translucent. Cleavage: complete. Fracture: uneven, brittle. Flame test: yellow. Pleochroic. Crystals: (monoclinic) columnar, acicular, tabular, vertically striped; usually intergrowth; often twinning. **Aggregates:** rough, fibrous, radial, granular; present in magmatites, pegmatites, seldom in metamorphic rocks. **Accompanied by:** arfvedsonite, feldspars, nepheline, sodalithe, zircon. **Found in:** Norway; Sweden; Portugal; Sardinia/Italy; Kola/USSR; Quebec/Canada; Arkansas, Montana/USA. **Similar to:** hornblende, arfvedsonite, actinolite.

Neptunite   ② California/USA 1:3

$Na_2FeTi[Si_4O_{12}]$

Streak brown. **Mohs' hardness** 5½. **Specific gravity** 3.2. **Characteristics:** black to dark brown, as splinter red. Lustre: strong vitreous; opaque to translucent. Cleavage: complete. Fracture: conchoidal, brittle; strong pleochroism. Crystals: (monoclinic) prismatic. **Aggregates:** none; only individual crystals, intergrowth and surface growth; present in pegmatites, natrolite deposits. **Accompanied by:** benitoite, natrolite, aegirine. **Found in:** Ireland; Kola/USSR; Greenland; Canada; California/USA.

Goethite   ③ Freisen, Saarland/Germany 1:3

$FeOOH$ ④ Chihuahua/Mexico

Streak brown to yellow. **Mohs' hardness** 5–5½. **Specific gravity** 3.8–4.3. **Characteristics:** brown to yellow. Lustre: strong vitreous; opaque, thin splinters translucent. Cleavage: complete. Fracture: uneven, brittle; soluble in hydrochloric acid. Crystals: (rhombic) prismatic, acicular, tabular, horizontally striped; rare; pseudomorphic. **Aggregates:** rough, radial, crusty, dense, crumbly, acicular, velvet-like; present in oxidized zones of sulfide-ore deposits. **Accompanied by:** lepidocrocite, hematite, pyrite, calcite, quartz. **Found in:** Siegerland/Germany; Czechoslovakia; England; Lothringen/France; Crimea/USSR; Canada; Alabama/USA; Cuba. **Similar to:** manganite, lepidocrocite, hematite.

Limonite   ⑤ ochre; Auerbach, Oberpfalz/Germany

$FeOOH \cdot nH_2O$ ⑥ Westerwald/Germany

Mixture of geothite and lepidocrocite. **Streak** brown. **Mohs' hardness** 4–5½. **Specific gravity** 2.7–4.3. **Characteristics:** yellow (yellow iron ore, ochre) to brown, black. Lustre: vitreous, adamantine, dull; translucent to opaque. Cleavage: indeterminable. Fracture: conchoidal, uneven, fibrous, brittle, soluble in hydrochloric acid. Crystals: (rhombic) cryptocrystalline, usually amorphous; often pseudomorphic. **Aggregates:** rough, crumbly, powdery, reniform; tuberous, bean-shaped, oolitic; present in oxidized zones of iron-ore deposits, as petrification medium. **Accompanied by:** pyrite, hematite, pyrolusite, psilomelane, calcite, quartz. **Found in:** Lower Saxony/Germany; Lothringen/France; Luxembourg; Elba/Italy; Ukraine, Urals/USSR; Utah, Arizona/USA; Cuba; Brazil; Zaire; India. **Similar to:** hematite and other ochre.

198 | betafite pg. 70, bronzite pg. 106, allanite pg. 140, hedenbergite pg. 142, hornblende pg. 142, hypersthene pg. 166, lepidocrocite pg. 186, pyrochlore pg. 200

Franklinite

① Franklin, New Jersey/USA

$ZnFe_2O_4$

Streak reddish brown. **Mohs' hardness** 6–6½. **Specific gravity** 5.0–5.2. **Characteristics**: iron-black. Lustre: metallic; opaque; very thin splinters deep red, translucent. Cleavage: incomplete. Fracture: conchoidal to uneven, brittle; slightly magnetic; soluble in hydrochloric acid. Crystals: (cubic) octahedral, edges mostly rounded; intergrowth. **Aggregates**: rough, granular to dense; present in zinc-ore deposits. **Accompanied by**: zincite, willemite, calcite, rhodonite, garnet, axinite, magnetite. **Found in**: New Jersey/USA. **Similar to**: magnetite, chromite, braunite, hausmannite.

Pyrochlore

② Minas Grais/Brazil 1:3

$(Na,Ca,U)_2(Nb,Ti,Ta)_2O_6(OH,F,O)$

Streak pale yellow to brown. **Mohs' hardness** 5–5½. **Specific gravity** 3.5–4.6. **Characteristics**: light yellow to dark brown, reddish. Lustre: vitreous, greasy, adamantine; translucent to opaque. Cleavage: none. Fracture: conchoidal to uneven, brittle. Often radioactive. Crystals: (cubic) octahedral; seldom cubes, mostly intergrowth. **Aggregates**: rough, granular to dense; present in foyaite (syenite), carbonatite, pegmatites, by-product of volcanic eruptions. **Accompanied by**: zircon, feldspars, nepheline, calcite, biotite, apatite, fluorite. **Found in**: Eifel/Germany; Norway; Sweden; Urals, Kola/USSR; Tanzania; Uganda; Greenland; Ontario/Canada; Colorado/USA. **Similar to**: betafite, zircon, scheelite.

Rutile

③ Namibia 1:2
④ in quartz crystals, Brazil

TiO_2

Streak yellowish brown. **Mohs' hardness** 6–6½. **Specific gravity** 4.2–4.3. **Characteristics**: brownish red, red, yellowish, iron-black. Lustre: metallic-like, adamantine; transparent to opaque. Cleavage: complete. Fracture: conchoidal to uneven, brittle; strong double-refraction. Crystals: (tetragonal) prismatic, dipyramidal; dendritic, acicular; thick columnar, often vertically striped; intergrowth and surface growth; twinning, polycrystalline sometimes with net-like intergrowth (sagenite). **Aggregates**: rough, granular, acicular, often intergrown with quartz; present in basic magmatites, pegmatites, metamorphic rocks, alpine crevices, alluvial deposits. **Accompanied by**: apatite, hematite, brookite, anatase, titanite. **Found in**: Tyrol/Austria; southern Tirol/Italy; Wallis/Switzerland; Norway; Urals/USSR; Virginia/USA; Mexico; Brazil; Namibia. **Similar to**: zincite, cassiterite, magnetite, zircon, tourmaline.

Braunite

⑤ Langban/Sweden 1:8

$Mn_7[O_8 | SiO_4]$

Streak dark brown, black-brown. **Mohs' hardness** 6–6½. **Specific gravity** 4.7–4.8. **Characteristics**: black to brownish black. Lustre: metallic; opaque. Cleavage: complete. Fracture: uneven, brittle; solubility in hydrochloric acid difficult. Crystals: (tetragonal) octahedroid, dipyramidal, usually very small; twinning. **Aggregates**: crystalline crusts, rough, granular, dense; present in manganese deposits. **Accompanied by**: hausmannite, manganite, pyrolusite, psilomelane, magnetite, barite, calcite, quartz. **Found in**: Thüringen/Germany; Piemonte/Italy; Sweden; Griqualand West/South Africa; Namibia; Kazakhstan, Urals/USSR; Texas, California/USA; Minas Gerais/Brazil; Chile. **Similar to**: hausmannite, magnetite, bromite, franklinite, bixbyite.

Streak

gold and
brown

Mohs'
hardness 1 ◄

2 ◄

3 ◄

4 ◄

5 ◄

6 ◄

7 ◄

8 ◄
-
9 ◄
10 ◄

Specific
gravity 1 ◄

2 ◄
-
3 ◄
-
4 ◄
-
5 ◄
-
6 ◄

7 ◄

Euxenite
① Madagascar 1:5

(Y,Ce,U,Ca)(Nb,Ta,Ti)$_2$(O,OH)$_6$

Streak yellowish to brownish, grey. **Mohs' hardness** 5½–6½. **Specific gravity** 4.3–5.9. **Characteristics**: black, greenish brown, often with a greenish cover. Lustre: metallic, resinous, greasy; opaque, thin splinters translucent. Cleavage: none. Fracture: conchoidal, brittle. Radioactive. Soluble in powder form in hot hydrochloric and sulfuric acid. Crystals: (rhombic) short prismatic, tabular, often striped, frequent twinning. **Aggregates**: rough, granular, fan-shaped; present in granite pegmatites, alluvial deposits. **Accompanied by**: monazite, ilmenite, magnetite, beryl, zircon, gadolinite. **Found in**: Hohe Tauern/Austria; Norway; Finland; Madagascar; Ontario/Canada; North Carolina/USA. **Similar to**: columbite, monazite, fergusonite, betafite.

Fergusonite
② Madagascar 1:3

Y(Nb,Ta)O$_4$

Streak light brown, grey-green. **Mohs' hardness** 5–6½. **Specific gravity** 4.7–6.3. **Characteristics**: black to brownish. Lustre: vitreous, dull, on fresh surfaces greasy and metallic; opaque, thin splinters translucent. Cleavage: none. Fracture: conchoidal to uneven, brittle. Crystals: (tetragonal) prismatic, dipyramidal; always intergrowth. **Aggregates**: rough, granular to dense; present in granite pegmatites, alluvial deposits. **Accompanied by**: monazite, euxenite, gadolinite. **Found in**: Norway; Sweden; Finland; Urals/USSR; Tanzania; Zimbabwe; Madagascar; Greenland; Texas, California/USA; Sri Lanka. **Similar to**: columbite, gadolinite, monazite.

Chromite
③ Guleman/Turkey

(Fe,Mg) Cr$_2$O$_4$

Streak brown. **Mohs' hardness** 5½. **Specific gravity** 4.5–4.8. **Characteristics**: black to brownish black. Lustre: greasy to metallic; opaque; thin splinters brown, translucent. Cleavage: none. Fracture: uneven to conchoidal, brittle; sometimes slightly magnetic. Crystals: (cubic) octahedral; rare and small. **Aggregates**: rough, granular, in clumps, dense, scattered; present in peridotite, serpentinite, banded complexes. **Accompanied by**: olivine, bronzite, uvarovite, magnetite, pure platinum, kämmererite. **Found in**: Steiermark/Austria; Silesia/Poland; Serbia/Yugoslavia; Turkey; Norway; Transvaal/South Africa; Urals, Altai/USSR; California, Oregon/USA; New Zealand. **Similar to**: magnetite, franklinite, braunite, ilmenite.

Hausmannite
④ Langban/Sweden

Mn$_3$O$_4$

Streak brown to reddish. **Mohs' hardness** 5½. **Specific gravity** 4.7–4.8. **Characteristics**: iron-black with brownish tint. Lustre: metallic; opaque; thin splinters deep red, translucent. Cleavage: complete. Fracture: uneven, brittle; soluble in hydrochloric acid. Crystals: (tetragonal) pseudo-octahedral, pyramidal, often horizontally striped; intergrowth and surface growth; frequent twinning, particularly quintupling, pseudomorphic. **Aggregates**: rough, granular, dense; present in manganese deposits. **Accompanied by**: braunite, pyrolusite, psilomelane, manganite, piemontite, magnetite, barite. **Found in**: Harz mountains, Thüringer Forest/Germany; Graubünden/Switzerland; Sweden; Bulgaria; England; Urals/USSR; Nevada, California/USA; Brazil; India. **Similar to**: braunite, magnetite, franklinite, psilomelane.

hematite pg. 186, zincite pg. 194, goethite pg. 198, limonite pg. 198

Streak

gold and
brown

Mohs'
hardness 1 ◄

2 ◄

3 ◄

4 ◄

5 ◄

6 ◄

7 ◄

8 ◄

9 ◄

10 ◄

Specific
gravity 1 ◄

2 ◄

3 ◄

4 ◄

5 ◄

6 ◄

7 ◄

Huebnerite
MnWO₄

① Silverton, California/USA 1:7

Streak reddish brown. **Mohs' hardness** 4–5½. **Specific gravity** 7.2–7.3. **Characteristics**: yellow, red to dark brown, brownish black. Lustre: metallic, resinous; transparent to opaque. Cleavage: complete. Fracture: uneven, brittle. Crystals: (monoclinic) short to long columnar, tabular, vertically striped; rare; twinning, pseudomorphic. **Aggregates**: parallel or radial arranged crystals; present in pegmatites, veins. **Accompanied by**: wolframite, scheelite, rhodochrosite, fluorite, quartz. **Found in**: Erzgebirge/Germany; Czechoslovakia; France; Transbaikal region/USSR; Colorado, New Mexico/USA; Peru; Australia. **Similar to**: goethite.

Wolframite
(Fe,Mn)WO₄

② Erzgebirge/Germany

Streak brown to black. **Mohs' hardness** 5–5½. **Specific gravity** 7.1–7.6. **Characteristics**: dark brown to black. Lustre: metallic, greasy; transparent to opaque. Cleavage: complete. Fracture: uneven, brittle; soluble in hydrochloric acid; powder will turn blue in concentrated sulfuric acid. Crystals: (monoclinic) thick tabular, prismatic, acicular, mostly vertically striped; surface growth and intergrowth; twinning, pseudomorphic. **Aggregates**: rough, bladed, radial, as impregnation; present in veins, pegmatites, alluvial deposits. **Accompanied by**: cassiterite, zinnwaldite, molybdenite, fluorite, apatite, quartz. **Found in**: Erzgebirge/Germany; Spain; Portugal; England; China; Malaysia; Burma; Canada; Colorado/USA; Bolivia; Queensland/Australia. **Similar to**: sphalerite, columbite, cassiterite.

Niccolite   nickeline
NiAs

③ St. Joachimsthal, Erzgebirge/
Czechoslovakia

Streak brownish black. **Mohs' hardness** 5–5½. **Specific gravity** 7.5–7.8. **Characteristics**: bright copper-red, often tinted greyish black or with a green crust (annabergite). Lustre: metallic, dull; opaque. Cleavage: incomplete. Fracture: conchoidal to uneven, brittle; gives off garlic odor when fractured; soluble in nitric acid with a green color. Crystals: (hexagonal) tabular, pyramidal; very rare and small; occasionally twinning. **Aggregates**: rough, botryoidal, knitted, dense, scattered; present in ore veins, gabbros. **Accompanied by**: chloanthite, skutterudite, bismuth, silver, proustite, arsenic, galena, barite. **Found in**: Black Forest, Erzgebirge, Harz mountains/Germany; Czechoslovakia; Ontario/Canada; California/USA; Japan. **Similar to**: breithauptite, maucherite, pyrrhotite, linneite, pure bismuth.

Breithauptite
NiSb

④ St. Andreasberg/Germany 1:10

Streak reddish brown. **Mohs' hardness** 5½. **Specific gravity** 7.5–8.5. **Characteristics**: bright copper-red, tinted blue-violet. Lustre: metallic; opaque. Cleavage: incomplete. Fracture: uneven to conchoidal, brittle; soluble in nitric acid and aqua regia. Crystals: (hexagonal) thin tabular, columnar, acicular; rare; twinning. **Aggregates**: rough, granular, bladed, dendritic; present in ore veins. **Accompanied by**: chloanthite, niccolite, ullmannite, pyrargyrite, silver. **Found in**: Harz mountains/Germany; Sardinia/Italy; Sweden; Norway; Ontario/Canada. **Similar to**: maucherite, niccolite, bismuth.

204 | cassiterite pg. 128, uraninite pg. 174, columbite pg. 176, maucherite pg. 17
fergusonite pg. 202

Streak

blue

Mohs'
hardness

1 ◄

2 ◄

3 ◄

4 ◄

5 ◄

6 ◄

7 ◄

8 ◄

9 ◄

10 ◄

Specific
gravity

1 ◄

2 ◄

3 ◄

4 ◄

5 ◄

6 ◄

7 ◄

Liroconite
$Cu_2Al[(OH)_4 | AsO_4] \cdot 4 H_2O$

① Cornwall/England 1:2

Streak blue, blue-green. **Mohs' hardness** 2–2½. **Specific gravity** 2.9–3.0. **Characteristics**: sky blue to greenish. Lustre: vitreous, greasy; transparent to translucent. Cleavage: incomplete. Fracture: conchoidal to uneven, brittle; soluble in acid. Crystals: (monoclinic) pseudohexagonal, lens-shaped; small and rare. **Aggregates**: rough, granular; present in oxidized zones of copper deposits. **Accompanied by**: azurite, malachite, chalcophyllite, olivinite. **Found in**: Saxony/Germany; Czechoslovakia; England; Urals/USSR; California/USA. **Similar to**: azurite, malachite, chalcanthite.

Vivianite
$Fe_3[PO_4]_2 \cdot 8 H_2O$

② Trepca/Yugoslavia

Streak light blue, white, brownish. **Mohs' hardness** 1½–2. **Specific gravity** 2.6–2.7. **Characteristics**: white, blue when exposed to air, black, brown. Lustre: vitreous, on cleavage face mother-of-pearl; transparent to translucent. Cleavage: complete. Fracture: bladed, fibrous, soft; thin blades malleable; strong pleochroism; readily soluble in hydrochloric and nitric acid. Flame test: blue-green. Crystals: (monoclinic) long prismatic to tabular; surface growth; usually small, rare. **Aggregates**: radial, fibrous, spheroidal, botryoidal, crumbly to powdery; present in ore-deposit sediments, on pegmatites, in clay, bogs, brown coal deposits, as impregnation, in bones and teeth of fossils (odontolite). **Accompanied by**: pyrrhotite, pyrite, siderite, triphyline. **Found in**: eastern Bavaria, Thüringen/Germany; Cornwall/England; Serbia/Yugoslavia; Crimea/USSR; Colorado/USA; Bolivia, Cameroon. **Similar to**: azurite, lazulite, turquoise.

Chalcanthite
$Cu[SO_4] \cdot 5 H_2O$

③ Laurion/Greece 1:3

Streak blue, also colorless. **Mohs' hardness** 2½. **Specific gravity** 2.2–2.3. **Characteristics**: light to dark blue, greenish blue. Lustre: vitreous; transparent to translucent. Cleavage: incomplete. Fracture: conchoidal, brittle; readily soluble in water; repulsive taste. Crystals: (triclinic) short prismatic; thick tabular; many different shapes; rare and small. **Aggregates**: rough, stalactitic, fibrous, crusty, botryoidal, surface growth, also granular and dense; present in oxidized zones of copper deposits in arid climates, in old mines. **Accompanied by**: chalcopyrite, atacamite, bronchantite, malachite, pyrite. **Found in**: Harz mountains, Erzgebirge/Germany; Slovakia/Czechoslovakia; Spain; England; Ireland; Chile; California, Arizona/USA. **Similar to**: azurite, liroconite.

Cyanotrichite
$Cu_4Al_2[(OH)_{12} | SO_4] \cdot 2 H_2O$

④ La Garone, Var/France 1:5

Streak blue. **Mohs' hardness** 1–3, difficult to determine. **Specific gravity** 2.7–2.9. **Characteristics**: sky blue to dark blue. Lustre: silky to vitreous; transparent to translucent. Cleavage: incomplete. Fracture: uneven; soluble in acid. Crystals: (rhombic) filamentary, acicular, long tabular; rare. **Aggregates**: radial tufts, velvet-like; present in oxidized zones of copper deposits. **Accompanied by**: brochantite, malachite, azurite, smithsonite. **Found in**: Var/France; Elba/Italy; Attica/Greece; Rumania; Scotland; Urals/USSR; Namaqualand/South Africa; Arizona, Nevada/USA. **Similar to**: azurite, aurichalcite, connellite.

anabergite pg. 44, tirolite pg. 132

Linarite

PbCu[(OH)$_2$|SO$_4$]

① New Mexico/USA

Streak light blue. **Mohs' hardness** 2½. **Specific gravity** 5.3–5.5. **Characteristics:** azure blue. Lustre: adamantine; translucent. Cleavage: complete. Fracture: conchoidal, brittle; when touched with hydrochloric acid color turns light blue to white; soluble in diluted nitric acid. Crystals: (monoclinic) prismatic, less often tabular; often multifaceted; surface growth, usually small; frequent twinning. **Aggregates:** in crystal groups and crusts, also radial, fibrous, matted, crumbly, powdery; present in oxidized zones of copper-lead deposits. **Accompanied by:** galena, cerussite, anglesite, brochantite, chalcopyrite, malachite, azurite, calcite. **Found in:** Black Forest, Harz mountains/Germany; Sierra Moraina/Spain; Kärnten/Austria; Sardinia/Italy; Cumberland/England; Namibia; Arizona, Utah/USA; Argentina; New South Wales/Australia. **Similar to:** azurite, caledonite, lapis lazuli, serpierite.

Diaboleite

Pb$_2$[Cu(OH)$_4$Cl$_2$]

② Mendip Hills/Wales 1:2

Streak blue. **Mohs' hardness** 2½. **Specific gravity** 5.42. **Characteristics:** light blue to deep blue. Lustre: vitreous; transparent to translucent. Cleavage: complete. Fracture: conchoidal to bladed, brittle. Crystals: (tetragonal) tabular, prismatic, usually with square contours, small. **Aggregates:** rough, granular, bladed; present in oxidized zones of copper-lead deposits. **Accompanied by:** boleite, linarite, cerrussite, phosgenite. **Found in:** Summerset/England; Attica/Greece; Arizona/USA. **Similar to:** boleite.

Caledonite

Pb$_5$Cu$_2$[(OH)$_6$|CO$_3$|(SO$_4$)$_3$]

③ Lead Hills/England 1:12

Streak blue, also white, greenish. **Mohs' hardness** 2½–3. **Specific gravity** 5.6–5.7. **Characteristics:** blue, light green to bluish green. Lustre: vitreous, greasy; transparent to translucent. Cleavage: complete. Fracture: uneven, brittle. Crystals: (rhombic) prismatic, fibrous, acicular; rare, small. **Aggregates:** tuft-like, as surfaces covering, rough; present in oxidized zones of copper-lead deposits. **Accompanied by:** anglesite, leadhillite, linarite, malachite, cerussite. **Found in:** Scotland; Cumberland/England; Sardinia/Italy; Rumania; Urals/USSR; Namibia; Arizona, California/USA; Chile; Japan. **Similar to:** linarite.

Aurichalcite

(Zn,Cu)$_5$[(OH)$_3$|CO$_3$]$_2$

④ Mapimi, Durango/Mexico

Streak light blue, also white and blue-green. **Mohs' hardness** 2. **Specific gravity** 3.6–4.2. **Characteristics:** pale green to sky blue, greenish blue. Lustre: mother-of-pearl, silky; translucent. Cleavage: complete. Fracture: bladed, soft; soluble in acid and ammonia. Flame test: green. Crystals: (rhombic) finely fibrous, acicular, tabular, indistinct faces; very rare and small. **Aggregates:** bladed, rosette-shaped, crumbly, dense, as crusts, surface covering; present in oxidized zones of nonferrous deposits. **Accompanied by:** malachite, azurite, smithsonite, sphalerite, hemimorphite, chalcopyrite, cuprite, limonite. **Found in:** Attica/Greece; Sardinia/Italy; Rumania; Santande/Spain; Lyon/France; Altai/USSR; Namibia; Arizona, Utah/USA; Mexico. **Similar to:** chrysocolla, cyanotrichite.

annabergite pg. 44, tyrolite pg. 132, covellite pg. 144

Streak

blue

Mohs'
hardness 1 ◀
—
2 ◀
—
3 ◀
4 ◀
5 ◀
—
6 ◀
—
7 ◀
—
8 ◀
9 ◀
10 ◀

Specific
gravity 1 ◀
—
2 ◀
—
3 ◀
—
4 ◀
—
5 ◀
—
6 ◀
7 ◀

Azurite
$Cu_3[OH|CO_3]_2$

① on malachite, Arizona/USA

Streak light blue. **Mohs' hardness** 3½–4. **Specific gravity** 3.7–3.9. **Characteristics:** deep blue. Lustre: vitreous, adamantine; transparent to almost opaque. Cleavage: complete. Fracture: conchoidal to uneven, brittle; soluble in ammonia and nitric acid (effervescence). Crystals: (monoclinic) mostly short columnar to thick tabular; intergrowth and surface growth; often multifaceted, pseudomorphic; seldom twinning. **Aggregates:** rough, radial, reniform, stalactitic, spheroidal, dense; crumbly, as dusting; present in oxidized zones of copper deposits, in porous sandstones. **Accompanied by:** malachite, chalcocite, cuprite, enargite, chrysocolla, chalcopyrite, pure copper, cerussite, anglesite, limonite, calcite, aragonite. **Found in:** Eifel, Spessart/Germany; Lyon/France; Cornwall/England; Attica/Greece; Sardinia/Italy; Urals/USSR; Namibia; Arizona, New Mexico/USA; Chile; New South Wales/Australia. **Similar to:** linarite, vivianite, lapis lazuli, cyanotrichite, liroconite, chalcanthite, charoite, tyrolite.

Boleite
$5 PbCl_2 \cdot 4 Cu(OH)_2 \cdot AgCl \cdot 1½ H_2O$

② Baja California/Mexico 1:4

Streak blue, also greenish. **Mohs' hardness** 3–3½. **Specific gravity** 5.10. **Characteristics:** deep blue. Lustre: vitreous, on cleavage faces mother-of-pearl; transparent to translucent. Cleavage: complete. Fracture: conchoidal, brittle; soluble in nitric acid. Crystals: (tetragonal) cubic, or octahedroid. **Aggregates:** botryoidal, rare; present in oxidized zones of copper-ore deposits. **Accompanied by:** malachite, azurite, diaboleite, cuprite, atacamite. **Found in:** Baja California/Mexico; Chile; Arizona/USA; New South Wales/Australia. **Similar to:** diaboleite.

Serpierite
$Ca(Cu,Zn)_4[(OH)_3|SO_4]_2 \cdot 3 H_2O$

③ Bad Elms/Germany 1:4

Streak bluish, also white. **Mohs' hardness** 3½–4. **Specific gravity** 2.5–3.1. **Characteristics:** sky blue. Lustre: vitreous, on cleavage faces mother-of-pearl; transparent. Cleavage: complete. Fracture: uneven, brittle; soluble in acid. Crystals: (rhombic) thin tabular to acicular; only very rare. **Aggregates:** tuft-shaped, crusty, botryoidal; present in oxidized zones of sulphide deposits. **Accompanied by:** smithsonite, cyanotrichite, linarite. **Found in:** Sauerland/Germany; Attica/Greece; Ireland; Kazakhstan/USSR; Ross Island/Antarctica. **Similar to:** linarite.

Connellite
$Cu_{15}[Cl_4(OH)_{32}|SO_4] \cdot 3 H_2O$

④ Cornwall/England 1:15

Streak light blue. **Mohs' hardness** 3. **Specific gravity** 3.41. **Characteristics:** greenish blue, blue-green, azure blue. Lustre: vitreous; translucent. Cleavage: indeterminable. Fracture: conchoidal, brittle. Crystals: (hexagonal) finely acicular, horizontally striped. **Aggregates:** bark-like, tuft-shaped, matted; present in oxidized zones of copper-ore deposits. **Accompanied by:** azurite, malachite. **Found in:** Cornwall/England; Sardinia/Italy; Algeria; Namaqualand/South Africa; California, Utah, Arizona/USA. **Similar to:** cyanotrichite.

cyanotrichite pg. 206, caledonite pg. 208

Streak

blue

Mohs'
hardness

1

2

3

4

5

6

7

8

9

10

Specific
gravity

1

2

3

4

5

6

7

Glaucophane

① Aostatal/Italy 1:2

$Na_2Mg_3Al_2[OH\,|\,Si_4O_{11}]_2$

Streak light blue. **Mohs' hardness** 5½–6½. **Specific gravity** 3.0–3.3. **Characteristics:** blue-grey, blue-lavender, blue-black. Lustre: vitreous; translucent. Cleavage: complete. Fracture: conchoidal to uneven, brittle; strong pleochroism. Crystals: (monoclinic) prismatic, acicular; intergrowth; end-faces seldom well-developed. **Aggregates:** rough, dendritic, fibrous, granular; present in metamorphic rocks. **Accompanied by:** chlorite, muscovite, biotite, paragonite, clinozoisite, jadeite, epidote, garnet, albite, calcite, quartz. **Found in:** Piemonte/Italy; Wallis/Switzerland; Bretagne/France; Euböa/Greece; Ukraine, Kazakhstan/USSR; California/Colorado/USA; Japan. **Similar to:** kyanite.

Arfvedsonite

② Macedonia/Yugoslavia 1:2

$Na_3Fe_4Al[OH\,|\,Si_4O_{11}]_2$

Streak grey to blue, also colorless. **Mohs' hardness** 5–6. **Specific gravity** 3.0–3.5. **Characteristics:** blue to greenish black, black. Lustre: vitreous; opaque to translucent. Cleavage: complete. Fracture: uneven, brittle; strong pleochroism. Flame test: yellow. Crystals: (monoclinic) long columnar, tabular; rare. **Aggregates:** rough, dendritic, granular; intergrowth; present in basic pitonite, less often in schist. **Accompanied by:** aegirine, nepheline, sodalite, eudialyte, zircon. **Found in:** Odenwald/Germany; Norway; Finland; Pantelleria/Italy; Ukraine, Kola/USSR; Greenland; Quebec/Canada; Colorado, New Hampshire/USA. **Similar to:** aegirine.

Odontolite

③ Kitzbühl, Tyrol/Austria 1:½

Mixture of apatite, calcite, organic substances, and vivianite.

Streak blue, white. **Mohs' hardness** 5. **Specific gravity** 3.0–3.5. **Characteristics:** turquoise blue, in artificial light blue-grey. Lustre: waxy; translucent to opaque. Cleavage: indeterminable. Fracture: conchoidal; light effervescence when in contact with hydrochloric acid. Crystals: (monoclinic) microcrystalline; present as fossil teeth and bone substances of extinct prehistoric animals (mammoth, mastodon, dinosaurs) in sedimentary rocks. **Found in:** Siberia/USSR; Gascogne/France; has become very rare. **Similar to:** turquoise, colored ivory.

Lapis Lazuli   lazurite

④ Chile 1:2

$(Na,Ca)_8[(SO_4,S,Cl)_2\,|\,(AlSiO_4)_6]$

Streak pale blue. **Mohs' hardness** 5–6. **Specific gravity** 2.4–2.9. **Characteristics:** glazed blue, also greenish, violet, often spotted. Lustre: vitreous, on cleavage faces greasy, dull; opaque, edges translucent. Cleavage: incomplete. Fracture: conchoidal to uneven, brittle; soluble in hydrochloric acid with a foul odor; white fluorescence under ultraviolet light. Crystals: (cubic) rhombododecahedral, also octahedral; very rare; only intergrowth. **Aggregates:** rough, fine-grained, dense; always in combination with other minerals, such as pyrite, sodalite, calcite, haüynite; present in limestone, sometimes in lava and as a by-product of volcanic eruptions. **Accompanied by:** scapolite, enstatite, augite, hornblende, diopside, mica, humite. **Found in:** Alban hills, Vesuvius/Italy; Afghanistan; Baikal Lake region/USSR; Burma; Pakistan; Labrador/Canada; California, Colorado/USA; Chile; Angola. **Similar to:** sodalite, haüynite, lazulite, azurite, linarite, dumortierite.

 ludwigite pg. 140, riebeckite pg. 166

GLOSSARY

accessory minor and nonessential constituents in rocks

accompanying mineral sharing the same paragenesis (*see below*)

acidic rocks rich in silica, at least 65%

arid climate in a region where moisture is evaporating faster than can be replaced by precipitation

atoll coral island consisting of a reef surrounding a lagoon

basic rocks containing less than 52% silica

bituminous mass consisting of naturally occurring hydrocarbons (coal) or their derivatives (petroleum)

botryoidal resembling a cluster of grapes

cleavage angle the angle created between cleavage faces when a mineral is split

concretion spheroidal or tuberous body of mineral aggregate formed in sedimentary rocks

covering crystallized minerals forming a crust-like cover

crevice open or mineral-filled space in rock

crust thick covering of minerals

cut one-sided cutting

dense mineral aggregates whose individual components are so small that they cannot be detected with the naked eye

dendritic moss- and branch-like shapes or markings; developed during crystallization of ore and manganese compounds

deposit a particular layer of rocks within a rock formation

dike rock formation that infiltrates adjacent rocks like a foreign body substance, usually with upright contours. Usually igneous, but also sandstone

drusy cavities hollow spaces within a rock, such as volcanics, that are filled with a collection of secondary minerals

dusting extremely thin, sometimes crust-like mineral occurrence that appears as if the mineral were sprinkled as dust across its host

emery a mixture of finely granulated corundum, magnetite, hematite, ilmenite, and quartz

facet small surface displayed by a crystal either naturally occurring from growth, as in crystal faces, or cut, as on a precious stone

fahlerz group of olive–grey–yellowish (pale lustre) sulfide minerals comprising the series tetrahedrite–tenatinite

feldspars a group of rock-forming silicate minerals with the subgroups orthoclase and plagioclase

fluvial belonging to or produced by a stream or river

fossil remnant, impression, or trace of animals or plants of past geological ages that has been preserved in the earth's crust

foyaite a kind of syenite first described in Foya, Portugal. Related to Eläolite

fumarole volcanic vent of various gases with temperature of 200–800 °C

gangue the relatively worthless rock or vein material in which valuable metals or minerals occur

geode cavity within a rock that has been filled with a collection of minerals

glass bead–shaped reniform–botryoidal mineral aggregate with smooth, shiny surface

gneiss foliated metamorphic rock corresponding in composition to feldspathic plutonic rocks

gravel small pieces of rock, with edges rounded and surfaces smoothed through water movement

guano phosphate-rich bird droppings found especially on Pacific islands that receive little rainfall

heat-treated subjected to a process of heating (especially precious stones) to change the color

hook-shaped angular fracture, particularly in metallic minerals

host minerals that make up the bulk of a rock

hygroscopic readily taking up and retaining water

impregnation diffusely disseminated mineral in the pores of a rock

inclusion defect or foreign object, gas, or liquid contained within a mineral or rock

intermediate rocks with a 52–60% silica content

kimberlite pipe volcanic, pipe-shaped structure filled with kimberlite rock that might contain diamonds

knitted resembling knitted material

magmatite rocks, also called igneous, created from the molten substance of the earth (magma). Those developing in the earth's crust are plutonic rocks, those on the earth's surface are volcanic rocks.

metamorphic rocks rocks that have developed into new rocks due to changes in condition in the earth's crust; well-known examples are quartzite, gneiss, phyllite, marble, slate, schist, serpentinites, amphibolites.

nodule rounded or almond-shaped lump of mineral or aggregate, typically in siliceous volcanic rocks

nugget clumps of gold or platinum in alluvial deposits

ochre yellow-to-brown-colored mixture of different iron compounds such as hematite and limonite

oolite sedimentary rocks made up of very small spheroidal granules often of calcium carbonate cemented together

ore mineral material with usable mineral content; in petrology all metallic minerals

oxidized zone layers in ore deposits close to the surface, where weathering produces secondary minerals

paragenesis the formation of minerals in contact in such a manner as to affect one another's development

pegmatite magmatites with large, individual crystals

petrification the process by which the outer structure of plant or animal material buried in fine-grained sediments can be preserved as the organic material is replaced by mineral crystallization

piezoelectric characteristic of some crystals that become electrically charged when mechanically altered

pisolite rocks that look like a conglomeration of small pea-shaped spheres

placer accumulation of heavy, robust minerals in a sedimentary deposit, especially of fluvial origin

plutonic rocks igneous rocks within the earth's crust that were crystallized from magma; well-known examples are: greisen, granite, granodiorite, syenite, gabbro, peridotite.

pore space open or subsequently mineral-filled space between grains or crystals in a rock

powdery ground into powder form or having the appearance of powder

precious stone mineral or mineral aggregate with special characteristics, such as hardness, color, lustre; therefore considered particularly precious for gemstones

pure metallic minerals in their basic elemental condition

pyroelectric a characteristic of some minerals that become electrically charged when heated or cooled

rock-forming significantly present in the formation of rocks

rough minerals or mineral aggregates which occur without a regular crystal surface

salt dome mushroom-shaped structure of salt contained within other rocks, usually diapiric

scattered or dispersed larger minerals (xenoliths) with typical distinct shapes scattered throughout a deposit or magmatite

secondary mineral formed subsequently to the host rock and usually derived from the host

sedimentary rocks rocks developed in the weathering process; well-known examples are: marl, shale, sandstone, greywacke, limestone, dolomite, gypsum, bauxite

sinter mineral deposit in springs

sparlike aggregates having characteristically smooth, often shiny cleavage faces

stalactitic cone-like formations, similar to those suspended in dripstone caves

stalagmite column-shaped dripstone growing upwards from the ground or cave floor, or features resembling such columns

stratification the identifying, visible structure of a rock

syenite hornblende, feldspar plutonic rock allied to granite, with or without quartz

synthetic artificially created crystal, often used as precious stone

terrestrial referring to the earth's surface

tufa porous rock formed as a deposit from springs or streams

tuff porous rock formed as a byproduct of volcanic eruption

ultrabasic rocks with a silica content below 45%

vein refers to either a predominantly quartz hydrothermal crystallization or a usually horizontal, relatively narrow layer of minable mineral material—ore, lode

vent gas and steam exhalations of volcanic origin

volcanic rock igneous rocks developed from magma at or near the earth's surface, such as rhyolite, trachyte, phonolite, basalt, kimberlite

weathering the effect on rocks at the earth's surface under the influence of the elements

INDEX

222